Equality and Power in Schools

Based on a study of 12 single-sex and co-educational schools over a two-year period, this book explores issues of equality and power both in the classroom and in the staffroom. Through classroom observation, interviews with students and staff, focus groups and questionnaires the authors demonstrate how the micro politics and practices of school and classroom life can work quietly but systematically to perpetuate inequality, and to forestall change. The book also examines the dynamics of power in schools, both in terms of student–teacher relations and relations amongst teachers themselves. It demonstrates the importance of democratisation as an equality issue in education.

The authors' findings offer an insight into the way schools operate in terms of social class, gender, religion and ethnicity, and raise fundamental questions about the use and abuse of power in schools and how this affects the lives of students and staff.

This book will be of interest to those studying education, sociology, equality studies, gender studies and women's studies, and to policy makers and teachers in senior management roles.

Kathleen Lynch is Head of Research at the Equality Studies Centre, National University of Ireland, University College, Dublin. **Anne Lodge** is a Lecturer in Sociology of Education at the National University of Ireland, Maynooth.

Equality and Power in Schools

Redistribution, recognition and representation

Kathleen Lynch and Anne Lodge

RoutledgeFalmer
Taylor & Francis Group

LONDON AND NEW YORK

First published 2002
by RoutledgeFalmer
11 New Fetter Lane, London EC4P 4EE

Simultaneously published in the USA and Canada
by RoutledgeFalmer
29 West 35th Street, New York, NY 10001

RoutledgeFalmer is an imprint of the Taylor & Francis Group

© 2002 Kathleen Lynch and Anne Lodge

Typeset in Bembo by
Keystroke, Jacaranda Lodge, Wolverhampton
Printed and bound in Great Britain by
St Edmundsbury Press, Bury St Edmunds, Suffolk

All rights reserved. No part of this book may be reprinted or reproduced
or utilised in any form or by any electronic, mechanical, or other means,
now known or hereafter invented, including photocopying and recording,
or in any information storage or retrieval system, without permission in
writing from the publishers.

British Library Cataloguing in Publication Data
A catalogue record for this book is available from the British Library

Library of Congress Cataloging in Publication Data
Lynch, Kathleen, 1951–
    Equality and power in schools: redistribution, recognition, and
    representation/Kathleen Lynch and Anne Lodge.
        p. cm.
    Includes bibliographical references and index.
    ISBN 0–415–26805–2 (hard)—ISBN 0–415–26806–0 (pbk)
    1. Educational equalization—Ireland. 2. Discrimination in education—Ireland.
    3. Critical pedagogy—Ireland. I. Lodge, Anne, 1966– II. Title.

    LC213.3. I73 L93 2002
    379.2'6'09417—dc21   2002072407

ISBN 0–415–26805–2 (hbk)
ISBN 0–415–26806–0 (pbk)

For Ann Lynch, Bríd Cahill
and Mary Cahill

Contents

Figures

Tables

Acknowledgements

This book has had a long gestation and many people have contributed to its completion, both within and outside the education sector.

Our first vote of thanks is to the students, teachers and school principals who participated in the pilot study and in the main phase of the research. They gave generously of their time, often at considerable inconvenience to themselves. We gratefully acknowledge their co-operation, hospitality and support, especially that of the students and teachers who allowed us to observe their classes. We are also deeply indebted to the school principals who were so supportive of the project, and who facilitated us in whatever way they could at different stages of the work. We thank them and their teaching colleagues sincerely for reading drafts of texts, and commenting on our analysis. We also really appreciated the help of the students in giving us feedback on our interpretation of schools events. The feedback from all the research participants on our early draft research reports was invaluable, and greatly enriched our understanding of how schools work in equality terms.

Our colleagues in the Equality Studies Centre in University College Dublin have been a source of inspiration and support throughout the project; they have played a major role in enabling us to bring the work to its conclusion. We acknowledge in particular the invaluable help given to us by Marjorie Fitzpatrick and Eileen O'Reilly in undertaking the pilot study, by Susan Gibbons and Margaret Healy in the analysis of the data, and that of Maureen Lyons, Mary McEvoy and Emer Sheerin in reading drafts and commenting on the text. We are especially grateful to John Baker for helping us refine our understanding of the concept of equality. Our thanks also to Nora Clancy, Patricia Gantly, Margaret Larminie, Jenny Murphy, Phyllis Murphy and Claire O'Riordan for their practical assistance and personal support at various stages of the project, and to Anne Coogan for being so helpful in organising and preparing the final text.

Many other colleagues from both within UCD and other academic institutions assisted us throughout the project with comments and critiques of our work. We acknowledge the help and support of John Bissett, Sara Cantillon, Marie Clarke, Dympna Devine, Mel Duffy, Marie Flynn, Joan Hanafin, Emer

Smyth and Michael Shevlin. We also greatly appreciated the support of Anne's colleagues in the Education Department of the National University of Ireland, Maynooth who gave her considerable encouragement in completing the project.

No project of this size could be completed without financial support. We would like to thank the Research and Development Committee of the Department of Education and Science for their financial support for the project, and their encouragement throughout. We also wish to acknowledge the support of the Social Science Research Committee of the Royal Irish Academy for the grant they awarded us for the project.

Finally, we acknowledge the support of our families and friends who have seen a great deal less of both of us than they might have wished over the lengthy period of time that we have devoted to this study; their care and concern have made it possible to complete the task.

Part I

Setting the scene

Introduction

Formal education plays a foundational role in determining the character of the political, economic and socio-cultural life of any given society. Education is the institution in which everyone participates to a greater or lesser degree. It plays a key role not only in distributing cultural heritage, but also in defining the parameters of that heritage, in excluding as well as including; it is a key player in legitimating and ordering socio-cultural relations. Schools and other educational institutions are recognised arbiters of what constitutes the culturally valuable, not only in terms of what is formally taught, but also in terms of the manner in which it is taught, to whom, when and where.

The role of education is not purely cultural however; it is also deeply social and political. In a globalised geo-political order, in which knowledge, particularly credentialised knowledge, plays an increasingly powerful role in determining the pattern of occupational opportunities, education is a central player in the distribution of privilege. Those who receive much formal education are considerably advantaged over those who receive little, and those who receive their education in elite institutions are privileged over those who do not (Bourdieu 1996).

Given the central role that education plays in the ordering of political, economic and socio-cultural relations it seems imperative that we analyse how it works, especially in its compulsory phase. The purpose of this book therefore is to advance such understanding. Building on the work of colleagues both nationally and internationally, we try to explore the inside life of schools, in classrooms and staffrooms, in corridors and in recreational spaces where students and teachers live out the practice of education on a daily basis. Using a triangular research strategy, we go deep inside the culture of schools, by listening to what students and teachers tell us, by observing classes, and by checking out our interpretations with those whom we observed and to whom we spoke. We do not confine our analysis of equality issues to the micro-actions of the school, however. We also try to locate the micro within the macro, to locate the subjective interpretation within the wider structural frame.

Our approach to the subject of education is not that of detached and disinterested observers however. Although we are deeply committed to the principle of objectivity in the deployment of our research instruments, including the tools of interpretation, we are also keenly aware of the naïve character of claims to absolute objectivity. Like all social scientists, we work out of paradigmatic as well as domain assumptions that are deeply value laden no matter how much we protest to the contrary (Gouldner 1970). Consequently we are happy to declare that the purpose of this book is not just to advance understanding of how schooling promotes equality or inequality in different ways, its goal is also to contribute to change by offering insights into how inequalities and injustices can be addressed. It is hoped that it will not only stimulate debate about the multiple and interlocking ways in which schools operate to promote different types of inequality, of a distributive, recognition and representational kind, but that it will also encourage and promote egalitarian change.

Schooling is compulsory until the age of 16 years in Ireland. While it is not legally compulsory after that time, it is de facto compulsory for many students as they know that without completing second-level education to the Leaving Certificate (the equivalent of the Baccalaureate in France, Highers in Scotland or A levels in England) their chances of good employment, or indeed further or higher education, are limited (Smyth and Hannan 2000). If the State requires young people to stay in school by law then it is imperative that their education in school is an enabling and enriching experience. It is imperative that it not only develops their capabilities, but that it also reinforces their sense of well being and self-esteem. To achieve such an objective it must promote an egalitarian culture for both the teachers and the students. If teachers are undervalued, either by management or colleagues, the chances that they will promote a positive and supportive learning environment for students are severely constrained. If all students are not treated with equal respect and enabled to develop their capabilities to the full, this raises important moral questions about the right of the State to confine people in an institution that may have enduring negative effects, be that culturally, economically or socially (Epp and Wilkinson 1996). Because schooling has been normalised as a social practice in most societies, we reflect little on the fact that it is mandatory. Its mandatory and universal character, however, places the question of equality in education centre stage. It is not an optional extra, either for the students or for teachers.

In this book we examine the core relations of schooling from an egalitarian perspective. Our approach to the subject is holistic rather than sectional; we do not focus exclusively on any single equality issue, or on any particular aspect of school life. Taking an inclusive view of the equality project and of schooling, we try to isolate the discrete ways in which schooling works in the development of particular sets of social class relations, so-called 'ability' relations, gender relations, minority relations and power relations. Drawing on the work undertaken with our colleagues in the Equality Studies Centre at University College Dublin (Lynch *et al.* 2001), we identify three inter-related core contexts in which inequality is generated in education, namely the socio-economic, the socio-cultural and the political.[1] The data suggest that, in social class and in so-called 'ability' terms, the problem of equality in education is primarily a redistributive one, while in terms of ethnicity (Travellers), sexual orientation, disability and religion the generative cause of inequality is the lack of recognition or mis-recognition of differences; it is a problem of social status rather than of redistribution of wealth or resources per se. The way power relations operate in schools also poses serious equality questions for education, not only in terms of student–teacher relations, but also in terms of student–student, and teacher–teacher relations. It is not possible, however, to draw a neat dichotomy between power, status and economic inequalities, particularly in the case of social groups where each of the three generative contexts of inequality are operating simultaneously, with no evident priority. Gender inequalities are, we suggest, exemplary of types of inequalities that are multiply generated; gender is a paradigm case of a multivalent status in equality terms.

Outline of the book

Part 1 of the book sets the scene for the analysis in the succeeding chapters. It opens in Chapter 1 with a review of the equality debates in egalitarian theory. Here we outline the scope of the academic debate about equality, and suggest that there are at least three major types of social injustices that need to be addressed in education, namely redistributive, recognition and representational injustices. To address these effectively in the policy domain, there is a need to have a closer alliance between social scientists and egalitarian theorists. A closer alliance between ethical and analytical discourses would, we suggest, help critical scholars to develop paradigms for transformative action.

While Chapter 1 sets the theoretical context for the study, Chapter 2 outlines the empirical scope of the work. It explains the research design and methodology as well as profiling the twelve schools involved.

Part 2 of the book examines issues of distributive justice in schooling. Using data from multiple sources, Chapter 3 presents an overview of the ways in which social class inequalities are produced in schools. We suggest that social class inequality is produced like a play with at least four major stages: it begins at the pre-school market stage when income and wealth are stratified thereby ensuring that some have more educational choice and capacity than others; the selection stage of class stratification takes place when students from different classes 'choose' schools; the allocation stage occurs when students are tracked by tests of attainment that favour the already advantaged; while social class differentiated classroom experiences complete the class experience.

Chapter 4 focuses on how the grouping or allocation practices of schooling reinforce social class inequalities, while simultaneously creating new stratifications and divisions around so-called 'ability'.

Part 3 is the longest section of the book; it addresses not only the inequalities of recognition experienced by different minority groups in schools, but also the interplay between recognition and other inequalities that arise in the gender area. Three of the four chapters (Chapters 5, 6 and 7) are devoted to the analysis of how single-sex schools differ from each other, and from co-educational schools, in the formation of gendered identities. The reason that we focused on school types as a means of understanding individual experiences is because of the desire to explore the complex subject of gender differentiation across schools in depth, a differentiation that is quite unique at this time in Western Europe. The focus on gender, as opposed to other social differentiations, is also related to the salience of gender as a structural division within Irish society. In terms of its scale and depth it is comparable to social class. Our data suggest that while gender relations are deeply status differentiated, they are more than this; they are also a deeply socio-economic and political set of relations that generate inequalities not only in terms of social status or culture, but also in terms of power and economic relations. Gender is a paradigm case of a multivalent status. Chapter 8 examines the position of minorities in schools. It highlights the long history of segregation in schooling, as well as the silences that have hidden, and continue to hide, the reality of differences. The equality problem for different minorities is often one of mis-recognition and/or of non-recognition of differences, either in terms of ethnicity (especially for Travellers), sexuality, religion or disability.

Part 4 of the book is devoted to the analysis of power relations. It suggests that equality in education is neither simply an issue of redistribution nor of recognition, it is also a problem of power, and how power relations are managed in schools. Taking the views of the students (Chapter 9) and the teachers (Chapter 10) we explore the multiple ways in which the ordering of power relations exercises both groups, not only in vertical terms but also in horizontal terms. We name the power dimension of inequality, the 'representational dimension', the third of the 3Rs, because the representation of interests is a core issue in the equalisation of power. Having political equality is about ensuring that one's definition of the situation is not disregarded, that one's voice is equal to that of others, that one is given the space and capacity to act autonomously.

The book closes with a discussion of the three major sets of relations that need to be addressed in education, namely the relations of redistribution, recognition and representation. It explores the importance of these, not only as discrete entities but also as sets of overlapping practices and procedures that need serious reformation and change.

Chapter 1

The equality debates

When we set out to publish this book, and in particular to give it a name, we were advised that the language of equality originated in another time, another age, when naïve social scientists and political theorists failed to appreciate the complexity of the post-modern world, a world in which the grand narratives of Marxism, feminism and other normative discourses were redundant. Others suggested that to speak in terms of equality in education was to ally oneself too closely with the ethical assumptions of political theory, and too far away from the 'objective', analytical discourses of the social sciences. Writing about equality in education was to place oneself outside of fashion, not to be seen to be part of the contemporary debates where modernist and progressive ideals had been abandoned because of their innocent preconceptions. The arguments were not dissimilar to the arguments presented against the founding of Equality Studies itself over ten years ago (Lynch 1995).

Yet equality is a fundamental principle underpinning the operation of all democratic societies. It is enshrined as a core value in numerous international agreements, including the Universal Declaration of Human Rights, the European Convention on Human Rights, the Amsterdam Treaty of the European Union, the International Covenant on Civil and Political Rights and the International Covenant on Economic, Social and Cultural Rights. It is also a principle to which there is deep commitment in education, albeit one that is often ill defined and minimally implemented. Given the centrality of equality to the discourse of contemporary politics, including the politics of education, it seemed both credible and desirable that it be the focus of a study on education.

A further reason for making equality a central focus of this study is because inequality in education, howsoever defined, has been one of the core subjects of research in the social scientific analysis of schools in recent history (Lynch 2000a). What has become abundantly clear as this research has progressed is that schools are major players in the determination of patterns of inequality in society. As knowledge-based industries and services gain increasing pre-eminence in the global economy, schools have become increasingly powerful players in the determination of life's chances. Their role as producers and disseminators of cultural products has also meant that they play a powerful role in determining the ordering of cultural relations in society, and in elevating and denigrating different cultural forms.

This book is about the issue of equality in education in all its complexity. While it analyses questions of difference and diversity, issues of power, and questions of distributive justice, it defines and interprets these not as separate and discrete entities, but rather as core, interfacing problematics within the wider equality project. It is eclectic in its approach, both intellectually and empirically. Although it is informed in large part by research within the social sciences on education, it does not confine itself to these perspectives. In particular it draws on work in normative egalitarian and feminist theory, to understand the complex ways in which schooling can produce different, and often unequal, outcomes in education, and to identify options for change. Two core principles inform the work therefore, an ethical set of principles that assume that inequalities in education are unjust and must be changed, and a pluri-disciplinary analytical framework that recognises the multivalent and interlocking character of student identities as relational subjects. We cannot draw a neat dichotomy between the material and the symbolic, between class, ethnic, gender and other social relations, if we want to understand social reality, in particular if we want to understand how inequality is perpetuated (Cole 2000; Crompton 1998; Fraser 1995; Anthias 2001). One's materially defined structural location, in class terms, and one's place on the circuits of power, are also strongly influenced by one's gender, ethnicity and regional location in an increasingly global social order.

Given the fact that the debate about equality, in equality terms, as opposed to stratification terms, takes place in political theory rather than in sociology, we want to draw on the insights gained from normative egalitarian theorists, in particular from critical theorists, feminists and Marxist-inspired thinkers within this field. Egalitarian theory is not of a piece. It comprises authors from the very different intellectual orientations including conservative thinkers such as Nozick (1974); neo-liberal scholars such as Waltzer (1985) and Dworkin (2000); classical liberals such as Rawls (1971, 1993) and Miller (1995); a range of radical thinkers such as Tawney (1964), Nussbaum (1995a,b), Nielsen (1985), Baker (1987, 1997, 1998) Cohen (1995, 1997, 2000) and Sen (1992); and critical feminist scholars such as Fraser (1997, 2000), Young (1990) and Phillips (1995, 1999). In this book, the focus is on the value of having a dialogue with the more radical Marxist-inspired and feminist critical scholars. They have most to offer social scientists interested in substantive egalitarian change in education.

Defining equality – locating educational research within an egalitarian framework

Much of what is written about equality in education within the social sciences does not define what is meant by equality: the understanding of equality or inequality remains implicit in the text. Yet, educationalists work within particular egalitarian paradigms even if the intellectual foundations of their analysis are not made explicit. By naming the scope and limitations of different egalitarian frameworks, we hope to set out the scope of the equality debate in education more clearly.

Inequality in education is not generated from a single source. At times the generative source of the inequality may be economic relations, at other times it may be political, socio-cultural or affective relations. In many cases the causes of inequality for a given group or individual may be generated from multiple, interactive sources. Research and theory about equality reflect both the complexity and the diversity of the origins of inequality itself.

By far the most influential tradition is that which focuses on the material distribution of goods and services. A second major tradition is that which defines equality as a problem of status and the recognition of differences, while a third defines power relations as an equality problematic separate from material and status considerations. Finally, there is an emerging perspective that draws attention to the affective domains of life when defining the scope of the equality project.

The redistributive perspective

The concept of equality that has gained pre-eminence in egalitarian theory is one that gives primacy to the concept of having, either having or availing of material goods and services, or having opportunities to access, participate or succeed in particular spheres (see the work of Cohen 1995, 2000; Rawls 1971; Sen 1992; or Tawney 1964). Such a concept has strong roots in materialist and economically-based concepts of social justice (Young 1990). It defines equality as a distributive problem; a problem of redistributing resources or opportunities more equally between individuals in particular.

Given the over-riding concerns of educationalists and policy-makers with equality of opportunity over the last forty years, it is evident that the distributive view of social justice has dominated social scientific analysis. Education was defined as a 'good'; the more of it one received the better (Connell 1993). While the substantive content of what was taught did receive critical comment from critical theorists and feminists in particular (including Giroux and McLaren 1996; Harding 1991; Popkewitz and Fendler 1999), the over-riding concern has been with distributing education credentials – increasingly higher education credentials – more fairly among working-class people, ethnic minorities, women and other marginalised groups.

Moreover, it has been the weaker rather than the stronger model of distributive justice, that has gained pre-eminence. The focus has been on equalising opportunities rather than equalising resources (Arnot 1991; Middleton 1990). Large scale empirical studies, on the effects of schooling on life chances and status attainment, formed the intellectual and political backdrop for much of contemporary research on equality in education, especially in the USA (Davies 1995). Although these studies are not as numerous in the USA or Europe as they were twenty years ago (Weiss 1995, Lynch 2000a), they have exercised a powerful influence on intellectual thought and effectively focused the equality debate on questions of opportunity. The goal has been the proportionate representation of marginalised groups in either accessing, participating or achieving at different levels of education. It is generally assumed that equality is being attained when 'marginalised' groups or 'disadvantaged' groups are increasing their entry rates to advanced or honours 'tracks', to prestigious universities or to high status jobs. As the structural inequalities endemic to hierarchies of knowledge, tracks, jobs etc., are not the subject of investigation, the work can and does have a deeply conservatising effect on public policy (Lynch 1999a: 287–312).

Although the distributive view of social justice is grounded in the discourses of political economy, sociological debates about equality in education never really engaged with the parallel work in the egalitarian theory field. The work of radical egalitarian theorists (such as that of Cohen 1995; Baker 1987; Neilsen 1985; Tawney 1964; Young 1990; and Fraser 1995) was rarely or never deployed to critique equal opportunities policies although it was clear from such work that equal opportunities policies alone could not promote any substantive form of equality. The failure to dialogue across disciplines has meant that many of the insights from political theory regarding the logistical impossibility of promoting equality in education in highly economically and politically egalitarian societies were lost to social scientists.

The gain for critical sociologists of engaging with such work therefore is that they would have access to conceptual frameworks that would enhance their sociological insights regarding the futility of trying to promote equality of opportunity without equality of condition (Tawney 1964). Radical egalitarian theory underlines the impossibility of exercising civil and political rights without having social and economic rights protected.

Recognition of difference

Issues of differences in status, and problems of power and domination are seen as derivative rather than generative in the distributive tradition. Consequently the institutional contexts of unequal power and non-recognition that underpin unequal economic relations are frequently ignored (Young 1990: 18–33). For many groups, however, the inequality they experience is not economically generated or resolvable in distributive terms either economically or opportunistically. Status-related inequalities, such as those arising from sexuality, religious beliefs or ethnicity, can only begin to be resolved through status-related initiatives in the socio-cultural realm.

Since the early 1990s there has been an increased interest in what has been called the 'politics of recognition'. In response to social movements, a number of theorists have emphasised the importance for some groups of cultural domination, misrepresentation, stereotyping and disparagement. Iris Young identified cultural imperialism as one of five 'faces of oppression' (1990) and Charles Taylor (1992) drew attention in a North American context to the 'politics of recognition'. The idea of recognition has been analysed in depth by Axel Honneth (1995) and its relation to distributional issues theorised by Nancy Fraser (1997, 2000) and Anne Phillips (1999). Issues of recognition are prominent in discussions of multiculturalism (Parekh 2000). The second strand in egalitarian thinking therefore is one that focuses on the issue of status and the respect for difference. Following a Weberian tradition, most often implicitly, it treats status as a discrete entity, related to, but separate from, economic and political positions (Fraser 2000; Phillips 1999).

While there has been a strong research tradition in sociology of education addressing issues of difference and identity, (Arnot and Weiner 1987; Barton *et al.* 1996; Connolly 1998; Epstein 1994; Francis 1999; Gill *et al.* 1992; Harding 1991; Mac an Ghaill 1994; Mason 1990), what has not been given much attention is the complex interface between the recognition and the redistributive interpretations of social justice. This is a subject however on which there is an especially fruitful debate in egalitarian theory (see Baker 1987; Fraser 1995, 1997, 2000; Phillips 1999; Young 1990), one that would enable sociologists to explore more systematically the scope and limitations of identity-based solutions to educational difference.

The work of Fraser (1995, 2000) has been especially useful in highlighting the dangers associated with a Hegelian-styled culturalist model of identity politics, one that focuses on supplanting misrecognition by others with a positive self-representation of one's own making. She has highlighted the limitations of an identity politics that is divorced from institutionalised status inequalities in particular. Like Phillips (1999) she explores the many complex ways in which the problems of recognition are inseparable from the problems of redistribution in an economically unequal society. They both observe how the equality problems for many groups, such as women and ethnic minorities, are not simply problems of recognition but also problems of redistribution.

Fraser's work (1995) also highlights the intractable policy dilemma facing those working for egalitarian change at the present time. While many radicals are drawn to 'transformative' (radical) as opposed to 'affirmative' (more liberal) solutions to inequality, the problem is that the former strategy is often so divorced from the life world of the most marginalised that it leads to a sense of political impossibility. The affirmative strategy has an even graver danger of becoming counter-productive insofar as it requires perpetual interventions in both the distributive and recognition spheres; these, in turn, promote negative perceptions that undermine the distributive and recognition objectives being advanced in the first instance.

Power and the representation of interests

A third strand within egalitarian thinking focuses on issues of power as an equality problem inter-related with, but separate from, distribution and recognition issues. In some respects this is one of the least developed perspectives within egalitarian thinking as boundaries between academic disciplines and areas of specialisation have had a tendency to separate these issues from those relating to the distribution of opportunities and resources. Here again, Young (1990) has usefully reasserted the importance of power relations to issues of social justice, drawing on the work of Foucault and other post-structuralist writers, and the importance of this dimension of equality has recently been acknowledged by Fraser (2000). A more integrated conception of equality has also been developing among liberal theorists such as Dworkin (2000), whose work on political equality has been effectively criticised by Brighouse (1996). In the Equality Studies Centre's own research, power inequalities have emerged as central concerns within the educational system both in secondary schools (Lynch and Lodge 1999; Lodge and Lynch 2000) and in community education (McMinn 2000).

While social scientists have examined power as a key dynamic in educational relations at considerable length especially at the macro-levels of the State and related institutions (for example, Apple 1982; Arnot and Weiner 1987; Bowles and Gintis 1976; Connell 1993; Francis 1998; Gewirtz et al. 1995; Halsey et al. 1997; Torres 1990, 1995), far less attention has been paid to the micro-level power relations in classrooms between teachers and students. Although the work of Freire (1972) inspired much debate about issues of power in pedagogical relations (Aronowitz and Giroux 1991; Ellsworth 1989; McLaren 1995) there has been relatively little sociological analysis of the dynamics of the power relations between students and teachers of the kind undertaken by Cusick (1973), Pollard (1987), Waller (1932) and Woods (1980, 1990). The emerging children's rights discourse in the sociology and philosophy of childhood still remains quite separate from mainstream educational debates (Archard 1993; Devine 2000; James and Prout 1990; James et al. 1998; Epp and Wilkinson 1996).

What egalitarian theory has to offer sociologists first is an understanding of the discreteness of power as an equality problematic. It focuses attention on the issue of child–adult relations as an equality consideration in its own right, related to, but separate from, issues of gender, ability, social class, ethnicity, sexuality, etc. In that sense it introduces a new variable into the equality equation, the variable of age-related status and its impact on educational relations. It requires us to rethink the relations of dominance and subordinacy that are institutionalised in educational life.

The work of Phillips (1995) and Fraser (1997) is particularly valuable in problematising the way in which authority and power are exercised in democratic structures and the limitations of the same. Anne Phillips provides cogent arguments and evidence regarding the importance of institutionalising systems of power relations that enable subordinate groups to exercise political influence. She makes the case for a 'politics of presence' so that marginalized groups are directly involved in negotiating policies and procedures that affect themselves. While the themes and contexts discussed by Phillips refer primarily to the macro-institutions of society, the principles underlying a concept of presence can be applied in the micro-world of the school and classroom as much as in the broader political context of the State. They offer an interesting framework for making educational relations generally more egalitarian.

Equality considerations in the affective domain

In most of the writing internationally about equality the individuals involved are assumed to be free and equally autonomous agents (Kittay 1999: 100). This is evident in education in both the dominant distributive and in the recognition traditions; in neither case is there a discussion as to the role that affective considerations might play in determining the parameters of social justice. What this Rawlsian-inspired view of justice largely ignores is the fact that human beings are not just rational actors; they are also affective agents in social and political life. Dependency and interdependency are endemic to the human condition. There is no person who is not at some time, to a greater or lesser degree, dependent on others, while interdependence is an inevitable correlate of everyday human functioning.

Because dependence and interdependence are an integral part of the human condition, taking dependence and interdependence seriously is a prerequisite for social justice (Held 1995; Nussbaum 1995b). When one recognises the salience of the affective dimensions of social existence, it is evident that affective inequalities are significant social phenomena in their own right. They may exist when a person is deprived of the emotional nurturance she or he needs to develop and/or maintain intimate, trusting and solidarity-based human relations. They may exist when a child is deprived of close, trusting and loving relations, or when an adult is deprived of the intimacy they have the capacity to enjoy, or is denied opportunities for friendship, solidarity and belonging in their community, associational or work relations.

Teaching and learning are interdependent, and hence affective, enterprises involving a considerable amount of emotional investment on behalf of students and teachers. Yet much of education theory and sociological research gives little or no attention to the affective aspects of the learning environment. Students are generally represented in sociological research as if they were simply rational actors, purely cognitive beings learning 'subjects' in schools. In equality terms, differences or deprivations are analysed in terms of gender, disability, race, sexuality, etc., but not in terms of affective relations. The fact that students and teachers have an emotional history as well as a social class, gender or ethnic history is not addressed, yet there is ample evidence that learning cannot be divorced from affective engagement with the subject. While work by Reay (1998) has begun to name the place of emotional work undertaken by parents with students, there is as yet little discussion as to the effects of the students' own emotional capital on their learning, or that of teachers on their teaching. The denial of the emotional dimensions of the learning process means a denial of the totality of what it is to be a teacher and a learner in the first instance. By failing to engage with the affective we can do grave injustices to those students (and teachers) whose alienation from schooling stems from emotional considerations as well as, or apart from, considerations of social class, gender, disability, ethnicity or sexuality. We also ignore how recognition, resource or power differences and deprivations interface with those in the affective domain. The gaps in our understanding of affective relations are relevant for all learners but especially for those who have been consistently deprived of love and care or who have been traumatised by war, displacement or immigration.

Another way in which the affective dimensions of human life are disregarded in education occurs in the nature of the subjects studied in schools. The classical–liberal and the mathematical–scientific curricula form the basis of much of what counts as valued knowledge in most Western-style education (Gardner 1983). Little time or attention is given to the forms of knowledge or understanding that inform affective development. The work of psychologists, such as Gardner (1985, 1993) and Goleman (1995), has inspired a debate among educationalists about the different forms of human intelligence, and in particular about the intelligences that could be said to be largely in the affective domain, intra-personal intelligence and inter-personal intelligence. However, most educational research in sociology assumes that the inequality problem in education has little to do with the affective domain. Learners are defined as rational rather than affective actors; inequality is defined as a problem of cognitive difference or deficit. While there has been a recognition of the importance of emotional work in general sociological research (e.g. Hochschild 1983, 1989; Delphy and Leonard 1992), to date the emotional work involved in education has received relatively little attention.

What the work of egalitarian theorists such as Nussbaum (1995a, 1995b) and Kittay (1999) would bring to education is a deeper appreciation of the role of the affective dimensions of life in relation to understanding the nature and scope of what could and should be learned in schools. It would encourage us to challenge the view of the learner as a purely cerebral person. It would allow a deeper appreciation of the role of dependency and interdependency in the exercise of power and control in educational relations. Naming the emotional dimensions of social life would also provide new frameworks through which to explore the implications of developments such as the intensification of work and competition within and between schools.

Egalitarian theorists would, in effect, provide the ethical foundations for a theory of justice that incorporates the affective. As Nussbaum has observed, recognising the affective dimensions of social justice is important not only in its own right, but also in gender terms. It is a means of incorporating a different and more gender-inclusive view of the person into the justice debate.

Discussion

The dialogue with egalitarian theory suggests that inequality has at least four major generative roots, each of which presents separate but inter-related challenges for those interested in social change. Inequality is a distributive problem in so far as it is rooted in politico-economic systems in terms of patterns of ownership, control, distribution and consumption; it is a recognition problem in so far as it operates in culturally-based systems of recognition, non-recognition and misrecognition; it is a representational problem in all contexts where power is enacted, in the realms of decision-making, and in systems of inclusion and exclusion in the exercise of power; and it is an affective matter when it pertains to relations of dependency and interdependency. The relative significance of any one of these contexts for the generation of inequality for a given group can be empirically investigated.

Inequality in education: ethical considerations

The second lesson learned from the dialogue with egalitarian theory is that sociological reality is not simply a world of facts, it is also a world imbued with values. Human actions tend to be value-laden actions, howsoever defined. Yet the relationship between fact and value has received relatively little attention in mainstream sociological research. Ethical discourses, located primarily in norma- tive political theory, have been generally disregarded by positivist social scientists. Correlatively, normative theorists have shown little interest in the empirical findings of their social scientific colleagues (Young 1990). Normative political theory and positive social science are mutually estranged (Sayer 2000a: 186).

Yet it is desirable that research on education would engage with ethical issues as education is an ethical enterprise. As Freire (1972) reiterated many times, education is never neutral; it is either for domestication or for freedom. Any educational action involves a normative judgement, a decision as to what constitutes the educationally valuable, a decision as to who and what to include and when. It involves decisions and value judgements as to what to explore and what to ignore. Given the ethical foundations of education itself, research on the subject of education is ethically grounded and this makes it even more problematic for educational researchers to attempt to create a neat dichotomy between fact and value (Callewaert 1999; Griffiths 1998).

Even for those who do not subscribe to the modernist and enlightenment project of which education is such a central part, there is no denying that educa- tion is essentially about the realisation of change in terms of some predefined sense of an educational good. There is what Shilling (1993) calls a 'redemptive tradition', in education. The focus of much research on education and social stratification, for example, implicitly assumes that education is a social good with definite redemptive effects, even though it does not engage with the ethical foundations of its own thought. There is a fundamental assumption that the more education you get, the better, and that being deprived of education is an injustice (Erikson and Jonsson 1996; Shavit and Blossfeld 1993).

The work that has most openly recognised the value dimensions of education has been that of critical theorists and feminists (Apple 1986, 2000; Arnot and

Weiler 1993; Arnot and Barton 1992; Francis 1999, 2001; Giroux 1983; Griffiths 1998; Reay 1996; Weiler 1988). Despite the concern with normative issues, however, critical education theory has not really liaised with normative moral and political theory in any overt and direct sense. While critical social science implies a connection between positive (explanatory/descriptive) science and normative discourses such as those of moral or political philosophy, the normative or ethical dimension remains implicit rather than explicit. It is as if to 'pass' as serious researchers, normative orientations must be concealed or slipped in without naming them for what they are. To attempt to identify a vision of an alternative future is construed as utopianism, Platonic idealism, and a departure from 'real' social science. The job of analysis, even critical analysis, rarely offers a systematic opportunity to open up and explore different concepts of social systems. There is a reluctance to systematically explore the feasibility, desirability and operational rules of alternative systems. While there has been substantive critique, there have been few serious attempts to develop 'counterfactuals', serious and systemic outlines of alternative structures and systems (Sayer 1995). Some such attempts have been made in education by feminists, such as hooks (1994), Weiler (1988), and critical theorists, such as Aronowitz and Giroux (1991). Drawing on the work of Friere (1972, 1973) they have outlined concepts of counter-hegemonic resistance through a radical pedagogy of transformation. While this work has been important and inspirational for many activists, it did not develop the strong counterfactual framework of which Sayer speaks. Yet to begin to develop effective counterfactual proposals for a more egalitarian education system, a dialogue between scholars in related fields is essential (Wesselingh 1996).

The separation of analytical from normative discourses is detrimental to both intellectual traditions; it leaves crucial ethical questions unexplored in sociological research and crucial empirical questions disregarded in normative theory. Having a dialogue between ethical and explanatory discourses in politics and sociology respectively would help debates about the causes of inequality to also focus on the solutions to inequality. It would enable social scientists to explore counter-factual positions in relation to the diverse ways in which equality in education could be promoted. It would provide a new and conceptually rigorous language in which to name proposals for change.

Attempts to create a more integrated relationship between ethical and empirical analysis have been rejected recently by Foster et al. (2000). They outline a number of criticisms of case studies in education, especially research on inequality, that they deem to be drawing unwarranted practical value conclusions from empirical research data. They propose that 'all academic social and educational research ought not to draw practical value conclusions' (ibid.: 219). Their basic premise is that value disagreements cannot be resolved by science and they are therefore best left outside of it. Value statements must be conditional and contextualised relative to particular ideals, if addressed at all. Overall, their belief is that the main task of research is to describe, explain and develop theories (ibid.: 224), a position articulated by Hammersley on a number of previous occasions (1992, 1995).

While it is undoubtedly problematic when researchers suppose a set of values or ideals and implicitly use their research findings to endorse this position, the neat dichotomy that Foster and his colleagues draw between fact and value is not as simple as they claim it to be. Values influence what we choose to research, how we frame the research questions and how we interpret findings. Epistemological questions cannot be neatly separated from ethical questions, much as we may wish to do so (Midgely 1994; Taylor 1985). Moreover, our own biography influences our core theoretical assumptions more than we would care to admit. We operate not only out of paradigmatic assumptions but also out of the 'domain assumptions' formed by our lived experiences, a priori beliefs and values of which we may not be aware (Gouldner 1970).

Second, the 'problem' as defined by Foster *et al.* (2000) of not maintaining a clear distinction between fact and value, is not unique to one tradition within sociology of education. It is by no means the prerogative of case studies on inequality or indeed of work within the more critical and feminist traditions in sociology of education, as Hammersley (1992, 1995) has suggested. The numerous studies of social class stratification and its relationship to education published by the Nuffield group at Oxford, and their associates in other countries, do not receive any mention (Breen and Whelan 1995; Breen and Goldthorpe 1997; Erikson and Jonsson 1996; Goldthorpe *et al.* 1980; Goldthorpe 1996; Shavit and Blossfeld 1993). Yet, this work is deeply embedded in normative values about the importance of social mobility as a measure of inequality in society (Swift 2000). It ignores issues such as equality of condition (Tawney 1964; Lynch 1999a) and the extensive literature emanating from egalitarian theory that is critical of a simple distributive view of social justice (Young 1990; Phillips 1995).

Furthermore, the large body of work of 'the equality empiricists' that has dominated much of sociology of education for the last thirty years (Lynch 2000a), and which is deeply imbued with the values of political liberalism, has not been subjected to the same analytical scrutiny by Foster and his colleagues. Yet such work has several questionable normative assumptions. In particular it has tended to frame social class inequality in education in liberal terms, as a degendered and politically neutral issue, thereby foreclosing intellectual debate about the complex and variable character of class-related inequalities (Apple 1996; Apple and Weis 1983; Kerchoff 1984; Pink and Noblit 1995; Weiss 1995; Wexler 1987).

The point is not that values can be separated from analysis, but rather, how do values influence our research investigations and underpin our theories, and how can we subject them to more careful documentation, scrutiny and appraisal (Griffiths 1998). This is an especially pertinent issue in relation to inequality as it is a research subject that not only has a subjectively-situated meaning like all social phenomena, but is also a deeply value-laden subject.

Inequality is a social phenomenon that must be understood in terms of its three interrelated realities. It has an objective dimension in the sense that it can be observed by those outside of those experiencing it; it has a subjectively situated meaning for those who live with it and who know it experientially; and it has an ethically situated meaning, in that it can be assessed as creating greater or lesser injustice. Whether other social phenomena are ethically grounded is an open question; it needs to be answered in different cases. However, it is clear that many phenomena have ethical dimensions (including economic practices) even if this aspect of that reality has been ignored in recent history (Sayer 2000b).

Inequality is not a morally neutral subject because those who are subject to serious injustices experience serious damage and deprivation. In the case of those whose basic human rights to bodily integrity are violated, it leads to a profound physical and psychological harm. For those who experience deep economic inequality because of unequal terms of trade between the rich North and the poorer South, it frequently results in malnutrition or even starvation. At a more local level, inequalities of status arise for those whose sexualities are despised or whose abilities are hidden; they are subjected to inequalities of cultural recognition (Fraser 1995, 1997; Phillips 1999; Young 2000). One cannot treat the investigation of inequality as if it were the investigation of a relatively neutral ethical question therefore. When studying equality the ethical is deeply imbricated in the research. To ignore this is to ignore the totality of what injustice is; it is to ignore the total reality of the research subject itself. The key question therefore is not whether or not we should address the ethical dimension of the research subject but rather how we address it.

That progress has been made in relation to recognising the place of ethics in research is without doubt, especially in relation to research design and methodology. There is a growing realisation in the social sciences and cognate disciplines that unless we engage with the issues of ethics in research we may be part of the inequality problem rather than part of its solution (Bernstein 1983; Byrne and Lentin 2000; de Koning and Martin 1996; Harding 1991; Humphries and Truman 1994; Lather 1991; Mies 1984; Oliver 1992; Reason 1988; Smith 1987). It is increasingly recognised that unless research and theory on inequality develop some means of working towards an emancipatory goal for those with whom or about whom it speaks, there is a very real sense in which the research process becomes another tool of oppression. Without intent, researchers become colonisers, creating public images about groups and contexts of inequality (in both the academic and the policy world) over which most people participating in the pain and marginalisation of injustice and inequality have little or no control. Professional researchers know and own (as do the policy institutions, research foundations and state agencies that fund them) part of people's world about which people themselves know very little. By owning data about oppressed peoples, the 'experts' own part of them. The very owning and controlling of the stories of oppression adds further to the oppression as it means that there are now people who can claim to know and understand you better than you understand yourself; there are experts there to interpret your world and to speak on your behalf. They take away your voice by speaking about you and for you (Lynch and O'Neill 1994).

The first imperative dictating an ethical approach to research is therefore fundamentally a human rights one. It is the requirement that we do not colonise the injustices of others, and by so doing exacerbate their powerlessness and their susceptibility to manipulation and control. One of the strategies that would help preclude such a development is to institutionalise dialogical (in the Freirean sense) procedures between the academy and the community. This would allow for democratic dialogue between the researchers and those with whom (as opposed to just about whom) they write (Lynch 1999b).

There is a third and more political reason for engaging with the question of values in educational research. If the value dimensions of the research subject are ignored by all but a minority of critical thinkers and feminist scholars, this allows an intellectual space to open up and be claimed by uncritical and highly conservative voices in educational discourse. The rise of the New Right in the field of home schooling in the USA (Apple 2000) could be seen as an example of such a trend. Unless those with a more critical disposition to the subject of values engage with them, then the field remains entirely outside their control. The failure to address the issue of values in the field of economics for example has led to a situation where neo-liberal classical economics have become almost synonymous with the subject itself in many of the most prestigious economics departments throughout the Western world. The hegemony of one set of economic discourses in the academy has altered popular discourse; increasingly any dissent from neo-classical economic values is seen as a failure of common sense (Sayer 2000b).

There is a threefold imperative therefore dictating the investigation of the ethical in relation to equality issues in education, the nature of education, the nature of inequality and the nature of the politics of knowledge.

That there is resistance to the idea of creating closer links between normative theory (most of which is developed within political theory and philosophy) and sociological and related research is beyond doubt. The reasons for this resistance have been well documented by Sayer (2000a: 173–187). He points out that while some of this resistance is well grounded – arising from the political and sociological naïvete of much normative political and ethical theory, including its pre-social, atomistic conception of the individual – some of it is not. He challenges the Marxists in their unwarranted belief that Marx's rejection of the bourgeois ethics of his time meant the rejection of all ethics. While the historical context in which Marx was writing could justify his scepticism about ethics, to make such a claim in the early twenty-first century is untenable, not least because not all ethical argument is made in the interest of ruling classes. Feminist and disability studies are among the most visibly ethical forms of discourse; these are clearly not the ethical monopoly of a bourgeois class. Moreover, with the development of a growing anti-capitalist movement internationally, and the rise in global concern for human rights, especially among non-governmental agencies representing women and marginalised people, it is clear that the bourgeoisie do not control the ethical ground, especially on matters of equality and social justice.

Post-modernists reject the linking of the normative to the analytical because of its universalising intent. While the rejection of grand narratives is understandable in the wake of the colonising nature of so much globalisation undertaken in the name of 'development', nevertheless it must not be used to outlaw all ethical discourse. To do so is to play into the hands of powerful global economic interests whose profits and exploitative practices are threatened by ethical discourse (Sayer 2000b). There is a place for universalising, albeit a universalising that takes cognisance of all forms of difference, and of the political and cultural contexts of its own theorising.[1]

What is being suggested here is that to discount the ethical implications of inequality in intellectual analysis is to discount a substantive defining element of the research subject itself. The by-products of inequality, be these material or affective deprivation, powerlessness, non-recognition or abuse, can and do cause intense and prolonged human misery especially where they are deep and prolonged. To analyse inequality without regard for its degrading and exclusionary implications is to ignore a substantive part of what inequality is. It is to confine oneself to a partial analysis of the research subject.

Putting the study in context

This study was informed in its design and implementation by paradigms and frameworks derived from a number of different discourses and disciplines. The importance of recognising and naming the ethical implications of inequality in education arose from a dialogue with critical and feminist scholars in education, and from philosophical writings in egalitarian theory. It was the work of critical and feminist scholars on research design that also encouraged the employment of research methodologies that were co-operative and change-oriented, while work in more mainstream social scientific research demonstrated the importance of employing a triangular research strategy for understanding complex organisations such as schools, and a complex subject such as equality.

In the analysis of our findings we draw on a wide range of research traditions in education, especially sociological research. However, we also recognise the importance of psychological, political, feminist and policy analysis for understanding the why and how of inequality in education. Given the priority given to the analysis of inequality in political theory in particular, it has been the work of egalitarian theorists that has provided the broad conceptual framework for the study. Egalitarian theory has enabled us to explore the discrete character of inequality for particular groups and the interface between these inequalities for other groups. Our methodological and conceptual approach to the subject therefore is eclectic. We adopt this strategy in an attempt to understand the microphysics of inequality, and as a way of identifying contexts for action.

In taking our intellectual cue from the work in the Equality Studies Centre, we try to adopt a holistic approach to the research subject, rather than prioritising a particular equality theme (Baker 1997; Lynch 1995). That said, it is inevitable that certain equality themes emerge more strongly than others from the data. Inequalities arising in social class and gender relations in particular, and those arising in power relations between teachers and students, are the focus of much of the text as these were pervasive themes emerging from the data. While this undoubtedly reflects the limitations of our own paradigmatic and domain assumptions, it must also be said, in defence, that it reflects the depth and visibility of particular social divisions in our society over others. While inequalities experienced by ethnic, racial, ability, religious and sexual minorities are addressed in the research they are not analysed in as much depth as they might be in other studies, for a number of valid reasons. First, the scale of the racial, ethnic and religious differences in the Republic of Ireland is much less than in other European countries. Although there has been an increase in the number of immigrants in the last two years (since the data were collected), by international standards, Ireland remains a relatively homogeneous society in cultural terms. There was only one school in the study with an identifiable group of ethnically different students. Second, the way in which schooling for disabled students is provided in Ireland also mitigated against the compilation of data on the experience of students with different impairments in mainstream schools. While disabled students do attend second-level schools, most of those with severe or moderate physical and learning impairments attend separate schools. Consequently, there were very few disabled students in the study. However, we do address the complex issue of 'ability' and explore the ways in which students are stratified on the basis of their assumed abilities in different classes. Sexuality was a subject that we hoped to investigate in depth in relation to its equality implications. This was made difficult, however, by the unwillingness of school administrators and students to discuss the subject in a public way. We were not given permission by a number of the schools to ask questions about individual students' sexual orientation, although we could and did ask questions about attitudes to sexual differences in all schools.

Although we have identified four major contexts in which inequality is generated in society – the economic, the political, the socio-cultural and the affective – the study does not explore issues around affective relations and their implications for equality in education as a major theme. This is not because we regard affective relations as unimportant, but rather because the study was not designed to collect substantive data on the subject. It is clear from the data compiled however, especially on teacher–student relations and peer relations, that there is an important emotional dimension to the schooling experience that deeply affects the quality of the education received. Data provided by students on such issues as labelling, the use of sarcasm and what makes school a supportive and positive place, indicate that affective relations are a site of social experience in their own right.

Bourdieu's work suggests that schools cannot promote equality as currently structured. He proposes that we abandon 'the myth of the "school as a liberating force"' so that we can 'perceive the educational institution in the true light of its social uses, that is as one of the foundations of domination and of the legitimation of domination' (Bourdieu 1996: 5). If schools are, as Bourdieu suggests, endemically inegalitarian in their processes and outcomes, we must look for places and spaces where resistance is possible, no matter how difficult that may be. We must approach our research agenda with an honest and open admission of how unjust certain schooling practices are. By so doing we can generate a debate that allies explanatory and normative frameworks for change. We can create a dialogue of resistance to injustice.

Chapter 2

The design of the study and a profile of the schools

Aims of the study

In the 1980s, one of the co-authors was involved in a study of how the hidden curriculum of schools contributed to the reproduction of inequality in education (Lynch 1989). A number of other studies undertaken by the authors since that time, and by colleagues both at home and abroad, indicated that schools played a crucial role in matters of equality (Clancy 1995; Drudy and Ui Cathain 1999; Lee *et al*. 1994; Lodge 1998; Lynch and O'Riordan 1998; Lynch 1999a; Hannan *et al*. 1996; Mac an Ghaill 1994; Mortimore *et al*. 1988; Oakes 1985; Smyth 1999). Yet, there had been very few studies in education that focused simultaneously on the multiple ways in which schools promote equality or inequality for different groups and individuals. In particular, there had been few major studies that utilised a wide range of research tools to understand the role schools play in the equality 'game'.

The prospect of taking a holistic approach to the study of inequality was daunting, not least because schools are highly complex organisations (Ball 1997; Westoby 1988). Whether one adopted a traditional bureaucratic approach, a more interpretative approach, a critical poststructuralist or feminist perspective, the task of explaining how schools and classrooms operate remained equally demanding (Tyler 1988). We were aware that the theoretical and empirical lenses that we wore at any given time would only allow us to see parts of the picture. The analysis of schools is made difficult not only by the fact that schools are 'loosely coupled systems' with several overlapping quasi-autonomous subsystems (Weick 1988); it is also complicated by the highly contingent character of school and classroom life itself. The culture of schools varies with intake, tradition, cultural context, gender, social class, modes of assessment and grouping (tracking) practices. Moreover, the cultural climate of any given school is tempered by multiple micro-climates within particular classrooms, staffrooms and playgrounds (Darmarin 1995; Osborn and Broadfoot 1992; Swain 2000; Hammersley and Woods 1984). It is within this cautionary context that we set out to understand the ways in which schools may reproduce inequality.

The design of the study was inspired by both emancipatory principles and a realisation that understanding the complex life of schools requires a range of research strategies. We employed a range of ethnographic research tools, including interviews, observations and the compilation of documentary materials provided to us by the schools and the students (Hammersley and Atkinson 1995). It did not rely on these exclusively however, as there were factual data about schools' and students' profiles that required the use of more quantitative research tools including a structured questionnaire. There was therefore a deliberate attempt to engage in triangulation: different sources of data on the same phenomenon were used as means of challenging and corroborating different claims and interpretations (Seale 1999).

We also set out to have, what Burgess (1988) has termed, 'purposeful conversations' as well as utilising such structured methods of research as were appropriate. We were especially anxious to talk with young people in schools and with teachers, not just through the medium of questionnaires, but directly as persons involved in the mutual task of education. We wanted to hear the insider's passionate perspective as well as the so-called objective outside view (Ellis and Flaherty 1992). We wanted to hear the critical voices of those who are outside the framers of research theory and practice, to listen without rigid preconceptions. We wanted to hear the 'vernacular theories' of those living out and through schooling, to hear the voices of those who are not only powerless in schools but also in defining the research agenda (Herr and Anderson 1997). We also wanted to observe life inside schools, especially life in classrooms as it was lived day-in-day-out. Our research strategy was multifaceted, complex and undoubtedly overly ambitious. It was messy research in a very real sense (Smyth and Hattam 2001). Given the scale and complexity of what we were trying to do, it did not always have clearly defined boundaries; it appeared to be running away from us many times. Yet, having endured the long march from the initial pilot study to the editing and re-editing of the text in the light of comments from both research participants and colleagues, we think we do have a story to tell about equality in education, in particular a story about its complex and multifaceted character.

The research dialogue

As noted above, emancipatory research principles guided the research process from the outset (Heron 1981; Lather 1991; Humphries and Truman 1994). We set out to have a dialogue with schools, most especially students, but also teachers. We wanted to hear what they understood inequality to be in education, and when we had drafted an account based on what they told us, to check it out with them for accuracy and fairness. We also hoped it would become a generative force for change within schools and education generally.

All schools invited to be involved were sent an outline of the proposed research goals and research instruments at the design stage of the study. In addition, each school was visited prior to the study and teacher comments and views on the research design were taken into account. Unfortunately it was not possible to consult with students about the research design prior to the study, due mainly to a lack of resources but also due to our own realisation that schools were unlikely to co-operate with such a proposal. Our initial soundings with school administrations indicated that while they could facilitate a dialogue with staff about the research, the resources and time required to have a systematic dialogue with students were beyond their capacity. As it happened, establishing co-operative research arrangements with individual staff across twelve schools involved protracted negotiations, involving not only individual staff, but also teacher unions and school management and owners.

When our first draft of the findings for each school was completed, we made an oral and short written presentation on these to the whole staff in each of the twelve schools. The teachers made both oral and written responses to our data analysis and interpretations. We subsequently took these into account in our writing. After this event, as we drafted each stage of our research report, we sent them to the schools for comment and correction. It was a slow process, and one over which we exercised little control as time moved on. What we do know is that students had less influence on redefining interpretations than we would have wished for. The only real dialogue about our findings that we had with students was when we held focus groups after they had completed the essays and questionnaires. During these meetings, we were able to check out their understanding of our telling of their stories. Once we left the schools however, and relied on posting back reports to the schools and waiting for a response, it was mostly the views of school principals and senior teachers that we heard. Schools had autonomy and we had no authority to intervene in this.

Specific methodologies

The study involved a triangular approach to the research subject (Seale 1999). It employed a range of methodologies including informal interviews with students about school, classroom observation, general school observation, focus group interviews with students, a questionnaire survey of the pupils and teachers, and intensive interviews with school principals and other senior personnel in the twelve schools. All of the students were also invited to write an essay on their experience of inequality in their school.

The final data base for the study comprised the following:

- 1,557 questionnaires completed by the students.
- 1,202 completed essays on school by the students.
- 162 classrooms observed – across all subject areas.
- 70 focus groups (four students per group drawn from the original sample classes).
- Observational studies of meetings, social events, extra-curricular activities, etc., and informal conversations with staff and students at various school events and in staffrooms.

- The compilation of written information about the school.
- 380 teacher questionnaires – short questionnaires eliciting their views on equality.

The data were compiled in the following manner.

Phase 1: the pilot study

Before the main study began, a pilot study of one large school in the Dublin area was undertaken in 1994. This proved an invaluable exercise in terms of developing research priorities. Our research questions were refined and research instruments were modified on the basis of the lengthy dialogues, interviews and questionnaire material we collected in this school. The most important lesson learned was the need to listen to students, to allow them to speak in their own words about their equality priorities in school.

Choosing the schools

The selection of schools for the study took a considerable amount of time and involved written communications and telephone calls with a wide range of people in the second-level education sector. As the research involved classroom and school observation, it was essential to have a reasonable level of co-operation and interest in the research in the participating schools. If there had been a high level of opposition to the research among staff, it would not have been possible to conduct it successfully. In addition, it was necessary to involve a representative range of schools in different locations.

After consultations with administrative bodies in the second-level sector, teacher unions and other educationalists, a total of fifteen school principals were invited to get involved in the study. These schools were chosen because they were representative of different types of schools in the Republic of Ireland in terms of gender, social class, size, ethnic intake, management structures and ownership. Three of these declined, one because there was a new principal being appointed, another because extensive building was under way, and a third because the school was involved in a number of projects and the principal felt that staff involvement in another project might not be forthcoming. Two of these were boys' schools and one was co-educational. The final sample of schools for the study comprised four single-sex girls' schools, four single-sex boys' schools and four co-educational schools. There were three elite (fee-paying) schools and three designated disadvantaged schools included, one of each gender type. The reason why these schools were over-represented in the study was to ensure that social class differences in schooling practices could be analysed in depth.

Initial contacts and visits to the twelve participating schools were made between spring and autumn 1995. The gathering of data began in September 1995 and continued for the rest of the school year 1995/6. During this period, every school was visited on at least two separate occasions for a period of two working weeks per school. During these visits, a large amount of quantitative and qualitative data was collected. Discussions with students about the essays and questionnaires they completed also took place on the second visit to each school. The final visits to the schools, involving the dialogue with staff about preliminary findings, took place in the autumn of 1996 and the spring of 1997.

Phase 2: survey of students

The first task we undertook was to administer a questionnaire and essay title to students about the subject of equality. We personally administered it to each class and presented it on an overhead projector to explain any words that students might find difficult. We personally went through questions with students who had reading difficulties.

The students of one class from each school year in all the schools were asked to complete a questionnaire and essay about equality issues in their schools. Students could and did opt out. Care was taken to ensure that a representative range of classes in terms of measured academic attainment was selected in each school. Where a streaming or banding situation existed, classes were selected to give a broad representation of all tracks. If schools had mixed classes or a range of grouping systems, classes were selected across the years to reflect the academic profile of the school. The school principals, vice-principals and guidance counsellors assisted in the selection of a representative range of classes in each school.

A total of 1,557 (21 per cent) pupils in the participating schools filled out questionnaires. Within individual schools, the proportion of pupils who completed questionnaires varied, due to the variability in school size, but also to the fact that three schools did not have a six-year cycle at the time of the research. In all, 508 (33 per cent) of the student respondents to the questionnaire were in single-sex girls' schools; 527 (34 per cent) were in single-sex boys' schools, while 522 (34 per cent) (262 boys, 260 girls) were in co-educational schools. Just under half (49.3 per cent) of all respondents were female and 50.7 per cent were male.

The aim of the student questionnaire was to determine the views and experiences of students on equality issues within their school and their views on the school's social climate generally. A small number of questions on academic and personal self-concept were also included. The questionnaire obtained detailed background information on parental occupations, housing, students' part-time jobs and childminding responsibilities, their extra-curricular activities both in and outside of school, and subjects they were studying. It also explored their views on school climate, their self-image and their attitudes to issues of gender, social class, ethnicity, sexual orientation, disability, race, religion, the exercise of authority in the school and the method of grouping students. Finally, the students were asked to write two short one-page essays on (a) whether she or he ever experienced unfair or unequal treatment either from teachers or peers, and (b) how he or she would make the school a fairer and more equal place.

Phase 3: interviews with students

Focus group interviews were conducted with four randomly selected students from each of the classes given the questionnaire. In the co-educational school, two females and two males were selected from each class group. A total of seventy such interviews took place involving 278 students. All of these were audio-recorded. The focus group interviews were undertaken after the survey of each class and their purpose was to explore more fully with students the equality issues which arose in the questionnaires for that class. In particular, we wanted to explore with students if our understanding of what they had written in the questionnaires and in the essays was accurate and truthful.

Phase 4: classroom observation

One of the aims of the project was to obtain a clear profile of social life in the school organisation. It was essential therefore to engage in classroom observation if this were to be complete. All teachers in all twelve schools were invited to volunteer for the observation part of the study, although it was pointed out that only a small number could be observed in each school, given time and resources. It was also necessary to obtain data from classes in different subjects and across different age groups and tracks, and this also limited the options open for observation. Given that teachers in Irish second-level schools are rarely if ever observed once they become qualified, either for research or inspection purposes, undertaking observation and audio-taping classes was quite a sensitive matter. Only teachers who volunteered could be observed. We relied on teachers' good will and interest in the project. While this seemed highly problematic from the outset, not only because we feared that we would not get a representative range of classes, but also because we might get too few classes, our fears were somewhat exaggerated. As trust was built up with individual teachers in each school, more and more teachers offered to have their classes observed.

Given the voluntary nature of the classroom part of the study, we were not able to observe all seventy classes to which questionnaires had been issued in Phase 1. While some of the students who completed questionnaires were also observed in class, this did not apply in the majority of cases. We were pleased however that at least five teachers were observed in each school, and a total of 100 teachers were observed overall in 162 classes with the consent of the students. Ten teachers were observed on three occasions with different classes, 42 per cent were observed twice while the remaining 48 per cent were observed once. A slightly higher proportion of single-sex girls' classes, 34.6 per cent, were observed compared with single-sex boys, 31.4 per cent, and co-educational classes, 34 per cent. Female teachers were also slightly more likely to volunteer to be observed: while 64 per cent of teachers in the study were female, 70 per cent of the teachers observed in class were female. All types of subjects were observed, including all the major languages, humanities, mathematics, sciences, business subjects, technical subjects, religion, home economics, art, music and non-examination subjects. Classes were observed from all years and tracks ('ability' groups).

Most classes were audio-recorded. In a few cases, the teacher requested that no recording be made, and in a number of others recording was impossible for technical reasons (e.g. very high noise level). Extensive fieldnotes were written on each of the school visits in addition to the survey and classroom data collected.

Phase 5: survey of teachers and interviews

To obtain a profile of the school, its entrance policy, subject and curriculum plans, staff selection, grouping practices, etc., formal and informal interviews were carried out with key personnel (principals and vice-principals, guidance counsellors and remedial teachers). All written information available on the schools was also compiled. Informal discussions were also held with as many staff as possible during the visits to each school in order to obtain more general information about the social climate of the school from the teachers' standpoint.

There was a total of 560 teachers involved in the twelve research schools, of whom 147 (26 per cent) were teaching in single-sex boys' schools, 178 (32 per cent) were in single-sex girls' schools while 235 (42 per cent) were in co-educational schools. A total of 380 teachers returned questionnaires giving a response rate of 68 per cent. This short questionnaire sought background information on the respondent's teaching experience as well as views on equality issues regarded by the respondent as being of importance to students and to teachers. It also allowed each individual to make a written response to the data we presented from our findings on their school.

Phase 6: presentation of preliminary findings to the schools

During autumn 1996 and spring 1997, return visits were made to each of the twelve schools. Data from the essay part of the questionnaires, from focus groups and some preliminary statistical data on attitudes and school climate were presented. There were two major reasons for this visit. First, the project was designed as both an action-research initiative and one in which we were trying to implement the emancipatory principles of dialogue. It was essential therefore that findings were returned to the schools for comment and to ensure that the schools had ownership of the data about themselves. This enabled school staff to address issues that arose in the research, and to plan and implement strategies within their own institutions to improve areas they might perceive as being problematic. It also gave the teachers the opportunity to comment on the research and to propose themes for more in-depth analysis. Second, it gave an opportunity for teachers to respond to the findings and to express their own views on equality issues. It was not possible to give feedback to students at these sessions due to resource constraints, although most of the schools did agree to involve students in any future presentation of findings. Although such visits were planned, they did not materialise due to lack of funding.

The dialogue with schools about the findings proved to be one of the most exciting and challenging parts of the project. While most of the schools were anxious in advance of the presentation of findings, and somewhat fearful of what students' perception of the school might be, the overall response to the data when presented was one of keen interest. Further fieldnotes were written about each of these visits. One important and somewhat unexpected outcome of these visits was that ten of the twelve schools were very interested in receiving more in-depth feedback and in using the information to develop and implement whole school equality policies and other changes in organisational practice.

School profiles

The twelve schools involved in the study educated students between the ages of 12 and 18 years. There was considerable variation in their profiles, reflecting the complex and varied nature of the Irish post-primary education system. They ranged in size from those catering for approximately 1,000 students to those with an enrolment of just over 250. They were located in six different counties, in cities, towns and rural areas. Four were co-educational while the remaining eight were equally divided between single-sex girls' and boys' schools. While three of the schools were designated disadvantaged[1] (St Peter's girls' school, St Dominic boys' school and Ballycorish co-educational school) and were predominantly working-class and lower middle-class in intake, three were fee-paying and were predominantly upper middle-class (St Cecilia's girls' school, St David's boys' school and St Ita's co-educational school). The remaining six schools were more mixed in their social class intake, although St Patrick's girls' school and Ballinroe boys' school were much more middle-class in intake than either Ollan and Ballydara co-educational schools, or Our Lady's girls' school.

Each of the participating schools is described in brief below. All the names of people and locations used throughout this text are pseudonyms. Given the fact that Ireland is a relatively small country, we have decided to describe these schools in very general terms to preserve their anonymity. (See Table 2.1, including Notes a and b.)

Girls' schools

St Peter's is a large, designated disadvantaged girls' free-scheme secondary school located in a city suburb. It is a Catholic school founded and managed by a female religious order. As in the great majority of Irish religiously-managed schools, the principal and almost all the staff are lay people. In St Peter's almost all the teachers were also female. The school was built to serve a large local community, but due to declining numbers in more recent years it now has a significant intake from outlying suburbs. This school has been granted disadvantaged status and is eligible for some additional resources and support. It also has a home–school community liaison programme in operation. The school is a large building situated in good grounds shared with the convent and the primary school.

At the time of the study 29 per cent of the sampled students in St Peter's were from middle- or upper middle-class backgrounds; almost half (48 per cent) were from lower middle-class or skilled manual backgrounds, and 23 per cent were from semi-skilled, unskilled and other backgrounds. The school used 'mixed ability' (for further discussion on the problematic character of the concept of 'ability' see Chapter 4), with setting for core subjects (Mathematics, Irish and English). The school did not have a Students' Council at the time of the study.[2]

Our Lady's is a single-sex girls' secondary school established over fifty years ago by a religious order of sisters. It is situated in a small town serving a large, relatively isolated rural area characterised traditionally by high levels of poverty, migration and emigration. Both the principal and the vice-principal of the school were women, as were almost all the staff. The school was very popular in the locality as it had a reputation for high academic attainment. In spatial terms, the school was quite over-crowded and was situated on a relatively small site. A new extension was being planned at the time of the study.

Thirty-two per cent of the students were from middle- and upper middle-class backgrounds while 23 per cent were from lower middle-class and skilled manual backgrounds. A further 26 per cent were from semi-skilled, unskilled and other backgrounds while 19 per cent were the children of farmers. The school operated a system of mixed grouping, with setting for core subjects (Mathematics, Irish and English). It had a Student Council with representatives from every class.

St Patrick's is a large, single-sex girls' free-scheme secondary school located in a large town. Like Our Lady's and St Peter's it is a Catholic school although almost all of the staff are lay people, including the principal. The school principal is male. It is a very popular school in the locality and has a lengthy waiting list due to its reputation for high academic attainment. The school was originally established in the nineteenth century; the original school buildings are small and quite cramped in terms of space. Plans for a new extension were under way at the time of the study.

Almost two-thirds (64 per cent) of the students were either middle- or upper middle-class, while 26 per cent were from lower middle-class or skilled manual backgrounds; 9 per cent were from semi-skilled and skilled backgrounds while 1 per cent were from farming backgrounds. The school operated a strict system of streaming in the junior cycle and it did not have a Student Council.

St Cecilia's is a fee-paying, single-sex girls' secondary school located in a city suburb. It is a Catholic school and is situated in large attractive grounds. It was founded by a religious order of sisters and has a female principal and vice-principal. The school fee was IR£800 per annum at the time of the study.

Table 2.1 Profile of participating schools organised by student intake size (*n* = 12)

Size	School name	Type[a] (code)[b]	Location	Gender intake	Notes
Large (751–1,000 students)	St Peter's	Free-scheme secondary school (ssg fr)	City	Single-sex girls	Disadvantaged status
	St Patrick's	Free-scheme secondary school (ssg fr)	Large town	Single-sex girls	
	Ballydara	Community college (co-ed Com Col)	City	Co-educational	
	St Ita's	Fee-paying secondary school (co-ed fp)	City	Co-educational	
Medium (500–750 students)	St David's	Fee-paying secondary school (ssb fp)	City	Single-sex boys	
	Ballinroe	Free-scheme secondary school (ssb fr)	Large town	Single-sex boys	
	Ollan	Community college (co-ed Com Col)	Large town	Co-educational	
	Ballycorish	Community school (co-ed Com Sch)	Rural	Co-educational	Disadvantaged status
Small (< 500 students)	St Cecilia's	Fee-paying secondary school (ssg fp)	City	Single-sex girls	
	Dunely	Free-scheme secondary school (ssb fr)	Large town	Single-sex boys	
	St Dominic's	Free-scheme secondary school (ssb fr)	City	Single-sex boys	Disadvantaged status
	Our Lady's	Free-scheme secondary school (ssg fr)	Rural	Single-sex girls	

Notes
[a] Second-level education is provided in four different types of schools, secondary schools, vocational/community colleges, community schools and comprehensive schools. Schooling is free, in the sense that there are no fees in all of these schools with the exception of a small number of fee-paying secondary schools. The latter comprise 7 per cent of all schools. To denote the difference between the two types of secondary schools, we refer to those that do not charge fees as 'free-scheme' secondary schools.

Secondary schools comprise 58 per cent of all second-level schools and cater for approximately 61 per cent of all students in the sector. Almost all these schools are denominationally controlled, most being under Roman Catholic management. Almost all of their current and capital expenditure however is provided by the Department of Education and Science. Secondary schools were traditionally the most academic school types and the most socially selective, although there are huge variations among them both academically and socially. Single-sex schools comprise a slight majority of schools in the secondary sector.

A small number of secondary schools charge fees in addition to the State grants provided for teacher salaries and buildings. Fee-paying secondary schools are heavily concentrated in the Dublin area, and in a few other large urban centres. Approximately 60 per cent of fee-paying schools are under Roman Catholic management while most of the remainder are under Protestant management.

Vocational schools (many of which are now known as community colleges) are administered by local Vocational Educational Committees. They comprise 32 per cent of all second-level schools and cater for 26 per cent of all second-level students. These schools are spread throughout Ireland and traditionally served working-class, small farming and lower middle-class children. As their original name implies, the schools were designed originally as being vocational rather than academic schools. This policy changed over 30 years ago when all second-level schools were enabled to pursue academic programmes. They are non-denominational schools and are entirely funded by public monies. community and comprehensive schools comprise 8 per cent and 2 per cent of schools respectively. Between them they educate 13 per cent of all students. These schools were all established since the late 1960s and are managed jointly by the local Vocational Education Committee and a designated religious authority. They are effectively denominational schools being either Catholic or Protestant. They offer the full range of subjects and in social class terms cater for the widest cross section of any school type. However, like all school types, there are significant variations between individual schools in their social profiles. Almost all community and comprehensive, and most vocational schools are co-educational although boys are disproportionately represented in vocational schools in particular.

A majority of students, 58 per cent, attend co-educational second-level schools. The 42 per cent in single-sex schools are mostly in the secondary sector, and a majority are girls (Table A2.1).
b The codes indicated in parentheses are used throughout the text as an abbreviated description of school type.

The majority of the students were living locally, and most (82 per cent) were from middle- and upper middle-class backgrounds. Just 13 per cent of the students were from lower middle-class and skilled manual backgrounds, while a minority (5 per cent) were from semi-skilled and unskilled backgrounds. The school operates a mixed 'ability' system with setting for core subjects (Mathematics, Irish and English). The school had a Student Council with representatives from every class.

Boys' schools

St Dominic's is a single-sex boys' school in an inner city urban area characterised by high levels of unemployment and poverty. It is a Catholic school managed by a religious community and it has designated disadvantaged status. While the majority of its students came from the immediate locality, due to falling enrolments, the school also recruited students from outlying suburbs. The school had very limited sports facilities being situated in small grounds in a built-up area. All training for team sports took place in facilities that were over a mile away from the school. There was no physical education offered due to the lack of available facilities the year we were visiting the school. The staff was reasonably gender balanced, although both the principal and vice-principal were male. There were very few young teachers.

Twenty-five per cent of the students were from middle- or upper middle-class backgrounds while 34 per cent were from lower middle-class and skilled manual backgrounds. The largest single group (41 per cent), were from semi-skilled and unskilled backgrounds. The school operates a system of streaming throughout the junior cycle. The system of streaming is designed to advantage those in the lower streams who are placed in small classes and whose teachers have received special training. The school did not offer the Transition Year and had no Student Council.

Dunely is a single-sex boys' Catholic secondary school located in a medium-sized town serving students from the town and those from the agricultural hinterland. The school had been founded during the nineteenth century by a male religious order. It had a strong sports orientation although it had limited sporting facilities. Most of the staff were male, including the principal and vice-principal.

In term of social profile, Dunely was quite mixed: 42 per cent were from middle- and upper middle-class backgrounds, while 23 per cent were from lower middle-class and skilled manual backgrounds. One-fifth (21 per cent) were from semi-skilled and unskilled backgrounds while the remainder (14 per cent) were the children of farmers. The school operated a streaming system for second and third years. It did not have a Student Council at the time that the data were being collected.

Ballinroe is a medium-sized free-scheme secondary school for boys in a large town. The school is an old one, founded by a Catholic religious order during the nineteenth century. At the time of the study, the school was growing and new buildings were planned as existing facilities were quite inadequate. The principal and vice-principal of the school were both male and neither was a member of a religious order. There was a reasonable gender balance in evidence on the staff, although most of the older teachers were male.

Almost two-thirds (63 per cent) of the students were either middle- or upper middle-class. Almost one-quarter (24 per cent) were from lower middle-class or skilled manual backgrounds while 11 per cent were from semi-skilled and unskilled backgrounds. A very small proportion of the students (2 per cent) were from farming backgrounds. The school operated a streaming system for second and third years. First years were mixed 'ability'. There was a Student Council in operation.

St David's is a medium-sized, Catholic fee-paying boys' secondary school located in a city suburb. The school has a strong sports profile and excellent sports facilities for a wide range of activities. Both the principal and vice-principal were male; the former was a member of the religious order that had founded the school. The school remains under the control of this religious order. The school staff had reasonably even proportions of female and male teachers. The fees at the time the research was being conducted were IR£1,500 per annum.

The social profile of the students was similar to St Ita's: 93 per cent were either middle- or upper middle-class. A very small proportion (5 per cent) were either from lower middle-class or skilled manual backgrounds, while a smaller percentage (2 per cent) were from semi-skilled or unskilled backgrounds. The school used mixed 'ability' throughout, with setting for core subjects (Mathematics, Irish and English). The school had a Student Council which was most active among senior students.

Co-educational schools

Ballycorish Community School is situated in a small town and serves a large rural area as well. It is a medium-sized co-educational school of relatively recent origin. It is managed jointly by the local Vocational Education Committee and a Catholic religious order. The school has disadvantaged status. The school had reasonable sports facilities and offered a wide range of vocational and academic subjects. The school principal was female and the vice-principal male. The staff was reasonably gender balanced.

A relatively small proportion (15 per cent) of the students attending the school were either middle- or upper middle-class. Almost 43 per cent were from lower middle-class and skilled manual backgrounds while a further one-third (33 per cent) were from semi-skilled and unskilled backgrounds. Almost one-tenth (9 per cent) were from farming backgrounds. The school operated a system of banding which included a remedial class in each year. Along with St Dominic's, this was the only school in the study that did not offer the Transition Year[3] – as students and parents were not generally in favour of it. The school had a Student Council with representatives from every class.

Ollan Community College is formerly a vocational school and is situated in a large town. It is a medium-sized co-educational school and serves students from the surrounding countryside as well as from the local town. A non-denominational school under the management of the regional Vocational Education Committee, the school was well established and had expanded over the years. It was situated on a relatively small site and lacked adequate playing fields and sports facilities. The school's principal and vice-principal were both male although women comprised a significant minority of the staff.

The social profile of Ollan was more working-class than most schools, with the exception of St Dominic's and Ballycorish. While 28 per cent were from middle- and upper middle-class backgrounds, almost 32 per cent were from lower middle-class and skilled manual backgrounds. A further one-third (33 per cent) were from semi-skilled and unskilled backgrounds while 7 per cent were the children of farmers. The school operated a system of streaming for junior cycle students in second and third year. The school did not have a Student Council.

Ballydara Community College is a large co-educational school located in a city suburb. The school is relatively new and it serves a large, expanding suburb. The majority of students live close to the school. The building is quite recently constructed, and has sufficient space for staff and students. The school provides a wide range of academic and vocational subjects both for its second-level students and for a range of adult evening education courses. There was a reasonable gender balance among the staff in the school and it was managed by a male principal and female vice-principal. The school is non-denominational and is under the control of the regional Vocational Education Committee.

Just over one-third (34 per cent) of the students were either middle- or upper middle-class while 45 per cent were from lower middle-class or skilled manual backgrounds; 22 per cent were from semi-skilled and unskilled backgrounds. The school organises students into mixed 'ability' groups and utilises setting for core subjects (Mathematics, Irish and English). The school had a Student Council involving representatives from every class.

St Ita's is a large fee-paying co-educational secondary school located in a city suburb. It has a wide catchment area and caters for students of several different beliefs. The building stands in large, secluded grounds with good facilities. At the time the research was taking place, the fees in this school were IR£1,500 per annum. It had a large, gender balanced teaching staff, a minority of whom are paid privately by the school. The school principal was male and the vice-principal female.

The social class of the students was overwhelmingly middle-class: 91 per cent were either from middle- or upper middle-class backgrounds. A small proportion (7.3 per cent) were either from lower middle-class or skilled manual back-grounds, while a tiny proportion (1.6 per cent) were from semi-skilled, unskilled and other backgrounds. The school used mixed 'ability' (for further discussion on the problematic character of the concept of 'ability' see Chapter 4) through-out, with setting for core subjects (Mathematics, Irish and English). The school did not have a Student Council.

Concluding remarks

This study was a mammoth task undertaken on a limited budget. Collecting the data took two years to complete, while the data analysis took a further two years. While the study took much longer to complete than one might wish, it also gave us time to think, time to give presentations at various meetings of teachers and researchers, and time to have a protracted dialogue with the study schools. What we have attempted to provide at the end of all this work is a map of how schools work in equality terms. We analyse the ways in which their processes and practices facilitate the educational development of some students much more than others. We have learned a lot about the role of schools in the generation of inequality in society, and at times of their resistance to that inequality.

Part 2

Issues of redistribution

From a materialist perspective education is a social good: it is a resource and opportunity that enables one personally and occupationally (Connell 1993). Not being able to access, participate and achieve in education on equal terms with others is therefore a major equality problem in distributive terms.

As in many other countries, the groups that are currently most advantaged in education in Ireland, in simple distributive terms, are the upper middle classes, while those who are most disadvantaged are those from unskilled working-class households (Clancy and Wall 2000; Layte and Whelan 2000). This pattern is not new in Ireland nor in other countries; with some minor exceptions, the same classes have retained their relative advantages in education for decades (Breen *et al.* 1990; Shavit and Blossfeld 1993). If equality is to be promoted, the redistribution of educational 'goods' needs to be achieved. The advantage of some at the expense of others needs to be eliminated; the benefits of education have to be distributed according to principles of social justice rather than by the principles of economic advantage. Ultimately, therefore, the realisation of distributive justice in education, especially viewed from a social class perspective, demands creating the material conditions in society that enable all individuals and groups to avail of education on equal terms with others.

Promoting distributive justice in education is not a simple matter. There is no doubt that the social classes that are currently advantaged by schooling will defend their privileges. There is ample evidence, as we outline in Chapters 3 and 4, that they are already doing so. In addition, the mechanisms by which distributive injustices are enacted do not simply occur in one context. They operate across a wide variety of spheres, both inside and outside schools, and inside and outside classrooms. Some of the procedures by which inequality is perpetuated are not visible to the public eye, while others are so normalised and accepted that it is difficult to challenge them.

Realising redistributive changes in education across classes therefore is a major challenge. Indeed Bourdieu (1996) regarded it in some ways as a logical impossibility, insofar as education itself has become an institution that is designed and managed to ensure the transfer of privilege to the already privileged under the guise of certified competence. While there is no doubt that education is designed to advantage the already advantaged in many ways, there are opportunities within it for resistance and change, something Bourdieu (1998) himself admits in other contexts. Resistance can begin by naming the injustice, by dissecting the mechanisms of its operations and by highlighting the ethical implausibility of unjust outcomes.

While the need to redistribute educational 'goods' across classes is a major distributive issue, it is not the only one. Issues of distributive justice also arise in relation to the way in which intelligences are appraised in schools and students are subsequently allocated to tracks, including higher and lower (ordinary) level courses, streams or bands. Students who are placed in higher tracks are given the opportunity to avail of different forms of learning to those in middle or lower tracks. This can and does advantage certain students and disadvantage others in terms of educational and occupational opportunities, and in terms of their sense of themselves as persons and as learners.

In the following two chapters, we examine the various means by which schools produce different distributive outcomes for students across different tracks, and across social classes.[1] We explore also the complex interface between grouping in school and social class in particular, and we examine the means by which distributive issues can arise within the same classroom. By dissecting some of the major contexts in which distributive injustices arise, we hope to highlight specific contexts for action and change.

Chapter 3

The Class Act

A one-act play in four stages

Prologue

The failure of education as a social institution to eliminate social-class-related inequalities of opportunity became even more evident in the 1990s than it had been previously. Studies across several countries indicated how little life chances had changed between social classes despite educational interventions cross-culturally (Ambler and Neathery 1999; Breen 1998; Clancy and Wall 2000; Connell 1993; Erikson and Jonsson 1996; Kashti 1998; Shavit and Blossfeld 1993). Moreover, there was increasing evidence that conservative policies in countries such as the USA and the UK throughout the latter years of the twentieth century, had led to increasing rather than decreasing patterns of class-related inequality (Fischer *et al.* 1996; Glyn and Miliband 1994; Mortimore and Whitty 1997).

The recognition, at the macro level, that education may be a net contributor to class inequality rather than a net detractor has led to a whole new series of studies on how classes are created in education, and how in particular powerful middle- and upper-class groups operate to maintain their class advantages through education (Ball *et al.* 1995; Brantlinger *et al.* 1996; Erikson and Jonsson 1998; Crozier 1997; Hanley and McKeever 1997; Kerckhoff *et al.* 1997; Smyth 1999; Wells and Serna 1996). What all of these studies indicate is that class inequality in education is endemic to the education process as currently constituted. Bourdieu (1996) claims that it is likely to remain so, given the intimate association between the perpetuation of class privilege via schooling and the State's project in Western capitalist societies in particular. Yet he also recognises that change is possible; there is always scope for resistance (Bourdieu 1998).

One means of identifying the means and paths of resistance is by dissecting the processes of domination and control. As Connell *et al.* (1982) have observed, class inequality in education is fundamentally about sets of social relationships that are institutionalised; understanding the means to change therefore is about understanding the dynamics of these relations and how they are constituted and perpetuated. Empirical research enables us to explore the dynamics of control and power in education, and by so doing to identify the contexts for challenging inegalitarian practices and structures.

In this study we set out to explore how class works through education. We set about exploring class practices at different stages within schools. We examined the contexts of schooling and school choice, the methods of allocating students to classes, the dynamics within classrooms, and students' own views of the class processes and how they worked. We arrived at a map that indicated the staged nature of social class selection and stratification through schooling. Our data suggest that social class stratification is a staged affair with discrimination occurring through a complex web of eliminations.

The Class Act, Stage 1: stratification through economic policies

The first stage of the class act does not take place in schools. It takes place in the market context of global and local capitalism, in the deliberate stratification of power and income through labour markets and property markets. Classes are not only economically situated, they are also culturally and politically situated within the policy and legislative frameworks of the State (Bourdieu 1996). Class stratifications are made effective through legitimating discourses of rights and duties, abilities and talents, as well as industrial relations laws, property laws, wage agreements and welfare codes. The terms of a given class situation are normalised; they appear as natural and inevitable at a given time and in a given place. Stratifications outside of schooling exercise considerable command over the events within, albeit in complex and diverse ways. Education is both a major player in the normalisation event and a creator of that event: it creates class stratifications but within a legitimised code of discrete selections, examinations, 'ability' grouping or tracking, etc. It is also a product of class stratification, being controlled and managed at crucial times by interests outside of itself.

The class-specific practices that take place in school must be situated therefore in the wider politico-economic event that is class. Whether one is assessing the ability of students to access a particular type of education, or examining how the curriculum and pedagogical practices are classed, the wider context is always crucial. School may be a relatively autonomous site in how it realises the events of selection and stratification; it is far from autonomous however in its engagement with the social class project. As numerous studies of middle- and upper-class power and influence on education are now showing, cultural capital, as credentialised through schooling, is now a major force in the realisation and maintenance of class position, hence the close interface between class and economy in education.

The extent to which education is a class project in Ireland is borne out not only by empirical studies demonstrating the close links between social class and education outcomes (Archer 2001; Breen 1998; Clancy and Wall 2000; Eivers et al. 2000; Lynch and O'Riordan 1998; Ryan 1999) but also by numerous policy statements and reports that accept that education has very definite class effects (Department of Education and Science 1995, 2000; Higher Education Authority 1996; National Anti-Poverty Strategy 1997; Combat Poverty Agency 1998).

What is remarkable about the debate about class inequality in education, however, is its almost ritualistic character. While there is probably no single subject that has been researched in as much detail as class inequality in education, there have been no serious attempts at policy level to radically alter the class outcomes of education. Reports are written, the facts are presented but there is little in the way of radical policy change to alter education outcomes. While interventions are made, such as home–school liaison schemes, early start programmes, etc., the evaluations of these indicate that their effects at national level are limited (Kellaghan *et al.* 1995). The economic inequalities in the funding of education remain (Archer 2001) and are compounded by deeper and more persistent economic inequalities between classes (Cantillon and O'Shea 2001; Nolan *et al.* 2000). New Right ideologies about the sacredness of the market underscore and legitimate these class divisions, making dissent from the new national project of economic growth (irrespective of distribution) appear almost heretical (Allen 2000; Lynch 2000c).

Within education the debate about class inequality has not so much been silenced as it has been sanitised. The language used to denote class inequality is that of 'disadvantage', or, but less often, 'socio-economic status' in most official policy documents, and indeed in much academic research. Within such codes it is difficult to raise and analyse questions of class inequality in their relational context. Euphemisms for class such as 'disadvantage', 'weak students', or, in the adult education sector especially, 'community groups', remove class issues from their relational power and economic contexts and make mobilising for change around class all the more challenging (Lynch 2000c).

Economic inequalities are growing in Ireland. This was shown especially in the late 1990s (Allen 2000; Nolan *et al.* 2000); given the close interface between economic inequality and class-related educational inequalities, it is clear that these can and will exacerbate educational inequalities as they have done in other countries (Shavit and Blossfeld 1993). Our analysis of what is happening in schools therefore is situated against this wider backdrop of intensifying economic inequalities between classes.

The Class Act, Stage 2: social choice

The development of educational markets in Britain and elsewhere has been presented as providing parents with the ability to have real choices regarding their children's education. The opening up of educational markets and school choice has, however, made parental financial and cultural capital a more significant factor in accessing schools (Carroll and Walford 1996). There is evidence that some charter schools in the USA require the parents of prospective students to make substantial monetary and time commitments to the school as a condition of enrolment (Whitty and Power 2000). This marks a move towards the voluntarism that has characterised Irish education over a long period (Lynch 1989).

The focus on individual choice and opportunity in government rhetoric renders invisible the impact of such markets on equality concerns (Cole and Hill 1995; Reay 1996). Privileged groups tend to be better able to utilise the education system in such a way as to ensure optimum benefit for their own children, thus maintaining class stratification (Ball 1993; Ball *et al.* 1995; Hanley and McKeever 1997; Bourdieu 1998). Professional parents are more likely to operate as active consumers in an education market (Crozier 1997). There is evidence from both the USA and Japan that schools feel pressured into providing advanced tracks mainly catering for middle-class students in order to maintain middle-class enrolments (e.g. Wells and Serna 1996; McGrath and Kuriloff 1999; Kariya and Rosenbaum 1999). From the schools' perspectives, middle-class students are more desirable as they are deemed more likely to perform well in examinations, thereby enabling the school to continue to compete successfully in the marketplace; working-class students are more likely to be perceived as a liability, a risk to the status of the school in the so-called education market (Reay and Ball 1997).

School choice, voluntary contributions, fees and social class

Under the Irish Constitution, parents are defined as the primary and natural educators of their own children. They are free to send their children to any school they wish. Half of all second-level students do not attend their nearest school; those who are most mobile are middle-class children (Hannan *et al.* 1996).

Within our study social class-specific economic inequality manifested itself first in terms of one's ability to choose a school that was deemed to be most educationally advantageous. The most high status, academic schools were disproportionately subscribed by upper middle-class students. The most extreme examples of such 'class-related choices' were in the small but elite fee-paying sector. (These comprise approximately 7 per cent of all second-level schools nationally.)[1]

Three of the twelve schools in our study were fee-paying. Almost 90 per cent of the intake to these schools were drawn from social classes 1 and 2, the professional and managerial group. Only a tiny minority, 3 per cent, were from the classes 5, 6 and 7, the semi-skilled and unskilled group (Table 3.1). In contrast, 30 per cent of students in the three designated disadvantaged schools (two of which were secondary and one was a community school) were from social classes 6 or 7 while 24 per cent were from social classes 1 or 2, with four out of five of these being from social class 2. The remaining six schools occupied an interim position between these two extremes with the secondary (originally more academic and selective) schools being considerably more middle-class than the community colleges/schools (originally the more vocationally oriented and working-class). Although all schools have taught the same curriculum since the early 1970s, our data concur with research by Hannan *et al.* (1996) that secondary schools are still much more middle-class in their intake than community colleges.

Table 3.1 Social class profile of school types (Total n (questionnaires) = 1411)

School type	Prof./ man. (%)	Lower white collar/ skilled (%)	Semi/ unskilled/ other (%)	Farmers (%)	TOTAL (%)
Designated disadvantaged St Peter's (sec) St Dominic's (sec) Ballycorish (comm)	23.7 (8.6)a	43.4 (32.8)	29.9 (34.7)	2.9 (14.0)	19.4
Fee-paying secondary St David's St Ita's St Cecilia's	88.6 (47.4)	8.4 (9.4)	3.0 (5.1)	0 (0)	28.6
Free-scheme secondary schools St Patrick's Ballinroe Dunely Our Lady's	51.6 (34.3)	23.9 (33.1)	16.1 (34.3)	8.4 (73.7)	35.6
Community Colleges (formerly vocational schools) Ollan Ballydara	31.6 (9.7)	39.0 (24.8)	26.4 (25.8)	3.0 (12.3)	16.4
Total (%) Total n	53.5 755	25.7 363	16.7 236	4.0 57	100 1411

Note
a Column percentages in parentheses.

The way in which funding procedures reinforce social class-based 'choices' is also significant. Although all Irish schools are state funded, in terms of major capital and current costs (teacher salaries), many schools also rely to some degree on voluntary contributions requested from parents, or in the case of an elite number of schools, on fees. The amount that parents pay on the voluntary scheme varies greatly with the social class composition of the school intake. Thus schools with a high proportion of well-off parents contribute a disproportionately higher amount to the school annually resulting in differences in extra-curricular activities, sports and related facilities, and the number of additional staff employed (see Appendix A, Tables A2, A3 and A4).

Our findings reinforce evidence from the ASTI (1996a) regarding disparities in funding via voluntary contributions and fees. While designated disadvantaged schools do receive some extra financial support from the State in the light of their designated status, the income they receive is not remotely comparable to the income fee-paying schools command directly from parents. The fees charged in certain schools are also several multiples of what most schools would ask for, or receive, in terms of voluntary contributions.

From Table 3.2 it also clear that those who attend fee-paying schools pay whatever is required. However, other schools either do not ask for a contribution or, if they do, it is often unpaid, especially in the designated disadvantaged schools.

The system of funding Irish schools reinforces class inequality in a direct and highly visible manner. A small minority of elite secondary schools receive most of their capital and current funding from the state but are allowed to charge fees. While approximately half of these schools were originally established to serve minority religious groups (mostly Protestant denominations), this objective operates in close proximity to objectives of class perpetuation in both Roman Catholic and minority religion schools.[2]

The majority (approximately 60 per cent) of schools in Ireland are secondary schools. These are called 'voluntary schools' in the sense that they are operated voluntarily by religious orders and bodies, and a small number of private trusts. While they are mostly state funded, they are free to ask for a voluntary contribution from parents. As is evident from Table 3.2, and from research by the ASTI (1996a), the extent to which schools ask for a contribution varies considerably as does the amount that they request. While the voluntary character of the contribution may make it appear to be class neutral, this is far from being the case. The existence of a voluntary contribution can and does operate as a social class barrier when parents are unfamiliar with the school and are unsure of what they will be asked to pay, or indeed where they do know the amount of the voluntary contribution and cannot afford to pay it. While schools claim to be discreet in the manner in which they operate the voluntary scheme, and that they emphasise the voluntary nature of the contribution, this is not necessarily the perception of parents. Teachers in our study pointed out in their comments about inequality in education that the voluntary contribution operated as an indirect access barrier for those parents who felt they might not be able to meet the request. They noted that certain parents would feel that their children would be disadvantaged in a school if they could not pay the voluntary contribution; they would opt instead to send them to schools where no voluntary contribution was required. They also observed that although it was actually voluntary it was seen by some parents as a 'fee'. This was a psychological barrier to entry even though the amount involved was a relatively small one in many cases.

The net effect of the funding mechanisms in operation between schools is that a clear three-tiered system exists in terms of class stratification. The upper middle classes (including large farmers) can and do send their children to fee-paying

Table 3.2 Social class profile and voluntary contributions and fees levied by the schools (*n* = 12)

In social classes 1 and 2 (%)	School	Description	Amount 1996/7 (IR£)	Reported response rate
81.5	St Cecilia's[b]	ssg, city, fee-paying[a]	800	Full payment
93.2	St David's	ssb, city, fee-paying	1,400	Full payment
91.1	St Ita's	co-ed, city, fee-paying	1,400	Full payment
29.1	St Peter's	ssg, city, vol. contrib. (disadv)	60	Circa 15% pay
64.2	St Patrick's	ssg, town, Vol. Contrib.	60–100	Good response
34.1	Ballydara	co-ed, city, Com College	No levy	Not applicable
62.9	Ballinroe	ssb, town, vol. contrib.	100	Good response
28.4	Ollan	co-ed, town, Com College	No levy	Not applicable
42.3	Dunely	ssb, town, vol. contrib.	20	Good response
15.4	Ballycorish	co-ed, rural, Com Sch (disadv)	No levy	Very poor response to IR£8 fee for photocopy materials
25.0	St Dominic's	ssb, city, vol. contrib. (disadv)	10	Approx. 5% response
33.0	Our Lady's	ssg, rural, vol. contrib.	20	Discretion exercised in collection by class tutors

Notes
[a] Almost 7 per cent of Irish second-level schools charge fees. The remainder do not, but a number of these other schools do ask for a voluntary contribution from parents, and the amount requested varies considerably. However the voluntary contribution would never be anything near the cost of attending a fee-paying school.
[b] All names are pseudonyms.
ssb = single-sex boys, ssg = single-sex girls, co-ed = co-educational
disadv = designated disadvantaged, which means the school has a high proportion of students from low-income households. Approximately 25 per cent of all schools nationally have this designation.

schools where this is feasible (as many of the fee-paying schools are in Dublin and fewer and fewer are boarding schools, this is not always an option); less well off middle-class families are heavily concentrated in secondary schools, while working-class families are the most likely group to attend community colleges in particular (these were formerly vocational schools).

The cost of uniforms

The economic impact of class does not just operate through the existence of fees and voluntary contributions, it also impacts via other hidden costs such as school uniforms and transport.

The cost of school uniform varied considerably across the study schools. School uniforms in some of the participating schools were relatively simple and inexpensive, comprising a specified colour shirt/blouse, a jumper and a skirt/trousers. Junior cycle students in Ballycorish (co-ed Com Sch), for example, calculated the cost of their full school uniform at between IR£49 and IR£73, depending on whether they bought a pair of trousers or a skirt. Place of purchase was not specified, and uniform items were possible to acquire in any of the low cost chain stores. Other aspects of appearance such as coat, jacket and footwear were unspecified. This was the case in both of the community colleges in the study as well. There were no negative comments in student essays regarding the cost of school uniform in any of these three schools.

However, in other schools, all of which were secondary, uniform was much more tightly controlled and was a more complex affair. Each of the fee-paying schools had uniforms that were highly specific and costly. In conjunction with the standard dress of shirt/trousers/skirt, they also had school blazers and coats; the school also specified the type of footwear and stockings/socks that were to be worn. In St Ita's (co-ed, fp), for example, junior cycle students calculated the cost of the uniform purchased at the beginning of that school year at between IR£250 and IR£300, inclusive of all the auxiliary items, such as physical education attire. The school blazer alone cost IR£80 and was available only in a specified department store. St Cecilia's (ssg fp) required students to have two pairs of school shoes, one for indoors and the other for outdoors, for the purpose of protecting the school flooring. In this school, the extra expense incurred in buying the complete school uniform was noted by students as a problem for some pupils although the school was fee-paying.

Although uniforms in free-scheme secondary schools were not at all as expensive as those in the fee-paying schools, they were more expensive than those required in the community school and colleges. They also varied between each other in cost depending on the tradition and location of the school. Uniform specifications in St Patrick's (ssg fr) included school blazer, school gabardine coat and a school jacket. Students were not permitted to wear their own jackets or coats to school. This school had at one time been a girls' boarding school and had retained some of the dress regulations of that time. Some students resented both the cost and appearance of these:

> The school coats are so horrible and you have to wear them or else it's a note in your journal and some families don't have money for the coats or black shoes.
>
> (A second year student, St Patrick's [ssg fr])

The school makes us wear uniform coats and I think that is unfair, some parents refuse to buy them for students as they are very expensive and make them wear their own jackets but when they come to school wearing them they get into trouble through no fault of their own.

(A third year student, St Patrick's [ssg fr])

In contrast with St Patrick's, St Dominic's was a secondary boys' school in an inner city area. It had a long tradition of educating working-class boys. The cost of the uniform was low, more on a par with community colleges, and much less specific than in girls' schools like St Patrick's which was much more middle-class in intake (see Table A5).

School uniform was therefore both a signifier of the class status of the school and a creator of that status. It operated as an indirect cost barrier to parents on low income discreetly serving to discourage them from 'choosing' that school. It had the opposite effect on middle-class parents, serving as an indicator of both the higher status of the school, and the likelihood that there would be fewer students from working-class backgrounds attending.

Transport

School fees, voluntary contributions or uniform requirements are not the only barriers to school choice; transport is also an important consideration in both rural and urban areas. While there is public transport to school at a nominal cost for all second-level students, many parents choose not to avail of it for all types of reasons – such as the times and routes of buses, the length of the school journey by bus, place of work of parents, etc. It is the parents with access to private transport (and the time to use it) who can choose most freely to take their children to a school outside their own immediate area. However, in large surburban and urban areas, having access to particular public bus or train routes also enables parents to choose schools that are a long distance from their home.

Students were asked to name their most frequent mode of transport to and from school. Over one-quarter (28 per cent) of all these students reported travelling to and from school by car most days. While those attending schools in towns with a large rural catchment area reported a higher level of dependence on private motor transport than did their peers attending city schools generally, the highest rate of dependence on cars across school types was reported in the fee-paying, city schools. Well over half (58 per cent) the students in St Cecilia's and 46.1 per cent of those in St David's reported being brought to school by car although both of these were city schools on good public transport routes (Table A6). In the third fee-paying school, St Ita's (a city school with good public transport), 31 per cent were taken to school by car. This was the fourth highest level of car dependence, just lower than Our Lady's (ssg fr) which was a totally rural school with girls coming from a wide range of catchment areas.

The strong interface between social class and use of private car transport is also evident from Table 3.3. Students from social classes 1 and 2 were the least likely of all classes to walk to school, indicating that they were commuting to schools well outside their areas; only 27 per cent of them walked compared with 40 per cent of classes 5, 6 and 7. Car usage was also far higher in classes 1 and 2: over one-third (36 per cent) went to school most days by car compared with less than 20 per cent in all other social classes.

In interpreting the findings regarding transport to school, one needs to exercise caution. As public transport in rural areas is generally very poor, there is a relatively high level of car ownership even among families that are not very well off. Having a single car is not a signifier of social class position in this context (although type and age of car, and number of cars might well be). Thus many children in rural areas can and do travel to school by car for a host of different reasons that we did not investigate. In urban areas, however, cars are not as essential as public transport is much more accessible. However, it is clear that upper middle-class families tend to use cars much more than other social classes to transport their children to school. We did not investigate the reasons why they used cars, but our observational data and knowledge of the school contexts indicate that it was a combination of reasons, including having two cars so one parent was available to take the children by car; the school commute was a very long distance from the student's home; the school was on a parent's work route; or, in the case of girls especially, parents believed that travel by car was safer. Further research would be needed however to investigate the link between school choice, social class and the use of private transport.

School traditions

Social class stratification between schools is not entirely related to the demand side of the choice equation, it is also related to the supply side; it is also an outcome of how the school presents itself to parents. Although 93 per cent of schools are free and open to all students without fees, schools within the secondary school sector in particular vary greatly in their traditions and in their interest in educating different classes. Most schools are under the management of Catholic religious bodies that are social class stratified among themselves. Certain religious orders have focused on educating the upper middle classes (most notably the Jesuits and Holy Ghost orders for males and the Loreto and Sacred Heart orders for females) while others, such as the Christian Brothers and the Sisters of Mercy, traditionally educated the academically oriented working class and lower middle classes (Hannan and Boyle 1987). Protestant schools have also been disproportionately middle-class in intake in large urban centres in particular for a range of historical and cultural reasons.

Although the social class profile of many schools has changed over time, especially after the introduction of free second-level education for all in the 1960s, several schools that were traditionally socially and/or academically

Table 3.3 Students' mode of travel to school by father's social class (n = 1241)

	Prof./man (%)	Lower white collar/skilled (%)	Un/semi-skilled/ other (%)	Farmers (%)	TOTAL (%)
Walk	27.2	39.6	41.3	0	31.6
Cycle	7.6	4.8	2.1	12.3	6.1
Car	36.0	18.5	17.0	19.3	27.7
Public transport	25.0	26.4	28.9	57.9	27.4
Other/ combination	4.2	10.7	10.7	10.5	7.2

selective still retain relatively elite profiles. Even though these schools do not charge fees and cannot select overtly on academic grounds, they often promote themselves in their prospectuses as academically oriented schools and/or schools that encourage types of extra-curricular and sporting activities that are more associated with the middle classes. Three of the schools in the study (St Patrick's [ssg fr], Ballinroe [ssb fr] especially, and Dunely [ssb fr]) were of this type. Each of these had been involved in the past in selecting on the basis of academic attainment (St Patrick's had had a boarding school as well) although these were now free-scheme secondary schools. Both staff and students in these schools noted that although the schools were now non-selective free-scheme schools, the perception among many local people in the areas in which they were located was that they were still designed to cater for a relatively socially select and academically-oriented intake. The fact that both St Patrick's and Ballinroe had some 60 per cent of their intake from social classes 1 and 2 while Dunely had 42 per cent from these groups (Table A5) indicates clearly how social class traditions lived on in these schools and how correct prospective parents were in their assessment of the school's social profile. Teachers commented on this matter in our discussions with them. They claimed that the identity of the school would discourage some low income parents from applying. In each case, these schools co-existed in towns with other second-level schools that continued to serve disproportionately higher numbers of working-class students.

One of the community colleges in the study (Ollan) was also very visibly affected by its historical profile. It had been the only non-selective school in a particular urban neighbourhood for over thirty years; it was therefore identified in the public mind as being neither socially nor academically selective. The principal and staff in this school claimed that many people (from middle and upper classes especially) would not send their children there because it was profiled in the public mind as a school that traditionally served high numbers of students from working-class and small farm backgrounds. This remained the case despite the expansion and development of the school in terms of student intake, and in spite of its academic and extra-curricular achievements.

The social class project of a school was visible in many ways, most conspicuously in the quality of the school environment, including the quality and range of school facilities. It was also visible in more subtle ways: in the types of sports and extra-curricular activities promoted in the school; in the presence or absence of prospectuses; in the quality of design work, printing and paper used for year books, magazines or prospectuses; in the images presented of 'successful' past pupils; in the types of plays/musicals that were staged (if at all); and in the language used to describe events. The extent to which a school used its historical image to present itself in the present also indicated its status: the more socially selective schools were those that were most likely to record the origins of their school and its importance as an education institution in their published material.

It is clear therefore that the history of a school is part of what it is in the present. It is not easy for a school to escape a given identity, especially when the historical profile is a low status one. Where a school has had a strong selective profile historically (in academic and/or social terms) this also appears to affect the current intake, especially when schools do not take any steps to dispel the selective image. As Reay (1996) has observed, parents read the school messages clearly, they know from the way schools project themselves that some children are more welcome than others and they 'choose' one where they know their child will fit in best.

The classing of schools takes place therefore through a complex series of social engagements and practices. First it is evident that access or lack of access to resources impacts on people's ability to make choices, both in terms of their ability to pay fees or voluntary contributions, as well as their ability to buy uniforms or transport their children to the schools of their choice. In a society in which there are still major differences in wealth and incomes (Cantillon and O'Shea 2001; Nolan *et al.* 2000), what this means, in effect, is that those who have resources can exercise choices and those without resources generally cannot, or have relatively restricted choices depending on the area in which they live. The exclusions occurring through lack of resources are compounded by the way schools profile themselves and are profiled publicly by their past. Schools can and do remain social class selective by living off a socially and academically elite trajectory. They can and do fail to dispel beliefs about the need to belong to a particular class, or the need to have reached certain levels of academic attainment to have access to a given school. By so doing they indirectly exclude students from particular social class backgrounds. Schools that are known historically to have a working-class profile face the opposite type of social class problem; in spite of creating more academic and middle-class profiles, they live with the legacy of their working-class identity. This acts as a disincentive for middle-class parents to choose that type of school for their child.

The Class Act, Stage 3: 'ability' grouping

If one were to find a generative theme, a dominant word that would encode the class selection and exclusion process in its class-neutralised form it would probably be 'ability' (see Chapter 4 for a more detailed discussion of this problematic concept). 'Ability' is frequently a euphemism for class; it neutralises class debate within a culture and an education system that prides itself on its meritocratic values. As Department of Education policy prohibits schools from selecting students on the basis of academic attainment, 'ability' only comes into play however when prior selections have been undertaken.

Stage 3 of the class stratification business begins when students are grouped in school on the basis of so-called 'ability'. Although streaming, tracking or banding are theoretically class-neutral systems of organising learning groups, this is not the case in practice. Our data suggest that the social class profile of the school influences both the type of grouping system that prevails in the school and allocation across groups.

The grouping of students in Irish schools is directly related to the way the curriculum and assessment systems operate. At both junior and senior level almost all subjects are offered and assessed at two levels, higher and ordinary. At junior level, three core subjects (Irish, English and Mathematics) are offered at a foundation level as well. In most schools, from second year onwards, students tend to be either set, streamed or banded, therefore, according to the level at which they take a subject. The nature, level and extent of grouping does vary considerably however according to school policy, size, gender composition, tradition and other variables (Hannan and Boyle 1987; Hannan et al. 1996; Smyth 1999).

As grouping is a complex affair, it can be difficult to decipher how it operates within a given school. The difficulty is exacerbated by the sensitivity of the subject involved. Because many school principals and guidance teachers are aware of the limitations of rigid streaming or tracking (from well publicised research studies such as those cited), they can be and are quite cautious in their disclosures on the subject. The sensitivity and complexity of the practice of grouping were demonstrated by the fact that in a number of schools, teachers, school principals and students varied to some degree in their accounts of the grouping procedure. To ensure that we had accurate data on grouping therefore we used a range of sources including official school records, as well as student and teacher views on how grouping worked.

All twelve schools in the study grouped pupils for at least some subjects according to some measure of attainment at both junior and senior cycle levels. While setting by level of subject taken was the most common form of grouping in the senior cycle, it was also the mechanism used to group students in the junior cycle in the six schools that did not have a more general form of streaming or banding.

The three fee-paying schools (and these were almost entirely middle-class, being mostly upper middle-class) had no streaming or banding. Each operated so-called 'mixed ability' systems throughout the junior cycle with setting for core subjects (Irish, English and Mathematics, and, sometimes, heavily subscribed subjects such as French, depending on the number of students in each class). While three secondary (non-fee) schools operated similar systems, two of these indirectly streamed classes by encouraging more academically oriented students to make particular subject choices, and by grouping students accordingly. In all, six schools had some direct form of banding or streaming: three boys' and one girls' secondary (free-scheme) schools, one community college and one community school (the full details on how schools grouped students are presented in Chapter 4, Table 4.2 when grouping is discussed in detail).

The grouping of students into bands or streams on the basis of so-called 'ability' (in reality according to some measure of attainment) is predominantly a junior (12–15/16 years) phenomenon as students in senior cycle are generally either set according to whether they are taking higher or ordinary courses, or in mixed classes (Smyth 1999). Senior cycle students also have more choice about the level at which they take the subject, depending on their junior cycle performance; it is easy to move from higher to ordinary but not vice versa.

Students from lower white collar/skilled (social classes 3 and 4) and semi/unskilled/other (social classes 5, 6 and 7) backgrounds were more likely to attend schools using streaming or banding as a method of class organisation than were those from the professional/managerial group (Table 3.4): 62 per cent of all students from the semi/unskilled aggregate social class grouping and 52 per cent of those in the lower white collar/skilled manual grouping were attending schools using streaming or banding compared with 37 per cent of students from the professional/managerial class.

Not only was the grouping system in a school related to the social class composition of the school, so was the band or stream to which one was allocated. Students from working-class backgrounds were disproportionately allocated to the lower status streams or tracks while those from the professional and managerial classes were more likely to be in mixed classes than in any other type of grouping: only 11 per cent of students from professional backgrounds

Table 3.4 The proportion of students from different social classes in schools with different types of grouping in the junior cycle (n = 799)

Type of grouping	Prof./man. (%)	Lower white collar/skilled (%)	Semi/ unskilled other (%)	Farmers (%)	Total (%)
Streamed/ banded	36.7	52.1	62.1	60.7	46.1
'Mixed ability' and setting	63.3	47.9	37.9	39.3	53.9
n	420	211	140	28	799
TOTAL %	52.6	26.4	17.5	3.5	100

were in low streams or tracks while almost 70 per cent were in mixed classes; the comparable figures for students from semi or unskilled backgrounds were 36 per cent in low bands/streams and 46 per cent in mixed classes. Students from semi or unskilled manual backgrounds were the least likely to be in a higher banded or streamed class (Figure 3.1).

Another way of assessing the relationship between social class and stream or band position is by examining the proportion of students in high and low stream/band classes who were from different social classes. While students from professional/managerial backgrounds made up over half (53 per cent) of the junior cycle sample, less than one-third (30.4 per cent) of those in lower streams or bands were from this class; by comparison, 18 per cent of the junior cycle sample were from semi- or unskilled manual backgrounds and almost one-third (32.3 per cent) of those in low bands or streams were from this class. Students from other white collar, non-manual and skilled manual classes were also disproportionately represented in lower streams and bands: they comprised 26 per cent of the sample but 34.2 per cent of those in lower streams and bands (Table A7).

The relationship between social class and the grouping of students in schools was recognised by a number of teachers in different schools:

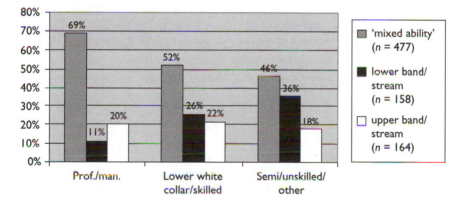

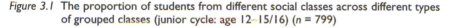

Figure 3.1 The proportion of students from different social classes across different types of grouped classes (junior cycle: age 12–15/16) (*n* = 799)

Key
The social class categories are aggregated as follows:
'Prof./man.' comprises Social Classes 1 and 2, higher and lower professional and managers;
'Lower white collar/skilled' comprises Social Classes 3 and 4, namely all white collar workers not in classes 1 and 2, Other non-manual and skilled manual;
'Semi/unskilled/other' comprises Social Classes 5, 6 and 7, semi-skilled manual, unskilled manual and occupation unknown;
'Farmers' have been assigned as a separate category as it was not possible to collect reliable information regarding farm size from school students.

There is certainly a concentration of lower social class levels in lower streams. This is a negative state of affairs in my opinion.

(Female teacher, St Patrick's [ssg fr])

Social class is the *final* deciding factor in deciding which class [ability level] a pupil enters.

(Male teacher, Ballycorish [co-ed Com Sch])

Unlike England and Wales, but similar to a number of countries in Europe, students in Ireland do not undertake national examinations during primary education; students' first public examination is in their mid-teens, when they do the Junior Certificate which is the examination at the end of compulsory schooling. However, most primary schools do administer standardised attainment tests in Mathematics and English (especially) and Irish, to students at different intervals during their primary career. At the end of primary school, a summary profile report, based on these tests and on related information regarding the student's overall performance across the curriculum, is compiled (and on her/his general attitude to learning and behaviour). It is passed on to second-level schools. In addition, most second-level schools also administer tests in Mathematics, English and Irish to primary school candidates prior to entry for the purposes of allocating the students to different classes. The class to which the student is allocated generally is an outcome of how the school assesses a student's primary record and/or their performance on pre-entrance tests. Little is known about how these various forms of information are utilised by the second-level schools to place students; the matter has never been subject to any serious study to date. Yet the decision about where to place a child in school is arguably one of the most serious decisions made about his/her educational future. The band, set or stream to which a student is allocated has profound implications for their educational and occupational futures (Lynch 1989; Smyth 1999). Very often, however, neither the students nor the parents are fully aware of the implications of the grouping system (Lyons *et al.* 2002).

While social class selection and division take place at the school choice stage, it also comes into play when students are being allocated to classes. Grouping operates as yet another mechanism for social class stratification, no matter how unwittingly that may happen. Upper middle-class students are the students who are least likely to be placed in low streams or bands within schools that track, but they are also the least likely to attend schools that group rigidly by band or stream in the first instance. The opposite is true for working-class young people, especially those from semi- or unskilled manual backgrounds: only 15 per cent of those in high streams or bands were from semi- or unskilled backgrounds compared with 51 per cent from professional and managerial backgrounds (Table A7).

The Class Act, Stage 4: classroom climates

The relative social class homogeneity of many classes meant that classrooms were not contexts in which class inequalities manifested themselves in terms of conflict. Prior exclusions and selection had made classrooms relatively homogeneous thereby ensuring that the learning environment of the classroom was relatively class–tight.

This is not to suggest that social class divisions are confined to either the school choice or class allocations stages of education. Life inside classrooms was also a mediator of social class effects, albeit very often via grouping practices. The learning environment in predominantly middle-class top streams or bands, and in mixed classes, was noticeably different to that of lower streams or bands where students from working-class backgrounds were more likely to be allocated. The way in which social class manifested itself within classrooms was in terms of differences in styles of control utilised with higher stream/band (and more middle-class) groups in comparison with lower streams/bands. While it is appreciated that lower stream/band classes were not at all exclusively working class in composition, working-class and lower middle-class students were disproportionately represented within them, while the reverse was true for higher bands/tracks and 'mixed ability' classes.

The lowest incidence of disruption was recorded in higher streams/bands: in all, almost one-quarter of all such classes had no disruptions that required the teacher to reprimand students or call for their attention. The comparable figure for low streams/bands was 4 per cent, while it was 14 per cent for mixed classes (Figure 3.2).

Not only were high streams/tracks and mixed classes the classes with least disruption, they were also classes in which the forms of control exercised were most work-focused. We observed how methods of control tended to vary across classes with some teachers deploying more work-oriented systems of control than others. The methods involved included the use of individual questioning,

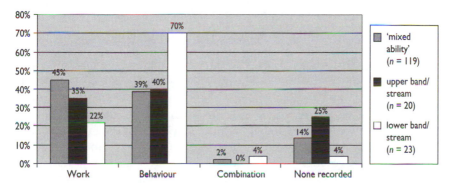

Figure 3.2 Overall methods of control employed by teachers in observed classrooms by grouping type (n = 162)

extra work allocations, and refocusing on the task in hand for the purposes of maintaining student attention. In other classes, the control mechanisms employed focused more heavily on student behaviour. It involved the correction of the student behaviour as a group, the correction of individuals in terms of appearance or behaviour, or giving punishments such as detention.[3]

Behaviour-related corrections and sanctions were employed in 40 per cent of the observed high stream classes and 39 per cent of the 'mixed ability' classes. The comparable figure for low streams was 70 per cent (Figure 3.2). In contrast, 35 per cent of the controls employed in high streams/bands and 45 per cent of those in mixed tracks were work-related while this was true in only 22 per cent of low streams/bands.

The use of work-related methods of control rather than the correction or sanctioning of individual social behaviour or personal demeanour suggests that there is quite a different learning environment across tracks, notably that it is more work-centred in higher bands and mixed classes. This is something we examine in more detail in Chapter 4 where it is shown how more time is spent on-task in high stream and mixed classes and there is less negative teacher interaction with students than in low tracks (Figures 4.3 and 4.4).

The fourth stage of the class act takes place within classrooms therefore. Not only are upper middle-class students more likely to attend selective schools, and be allocated to less selective and higher status classes within these, they are also more likely to be in classes that are less disruptive and have a more work-oriented learning environment. Although it is evident that grouping procedures in school are not coterminous with social class stratification systems, they are none the less quite closely interfaced with them. Grouping on the basis of prior attainment (so-called 'ability') is an integral practice in the perpetuation of social class inequality in education.

Epilogue

As Allen (2000: 1) has observed:

> Ireland was supposed to be different. The two main political parties did not divide on left–right lines but were broad catch-all parties that garnered support from all quarters of society. The elite did not go to private schools and talk with different accents to the rest. They were 'self-made men' who had been to the Christian Brothers schools and followed their local GAA[4] teams. Class was a British thing, associated with grimy factories and aristocrats who spoke with a plum in their mouths. Maybe it was the memories of the War of Independence or the strength of Catholicism, but there was a sense of a 'national community' – not class division. . . . It was always a myth. The 'self-made men' usually turned out to be the sons of former captains of industry. . . . It was always much harder for individuals from a working-class background to 'move up' the ladder in Ireland than it was in Britain.

Class discourses: euphemisms and the individualising and personalising of class differences

In effect, social class differences in Ireland have been denied, hidden behind the language of nationalism, community and, more recently, social partnership. Although class permeates the micropolitics of our lives, it hides behind the face of 'differentials' in trade union language; it is catalogued in the form of 'careerism' among the middle classes; it is sidelined into debates about work versus welfare in the 'poverty' debates, and it is depoliticised in educational debates as 'disadvantage'.

People rarely talk about class politics; where social classes are named, it is in euphemistic terms (Lynch 1999c). For the last ten to twenty years, people in low income working-class households have been termed the 'disadvantaged', the 'socially excluded' or the socio-economically marginalised. The language of social class is not part of the vocabulary of either politics or education, a phenomenon that is by no means unique to Ireland at this period of global capitalism (Pakulski and Waters 1996). Moreover, working-class identity is in several respects a negative identity (Reay 1998; Skeggs 1997); it is increasingly one which can only be named or claimed indirectly.

It is not surprising therefore that when naming the inequalities that they experienced in education, very few students named the problem directly in terms of social class. Even though education is profoundly implicated in the social class project, students rarely defined education in class terms, even euphemistically. Only 4 per cent of all student essays named class-related inequality as a problem for them in their school (see Table A8), and the students who named class as an issue were not predominantly working-class. Even in schools such as St Dominic's (ssb fr) where students were visibly disadvantaged in resource terms by their social class, there was little talk of social class differences per se and their effect on students' lives. When we tried to probe students on this matter in focus groups, we were sometimes confronted by a denial of class differences. Students even seemed embarrassed by the subject, saying that they did not know why we were asking questions about 'social background':

> [The class background of other students] isn't important to most pupils. Like, they'd know alright, but they wouldn't care.
> > (Sixth year female student, focus group participant, Ballycorish [co-ed Com Sch])

Social class differences were individualised; they were seen as attributes of particular persons that only became important when someone tried to use her/his more powerful class position to dominate others in inter-personal relations. Social class was not named in political terms.

> [Social class background] isn't important. You'd only slag someone rich if they were picking on someone who wasn't as rich as them.
> > (First year male student, focus group participant, Ballydara [co-ed, Com Col])

> They [students in this school] wouldn't care about anyone's background.
>
> (Sixth year student, focus group participant,
> Dunely [ssb fr])

The denial of class was paralleled by an ambivalence about class. Students from low income working-class backgrounds generally named social class differences in terms of perceived social demeanour, including accent, and sometimes wealth: the 'other' were those who 'were posh', or 'snobs', or who had 'rich' parents. They also equated being middle-class with being 'swots' or 'brainy'. The equation of middle-class status with academic ability indicates how the concept of being 'good at school' has become synonymous with being middle- or upper-class in the eyes of some students.

The term 'social background' was the closest phrase to social class that was used, and even this term was used very rarely. Middle-class students (especially) defined students in terms of the housing they lived in; they referred to the fact that they lived in a 'good area' and that others were from 'rough' areas. In many cases the name of the housing estate or the address was a surrogate term for class.

Sometimes class designations were derogatory. In one of the fee-paying schools, students referred to students from a community college (with whom they were debating) as 'knackers' and 'scumbags'. On the other hand a person who was seen as socially elite in a school with a mixed social class intake was defined as a 'snobby cow':

> Some of the students are prejudiced against others. Say one person from our class who lives in . . . [local area] thinks she is brilliant and that people from . . . [outlying suburb] are poor. Which is not true. She is a snobby cow. She is always telling people they are poor because they don't have a new school jumper, etc.
>
> (A third year student St Peter's [ssg fr])

Teacher or school management preference for wealthier students or those with higher social status also led to occasional comments:

> A lot of students get treated better if their parents are richer or have more important jobs.
>
> (A fifth year male student in Ballycorish [co-ed Com Sch])

> I think that students should be treated equally regardless of their family or social background. In my school, students whose parents are teachers in the school are given more attention and encouragement. In class, when the teachers is explaining something he/she looks directly at them as if there was no one else present. They never seem to get anything wrong and when they occasionally do the teachers tries to cover it up and makes excuses for

them. Students who come from a poor social background are not treated with as much respect.

>   (A sixth year female student in Ballycorish
>   [co-ed Com Sch])

Comments about the impact of parental status or wealth on how one was treated in school also arose in the fee-paying schools:

> Everybody should be treated the same regardless of their parents' standing on committees, boards, etc.
>   (A female sixth year student, St Ita's [co-ed fp])

There was a perception that those who were wealthier or more important were more likely to be believed and supported by the school institution.

> One girl accused me of bullying her and because she was very rich, they believed her and they wouldn't believe me and I hadn't actually done anything so that all went on my records.
>   (A second year student, St Cecilia's [ssg fp])

The claiming and denial of social class

While students were aware of class, and status differences within classes, there was an ambivalence and uncertainty around class that found expression in the way in which students classified themselves in social class terms, especially among students who would be social scientifically defined as being from a working-class background. In general, middle-class identity was positively appropriated but working-class identity was not: 90 per cent of those in the professional/managerial class (Classes 1 and 2) defined themselves as middle-class with 30 per cent defining themselves as upper middle-class and 4.4 per cent as upper-class. Only 2.6 per cent of the professional/managerial group defined themselves as working-class. Almost 70 per cent of semi- and unskilled workers also defined themselves as middle-class, with only 21.6 per cent defining themselves as working-class (Table 3.5). In all, only 9 per cent of students claimed working-class status although three times that number were from groups traditionally defined as working-class: 13 per cent were from households where their parents were semi- and unskilled manual workers and 15 per cent were from skilled manual backgrounds.

The reluctance to claim working-class status was illustrated clearly in focus group discussions in St Dominic's (ssb fr), a boys' inner city school. Although boys in this school had not claimed they had experienced any unfair treatment in school due to their social class, they were none the less aware that where they lived was seen as a 'bad area' and something to be hidden from outsiders such as employers or potential friends:

Table 3.5 A comparison of students' self-defined class and their social scientifically designated class (*n* = 1,411)

Selected class identity (in italics)	Social scientific designated social class				
	Prof./ man. (%)	Lower white collar/ skilled (%)	Semi/ unskilled (%)	Farmers (%)	Total (%)[a]
Upper class	80.5	7.3	4.9	7.3	2.9
	4.4	*0.8*	*0.8*	*5.3*	
Upper middle class	77.6	11.9	8.8	1.7	20.8
	30.2	*9.6*	*11.0*	*8.8*	
Middle class	55.1	26.4	14.0	4.5	53.2
	54.8	*54.5*	*44.5*	*59.6*	
Lower middle class	28.7	43.4	25.4	2.5	8.6
	4.6	*14.6*	*13.1*	*5.3*	
Working class	15.6	35.9	39.8	8.6	9.1
	2.6	*12.7*	*21.6*	*19.3*	
Unemployed	0	20.0	80.0	0	0.4
	0	*0.3*	*1.7*	*0*	
Unsure	35.7	38.6	24.3	1.4	5.0
	3.3	*7.4*	*7.2*	*1.8*	
Overall % of the sample in that class – using social science classifications prof/man/small proprietors Classes 1, 2	53.5 of which 22% higher prof./ man./large proprietors 31.5% lower skilled manual Classes 1, 2	25.7 of which 10.5% were from other non-manual 15.2% were unknown Classes 3, 4	16.7 of which 8.8% semi-skilled 4.5% unskilled 3.4% class Classes 5, 6, 7	4.0	100 *n* =1,411

[a] The percentage of the whole sample that described themselves as being in that class.

> Miss, when you're on your holidays, I say I'm from Claremont not from Henry Street flats, because people are prejudiced against the flats. They see us all as scumbags.
> (Second year male student, focus group participant, St Dominic's [ssb fr])

Another boy in the same group said that if he was going for a job

> I would lie about my address at a job interview and when they ask me where are you from – I'm going to say Castleknock or something.
> (Second year male student, focus group participant, St Dominic's [ssb fr])

Given the strong meritocratic ideology that pervades education in particular and social life generally, students' reluctance to claim working-class status is not really surprising. After all, much of education is about social mobility, or the promise of social mobility out of one's class; middle-class jobs (especially in the professions) are presented as positive choices, while unskilled or semi-skilled jobs are not. In fact, such jobs are often used as examples of the failure that can follow from not doing well in school.

Unlike students in St Dominic's, students in the fee-paying schools displayed confidence in their social class and in particular in the schools they attended. They were quite interested in talking about their school, the positive light in which it was perceived and the privileges it bestowed on them.

In a second year focus group in St Cecilia's (ssg fp), the girls described how their school is viewed by those outside as 'the little posh one up on the hill'. Students in the fifth year focus group in the same school said that 'pupils have a good name partly because we are well-spoken'. They regarded their school as quite homogeneous in class terms: sixth years claimed that 'there is no real snobbery here – most of us would be in the same social class, the same backgrounds'.

Students in the sixth year focus group in St Ita's (co-ed fp) were aware that the school provided a socially exclusive environment. One of them explained that St Ita's was not the sort of school to welcome those outside a certain group in society – something she considered to be wrong. She explained that if a working-class student arrived at the school this person would be made unwelcome and would be excluded in subtle ways by both students and teachers because of obvious differences such as accent.

The third years who participated in the focus group discussion in St David's believed that attending a fee-paying school gave them a better education. One boy said 'My mum just thinks that if she pays for it, it's got to be good', while another said 'My mum just wanted to give me a chance. She didn't want me to be in a messer class.' There was also a perception that it would advantage them later on in life: 'I'll have a better chance of employers giving me a job.' While the fourth boy saw it as helping him get into a good university because it would 'probably be better recognised abroad, like in Oxford'. A sixth year focus group participant from St David's said that 'the place has a reputation for sending out gentlemen' and another agreed, saying that it was his mother who was keenest to send him there so that he would be a 'gentleman', and laughed saying that it impressed his grandmother and his aunts. Another explained that their parents like sending them to a school like St David's because 'they see it as their way of giving us the best chance'.

Sensitivity to class

The essays and focus group interviews with students suggest that most students did not think that teachers or peers in their school favoured students from one social class above another, and in that sense schools were seen to be internally neutral in class terms. The social class selection that occurs prior to second-level entry seems to diminish class conflict within schools. Yet there was a tendency for upper middle-class students to view teachers in particular as being more class neutral than did other students. In response to the statement 'In this school, where you live and how much money you have makes a difference to the way you are treated by teachers' (Q63), while 24 per cent and 25 per cent of students from Classes 1 and 2 respectively agreed with this statement, 31 per cent and 32 per cent of students from Classes 5 and 6 held this view as did 30 per cent of those from Class 7. Students from Classes 6 and 7 were also the most likely to strongly agree with the statement.

Although students displayed embarrassment and discomfort about social class, they were aware of its significance albeit in politically neutralised language. There was a deep sensitivity around class differences that only became visible on occasions. This was illustrated clearly in one critical incident involving two schools in the study. During the course of the research St Cecilia's (a fee-paying girls' school) and St Peter's (a designated disadvantaged girls' school) were involved in a debate. Although St Peter's won, the girls involved felt that in general the adjudicators in such debates were biased in favour of teams from 'private schools', because of 'the way they talked'. Their team had lost the final of a debating competition the previous summer to another fee-paying school. Both the team members and their teacher felt that there had been unfair bias on the part of the adjudicators. The girls from St Peter's and their teacher were also upset by what they perceived to be a slur on their social background by girls from St Cecilia's; they claimed that the captain of the losing team in St Cecilia's insulted them after the debate. The teacher from St Cecilia's who was in charge of the debating team explained that the captain of his team had gone up to congratulate her opposite number saying 'you were brutal to us'. This was meant as a compliment to the skill with which the St Peter's team had dispatched them. However, this remark was interpreted by the St Peter's girls and their teacher as insulting – they believed that their performance was being denigrated. This incident was discussed at some length by both students and teachers involved in the debate after the event and was obviously still the source of much upset for both teams and their teachers.

Like students, teachers were also invited to comment on what they perceived to be the greatest inequality that both students and teachers experienced in their current school. While the issue of authority, and its use and misuse by management, exercised teachers in the same way that teacher misuse of power and authority concerned students (see Chapter 9), the issue of social class (called 'social background') inequality was also cited as a contributor to inequality for students, albeit by a small minority of teachers; 8.4 per cent of teachers named it as a cause of inequality for their students.

Some teachers stated that their peers did not hold students from certain backgrounds in high regard:

> Certain teachers look down on kids and their background – [these teachers have a] total lack of understanding and bias. [Their] narrow-mindedness and inexperience of hardship in their own lives, never experiencing 'the other side of the fence' [is the problem].
>
> (Female teacher, St Peter's [ssg fr])

Others claimed that middle-class students got preferential treatment both within their school or in education generally:

> Middle class [students] and high achievers are given extra attention and opportunity. Teachers are prejudiced towards well off and/or high achieving students.
>
> (Male teacher, Ollan [co-ed Com Col])

> In Dublin, schools are extremely categorised into social classes. Different schools are predominantly lower/middle/upper middle class, etc.
>
> (Female teacher, St Patrick's [ssg fr])

> All now favours the fee-paying student.
>
> (Male teacher, St David's [ssb fp])

> [An important equality issue in education is] equality of resources, availability of teaching aids etc. [This] varies too much throughout the strata of 'classes' in Irish second level schools from vocational to fee-paying.
>
> (Male teacher, Ballinroe [ssb fr])

There was a tendency however for some teachers to use deficit explanations for social class differences, to imply that it was sometimes the family's personal fault:

> [There is a] lack of understanding shown by teachers when dealing with students from socially deprived backgrounds. [There is a] lack of understanding of poor parenting practices.
>
> (Female teacher, Ballydara [co-ed Com Col])

> Students from poor home backgrounds can have a 'reputation' attached to them. There is some evidence of teachers targeting them so they get into trouble. Some staff [are] uncomfortable with the social problems that confront them.
>
> (Male teacher, Ballydara [co-ed Com Col])

Given that none of the three major political parties actually use class-based language to mobilise politically, and that there is no real social scientific education in Irish schools, around social class as such, although there are frequent references to 'poverty' (see the Programme for the new Civic, Social and Political Education course), it was highly unlikely that students would have an analytical vocabulary for class analysis. In so far as they were named at all, social class issues are presented in individualised and personalised terms. While both students and teachers were aware of class as a category, the language they used to name the world of class was politically neutral in almost all cases.

In discussions with students and teachers there was, in many cases, a sense of resignation as to the inevitability of class-related outcomes in education. There was little evidence of anger at the injustices emanating from class although a minority of teachers and students expressed disquiet and concern. There was a sense of people 'knowing their place' (Allen 2000: 1). However, there was a language to name social classes, one that did not cause embarrassment or discomfort. It was a euphemistic discourse centred around place of residence, 'good' or 'bad' areas, 'rough' or 'posh' areas; around wealth, 'rich' and 'poor' or 'people with money'; around status, 'snobs', 'posh people' and 'knackers'; and around language and accent, being 'well spoken', having a 'strong accent' (the latter being seen as working class).

Closing remarks

The way in which the Class Act is produced in schools is complex but systematic. It operates through a series of stages that are rarely subject to critical examination. Stage 1 begins with a set of politics and practices institutionalised in law and in economic and social policy that advantage the economically powerful and reinforce their dominance (see Cantillon and O'Shea 2001, Healy and Reynolds 1998, Nolan *et al.* 2000 for a detailed examination of these). Public policy places upper- and middle-class families at a considerable advantage in education as they have the economic resources to exercise choice, in what is in many respects a free market education system. Stage 2 of the Class Act is set when parents 'choose' a school for their children. Low income working class households are seriously disadvantaged at this stage as they frequently lack the money, transport, time and, sometimes, even knowledge, to discriminate between schools. It is middle-class families who exercise the freest choice. They can and do buy into the types of schools that will advantage their own children (Hannan *et al.* 1996). Class exclusions are not only operating in the demand side of the choice equation, they are also operating in the supply side as schools position themselves to attract the most educationally attractive students through a host of mechanisms that are clearly class biased; requirements regarding voluntary contributions, costly uniforms, and selection mechanisms that favour past pupils' children and those attending certain primary schools serving specific catchment areas, are all examples of procedures that advantage students from middle class families.

The third stage of the Class Act opens with the grouping of students by so-called 'ability' in schools. This is a highly invisible stage of the play as it has never been subject to substantive research scrutiny. However, our data suggest that both the type of grouping one is likely to experience and the group into which one is allocated are influenced by social class. Middle-class students are least likely to be in low streams or bands within banded/streamed schools, and they dominate the fee-paying schools where mixed 'ability' is the normal form of grouping in the junior cycle. Stage 4 moves inside the classroom door. Given that the classroom environment in top tracks and in mixed classes is frequently more work-oriented and more positive than that in low bands/streams, this means that middle-class students are once again advantaged educationally, even if they have not attended one of the more socially elite schools.

Both students and teachers are aware of social class and its significance, although they speak about it in politically neutralised terms. There is a sense in which social class is a silent subject, one about which there is much embarrassment and denial. When trying to discuss the issues associated with class inequality, we sensed a great unease, especially about calling anyone 'working class'. It was as if it were a term of denigration, something that one might be ashamed of and so left unclaimed.

Chapter 4

The grouping process: selecting out, selecting in

Introduction: 'ability' and grouping

It is not possible to discuss the subject of grouping in schools without recognising the complexity of the subject of 'ability'. While most research on education treats the concept of 'ability' as an unproblematic singular entity, this is far from being the case (Nash 2001). Even a cursory analysis of psychological research on education indicates that what constitutes 'ability' is a hotly contested subject (Devlin *et al.* 1997; Gardner 1985, 1993, 1997; Murray and Hernstein 1994; Simon 1978; Sternberg 1998). While the IQ-generated view of ability has been largely discredited by developmental psychologists, most recently by Howard Gardner and his team in the Harvard Zero Project, the concept of fixed and immutable intelligence has a strong hold in public consciousness, including that of teachers (Fontes and Kellaghan 1983). Students are frequently classified as 'bright' or 'dull', 'gifted', 'slow' or 'weak' without any reference to the insights of developmental psychology or education research. Moreover, students themselves have internalised and accepted these codes as we will show below.

We do not subscribe to the singular definition of ability or intelligence, or indeed to the view that what constitutes ability is simply what is measured and tested in schools (Lynch 1985, 1987a, b, 1992, 1999a). However, given the pervasiveness of so-called 'ability' grouping in schools, we recognise the importance of the subject as a lived practice. Even though the students are unjustifiably labelled or grouped as 'weak' or 'able', especially when ability is assessed in narrow singular (most often, linguistic) terms, nevertheless what is defined as real is real in its consequences (Znaniecki 1973). We have to examine the implications of so-called 'ability' grouping even though it would be more accurate to define what happens in schools as grouping based on prior attainment in specific subjects. To signify our rejection of the singular, absolutist view of 'ability', we refer to the subject throughout in inverted commas. Following Gardner, our view is that there are several intelligences or abilities rather than a singular entity called 'ability' or intelligence, and that each of these is open to development and change.

Efficiency and stratification

The importance of educational efficiency has reasserted itself internationally during the last two decades (Lauder *et al.* 1999). The creation of educational markets and the use of league tables, in countries such as England, has put pressure on schools to achieve the best results in order to either maintain, or raise, their current status (Mahony 1998). Schools are judged on quantifiable outcomes, such as examination results, and streaming is being revisited as a potential means of raising educational standards in a competitive market system (Ireson and Hallam 1999). So-called 'ability grouping'[1] is seen as a means of attracting middle-class parents to send their children to a particular school (Reay 1998).

Within this product-driven climate, grouping by academic achievement is frequently recommended as a policy option because of its apparent efficiency. Although the concept of efficiency in education, in and of itself, remains under-scrutinised (Ball 1989), it is argued that 'ability' grouping simplifies the organisational work of the school. There is a widespread belief that it simplifies timetabling and curricular provision, and enables teachers to plan lesson content and pedagogical approaches for a relatively homogeneous group of learners (Bennett deMarrais and LeCompte 1999; Sukhandan and Lee 1998). 'Mixed ability' teaching, on the other hand, is often regarded by teachers as inherently problematic because of the increased demands of planning, and the limitations of whole-class teaching with a more hetereogeneous group (Drudy and Lynch 1993; Sukhnandan and Lee 1998).

While the efficiency arguments may be defensible from a narrow organisational perspective, they are not tenable from a student perspective. The classification of learners based on their ascribed academic ability reflects a narrow interpretation of ability and intelligence (Gardner 1985, 1993; Sternberg 1998). This holds whether students are organised into ability-segregated classes, or are individually labelled as 'good' or 'weak' within 'mixed ability' classes (Lynch 1999a). The stratification of learners creates a hierarchy among students, where some are deemed to be more academically capable and successful, and are thus regarded as the more valued members of the school community. Such a hierarchical organisation of learners, and the consequent differentiated education they experience, is an equality concern. Differentiated curricular practices are a close correlate of tracking: such procedures perpetuate the advantages of certain social groups by giving them access to superior educational credentials (Connell 1993). Rigid grouping also promotes a sense of alienation among those who are negatively evaluated (Hargreaves 1967; Lacey 1974; Oakes 1985; Boaler 2000). Students who are tracked into low streams or bands, or who are otherwise negatively labelled on ability grounds, are the most likely to disengage from school. The disruption and disengagement that emerge in the low streams or tracks are an inefficiency outcome of streaming and tracking that cannot be ignored.

'Ability' grouping and differentiation in school

Students in stratified 'ability' groups are provided with differentiated curricula depending on their perceived academic capability (Boaler 1997a). Students in higher track classes are more likely to experience challenging, quick-paced lessons encouraging critical, independent thinking, while their counterparts in lower groups are more likely to be encouraged to develop diligent working habits and to learn factual information (Oakes 1985; Hacker et al. 1991).

There is conflicting evidence as to whether the organisation of students into classes stratified by ability actually benefits learners in academic terms (Betts and Shkolnik 2000; Rees et al. 2000; Sukhnandan and Lee 1998). While work by Argys et al. (1996) claims, for example, that the abolition of stratified 'ability grouping' would result in increases in lower achieving students' examination achievements at the expense of those who are higher achievers, there is ample evidence to challenge this claim. Many researchers have demonstrated how 'ability grouping' particularly disadvantages those allocated to the lower tracks (Oakes 1985; Gamoran et al. 1995; Smyth 1999). Smyth's data (1999) suggest that placement in lower streams or bands has negative consequences for students without simultaneously advantaging their higher grouped counterparts.

Where there is some agreement is in relation to the outcomes of grouping, in terms of its effects on students' self-image and status. Student self-esteem differs across stratified ability groups (Oakes 1985; Smyth 1999). Those in lower tracks are more negatively perceived, both in terms of their behaviour and expected academic attainment, by teachers and by their higher tracked counterparts (Sorenson and Hallinan 1986; Taylor 1993; Wang and Haertal 1995; Hallam and Toutounji 1996); they are also more likely to experience greater alienation from school and have negative relationships with teachers (Murphy 2000).

Systematic grouping into streams or tracks also appears to have independent effects on educational expectations. Lower tracked students have lower expectations of educational outcomes, and demonstrate less commitment to school both in terms of academic work and extra-curricular involvement (Berends 1991, 1995; Jenkins 1997). They are also more likely to drop out of school early (Berends 1995). Where they are stratified by academic ability, students tend to form friendships only with those in similar 'ability groupings', thus leading to social as well as academic segregation of young people (Gamoran et al. 1995; Kubitschek and Hallinan 1998).

Academic and social segregation also impacts on internal stratification of students by social class within schools. There is a large corpus of evidence from a number of different education systems showing that students from lower socio-economic groups are more likely to be located in lower tracks in school (Ball 1981; Douglas 1964; Jackson 1964; Taylor 1993; Rees et al. 1996; Boaler 1997a, 1997b). Evidence from studies conducted in Irish second-level schools shows that working class students are more likely to attend schools that stratify classes by ability (Hannan and Boyle 1987; Lynch 1989). This link between social class and stratification by ability means that economically advantaged students are more likely to access the curriculum that enhances their educational and life chances than are their less advantaged peers (Oakes and Guiton 1995). The advantaged position of middle-class students is not merely the result of a bias by the school in their favour. It is partly the consequence of their parents' greater knowledge of the workings of the education system and of schools, as well as their ability to exert influence over, or manipulate, decision-making in the tracking system (Oakes and Guiton 1995; Brantlinger *et al.* 1996; Wells and Serna 1996; Crozier 1997; McGrath and Kuriloff 1999). In some cases, as international evidence demonstrates, economically advantaged parents simply buy their way out of a public system into the private educational market that stratifies classes by ability (Kariya and Rosenbaum 1999).

It would be unwise, however, to suggest that ability differentiation in schools is solely tied to streaming or banding. The study of primary schools by Barker Lunn (1970) demonstrated clearly how teachers can track students mentally and physically in mixed classes. Hierarchical value systems around ability and achievement can remain intact in mixed classes. Students can be negatively labelled as 'low ability' by peers as a result of having difficulties completing or understanding set class work (Pye 1988). Even young children demonstrate an ability to rank themselves and their classmates according to academic ability (Crocker and Cheeseman 1991).

Teachers and 'ability' grouping

Although there has been little attention given to the impact of 'ability' grouping on teachers, it is evident that it does have implications for them. Teaching students in higher tracks is seen as inherently more psychically rewarding by many teachers. Relationships between students and teachers in high track classes tend to be more positive, task-oriented and quick-paced (Oakes 1985; Sorenson and Hallinan 1986; Harlen and Malcolm 1997; Boaler 1997b). Teachers tend to invest more in preparation for, and delivery of classes to, these groups (Oakes 1991). They are also more likely to transmit positive expectations to students in higher streams or bands (Boaler 1997a, 1997b). Conversely, learners in lower tracks tend to be more negatively regarded by teachers, being seen as more difficult both to discipline and to teach (Taylor 1993).

The use of streaming or banding may also create a hierarchy amongst teaching staff, where those deemed to be most experienced and competent are most likely to be assigned the high tracks (Finley 1984; Oakes 1991; Taylor 1993). Conversely, there is some evidence that the least experienced, or least effective, teachers have been allocated to lower streams or bands (Elton Report 1989; Lynch 1989).

The national context

Parents in Ireland have a constitutional right to control the education of their children subject to certain minimal requirements. They may send their child to the school of their choice within the limits of availability and personal resources. While most primary school children attend their nearest school, 50 per cent of second-level students do not (Hannan *et al.* 1996). Not surprisingly, it is middle-class parents who exercise most choice.

Although parents have a choice of school, second-level schools are not permitted to select students on the basis of academic ability. While most undertake tests of primary students prior to entry in Mathematics, English and Irish, these tests can only be used to group students on entry, they cannot be used for selection. Second-level schools also receive primary school reports on new entrants, and these are used to group students, in combination with the entrance tests.

Despite the formal prohibition on selection on academic grounds per se, schools are allowed to select on the basis of other criteria, many of which have a similar effect on intake to selection on academic merit. Selection on the basis of catchment area, nominated feeder schools, and other informal selection mechanisms, such as the 'first come first served principle', family ties with the school, or siblings attending, are permitted. These lead to relatively homogeneous social class and academic achievement profiles in the intakes in several schools.

The extent to which schools can and do select entrants influences their grouping practices. However, this is not the only consideration as schools differ in their policies about grouping depending on their tradition and ethos. Boys' schools, for example, have traditionally had a stronger tradition of streaming than girls' schools regardless of the nature of their entrants (Hannan and Boyle 1987; Lynch 1989). In addition, the reasons why schools stream or band may differ. Some schools group students to ensure that there is a track that is strongly academic and will thereby attract educationally ambitious parents to send their children there – this is especially true of schools with a socially and academically diverse intake such as community colleges and vocational schools. Others group because it has been part of a traditional belief in the educational merits of a selective system.

While the reasons for 'ability' grouping differ, grouping on the basis of academic attainment is widespread throughout second-level schools in Ireland. Moreover, it is not a recent phenomenon although it varies both within and between schools in the manner in which it is practised (Hannan *et al.* 1996). With the introduction of free second-level education in the late 1960s and the consequent expansion of secondary education to all, schools managed differences by streaming, setting and banding students (Hannan and Boyle 1987; Lynch 1987). As all subjects at both the junior (age 12–15) and the senior level (age 16–18) are examined at higher and ordinary levels, the structure of the curriculum and assessment lends itself easily to 'ability' grouping. The introduction of a three-tier programme into the compulsory junior cycle subjects of Irish and Mathematics[2] (higher, ordinary and foundation) led to a renewed emphasis on 'ability' grouping in the junior cycle, the argument being that it was impossible to teach students of such different ranges in the one class. Although grouping by attainment (that is, in terms of higher and ordinary level) is widespread in the senior cycle where class sizes permit, it is widely accepted at this stage of education as senior cycle students are in the post-compulsory phase of education and their choice to do higher or ordinary level papers is partly their own. It is dependent, however, on their Junior Certificate performance in the relevant subjects. Ability grouping in the junior cycle is more problematic however as students have little or no say as to the set, stream or band in which they are placed. Moreover, when students take ordinary or, in particular, foundation-level, courses in the junior cycle this seriously restricts their future educational and occupational choices.

The implications of 'ability' grouping

Grouping procedures[3] in the case study schools

A general invitation was issued to all teachers in the case study schools to offer classes for observation. A representative range of classes was then chosen for observation and audio recording from those that were volunteered. In selecting classes the goal was to obtain as representative a range of age groups, subjects and abilities as was practicable. This objective was achieved although there was an understandable reluctance on the part of teachers to allow us to observe what they defined as their more 'difficult' classes. Teachers were clear that they felt more comfortable with observation taking place in classes they regarded as well-behaved or academically able. For example, in Ballinroe (ssb fr), one teacher had initially agreed to allow one of the researchers to observe two different classes, but changed her mind and cancelled one of the visits. She explained that she only felt comfortable about the planned visit to a high stream group as she was afraid the lower stream group would misbehave and 'let her down'. Despite the limitation imposed by high levels of teacher selection of observed classes, important differences were recorded in the climates of classes with different attainment levels.

Given that the majority of classes in the schools studied were 'mixed ability', it is not surprising that most of the classes observed and recorded were defined as 'mixed ability' (73 per cent). Just over one-quarter of observed classes were either banded, streamed or set into lower or higher groups (Table 4.1).

All twelve research schools used academic attainment as a means of organising classes to a greater or lesser degree. Six of the schools used either streaming or banding to organise junior cycle but not senior classes. The remaining six used 'mixed ability' grouping for most junior cycle classes along with the setting of the core subjects, Irish, English and Mathematics. At senior level, 'mixed ability' with setting for core subjects (and some highly subscribed subjects such as languages) was in operation in all of the schools (Table 4.2).

Table 4.1 Types of grouping in observed classes (*n* = 162)

Ability grouping type of observed class	Numbers by category	Total n
'Mixed ability' group		119
Total lower track groups:		23
lower stream	4	
lower band	5	
pass/foundation set	12	
remedial group	2	
Total higher track groups:		20
upper stream	6	
upper band	5	
honours set	9	
Total observed classes		162

It is evident from Table 4.2 that grouping practices were quite standardised in the senior cycle but more varied at junior level. The schools that were least likely to stratify pupils rigidly were the fee-paying schools, none of which operated a streaming or banding system in the junior cycle although their class sizes would have allowed it. However, these schools did set students in Irish, English and Mathematics so they did have some tracking. Three of the four boys' schools operated a streaming system for most or all of the junior cycle while none of the girls' schools had streaming, although one operated a banding system. The three community schools and colleges varied most in their grouping with one having 'mixed ability' and setting, one having banding and one operating a straight streaming system.

Banding, streaming, stratifying: equality concerns

While grouping on the basis of academic achievement is frequently portrayed as a technical procedure for managing learning and teaching efficiently, our data suggest that students or teachers directly affected by it do not regard it in this way. All forms of stratification by achievement are viewed problematically by students especially, but also by many teachers. Using multiple sources of evidence including student essays, focus groups and questionnaires, teacher questionnaires and classroom observations and recordings, we outline below the diverse ways in which stratification by so-called ability is operating in education.

Students displayed a keen awareness of the significance of ability grouping and academic stratification generally, both in terms of their ongoing educational experiences and their educational futures. Their concerns about grouping and academic differentiation were among the most significant equality concerns to emerge spontaneously from their essays; they were second only to concerns regarding the exercise of authority and power. Almost one-fifth (18 per cent) of all student essays outlining their experiences of unfair or unequal treatment in their school expressed concerns about various aspects of academic ability differentiation. This was true not only in relation to streaming or banding, but also in terms of how teachers in mixed classes differentiated in terms of perceived ability (see Table 4.3).

Ability differentiation and labelling

Concerns regarding grouping varied across schools, reflecting the method of class grouping in use as well as the prevailing school climate. Some students regarded the use of any form of grouping by attainment as a source of unfair treatment in and of itself.

> There shouldn't be any separate classes for students of different intelligence.
> (A fourth year student in Dunely [ssb fr])

Several students commented on the negative labelling associated with membership of lower sets or bands. Students in low streams and bands reported feelings of inadequacy and failure after being assigned to these classes. The language they used to describe themselves indicated at times that they had internalised the subordinating 'ability' codes about themselves:

> If you are not that brainy you are put in the lower [set] class and I think everyone should do the same level as you feel very low.
> (A fifth year male student who had been set in lower status, ordinary level, tracks [Ballydara co-ed Com Col])

> And all the teachers think we're dumb.
> (A first year female student commenting on her experience in a low stream class in Ollan [co-ed Com Col])

> I think all the classes should be equal. [We ought] not to have smart students in one class and have stupid students in another.
> (A third year male student in a low band class in Ballycorish [co-ed Com Sch])

Concerns about the unjust outcomes of grouping were not confined to students in low tracks; students in higher bands were also aware of the stigma attached to being in a lower group:

> The students who are not as academically gifted should be treated equally to those who are academically talented. I think that teachers are more sympathetic and patient with the higher grade classes. I am in a higher grade class. . . . The lower level classes are often referred to as 'weak students' which I think is extremely unfair. I would like to see these students being treated with more respect and patience.
> (A third year high band student in St Patrick's [ssg fr])

Table 4.2 Grouping procedures at junior and senior levels

School	Description	Procedure for grouping if applicable	Type of grouping in junior cycle	Type of grouping in senior cycle
	Mixed Ability at junior cycle			
St Peter's	ssg, fr (disadv)	Informal grouping promoted by subject choice	Mixed Ability + core setting[a]	Mixed Ability + setting for cores and highly subscribed subjects[a]
Ballydara	co-ed, Com Col		Mixed Ability + core setting	Mixed Ability + setting for cores and highly subscribed subjects
St Ita's	co-ed, fp		Mixed Ability + core setting	Mixed Ability + setting for cores and highly subscribed subjects
St David's	ssb, fp		Mixed Ability + core setting	Mixed Ability + setting for cores and highly subscribed subjects
St Cecilia's	ssg, fp		Mixed Ability + core setting	Mixed Ability + setting for cores and highly subscribed subjects
Our Lady's	ssg, fr	Informal grouping promoted by subject choice	Mixed Ability + core setting	Mixed Ability + setting for cores and highly subscribed subjects
	Streaming/ banding at junior cycle			
St Patrick's	ssg, fr	Use primary reports and entrance test to band in 1st yr. Top 40% in upper band; 60% in lower band. No shared classes across the 2 bands in junior cycle	Banding 1st, 2nd, 3rd yr; re-grouped at end of 1st year: 20% top band, next 20% 2nd band, 60% in 3rd low band	Mixed Ability + setting for cores and highly subscribed subjects
Ballinroe	ssb, fr	Grouped at end of 1st year based on end-of-year tests	Streaming 2nd, 3rd; mixed ability 1st yr	Mixed Ability + setting for cores and highly subscribed subjects
St Dominic's	ssb, fr (disadv)	Use of primary reports and entrance test to stream	Streaming 1st, 2nd, 3rd yr	Mixed Ability + setting for cores and highly subscribed subjects

Ollan	co-ed, Com Col	Use of primary reports and entrance test to stream	Streaming 1st, 2nd, 3rd yr	Mixed Ability + setting for cores and highly subscribed subjects
Ballycorish	co-ed, Com Sch (disadv)	Use of tests given in primary and early in 1st year to band	Banding 1st, 2nd, 3rd yr. 2 bands – upper band had 3 groups all mixed; lower band of 2 small classes	Mixed Ability + setting for cores and highly subscribed subjects
Dunely	ssb, fr	Grouped at end of 1st year based on end-of-year tests	Streaming 2nd, 3rd yr; mixed ability 1st yr	Mixed Ability + setting for cores and highly subscribed subjects

Note

[a] The core subjects referred to here are Irish, English and Mathematics. In addition, most students are required to take history, geography, civil, social and political education, a European language and science for the Junior Certificate (but not the Leaving Certificate). Students take an average of 9–10 subjects for the Junior Certificate Examination and 7–8 for the Leaving Certificate Examination.

Several teachers also expressed concerns about the poor self-esteem of students assigned to lower track classes, whether these were streamed, banded or set. Some also commented on the low institutional regard for, and labelling of, these students relative to their higher placed peers.

> I feel that streaming is unfair as it leaves *the weaker child* with very little self-esteem and thus they have little or no ambition to do well.
>
> (Female teacher, Ballycorish [co-ed Com Sch]. Emphasis is ours here, and in the following quotes)

> Banding for 2nd and 3rd years creates a poor self-image.
>
> (Male teacher in Ballinroe [ssb fr])

> Lower stream students are just *bricks in the wall*.
>
> (Female teacher in St Patrick's [ssg fr])

> Students of low ability are not being given enough attention and not being encouraged to do their best. A higher standard of effort should be demanded of students in low streams [sets].
>
> (Female teacher in Ballydara [co-ed Com Col])

> I suppose mainly the more academic student is perceived as the top group in the school so as a result the *weaker student* feels very inadequate.
>
> (Female teacher in Our Lady's [ssg fr])

Table 4.3 Proportion of student essays expressing concerns regarding 'ability' grouping and stratification (*n* = 1,202)

Ability grouping type used at junior cycle	Essays concerned with ability differentiation (%)	Total essays from school type
Schools with streamed/ banded junior cycle	15.5	547
Schools with mixed ability + set junior cycle	20.0	655
Total %	18.0	
Total *n*	216	1202

> *Weaker classes* I think have been treated as '*the duds*' referred to as '*stupid*' etc. Higher classes are referred to as 'the better students'.
>
> (Female teacher in Ballycorish [co-ed Com Sch])

While the empathy the teachers expressed with students assigned to low sets or bands is clear, their remarks also suggest they hold deep-rooted essentialist views of students' abilities. The most widely used expression to describe students in lower streams or bands is 'weak'. A binary code of 'the weak and the strong' seemed to inform teacher judgements about students' abilities, with those defined as 'weak' being regarded as educationally more demanding.

Grouping and academic self-image

When filling out their questionnaires, students were invited to describe and rate themselves in a range of different ways, including perceived cleverness and educational ability. There were clear differences across ability groups as to how students rated themselves in these categories. Almost 75 per cent of those in higher track classes regarded themselves as 'clever or very clever' compared with 37 per cent of those in lower bands; the figure for 'mixed ability' classes was 56 per cent (Figure 4.1).

Both students in 'mixed ability' and those in high banded or streamed classes were very unlikely to describe themselves as 'below average' – only 3 per cent and 2 per cent respectively did so. However, one in ten of those in the lower banded or streamed groups rated their intellectual ability negatively. There were interesting gender differences in the ways students rated their ability. In 'mixed ability' groups as well as in lower banded or streamed classes, boys were more likely to describe themselves positively than were their female peers. However, the reverse was the case in higher banded or streamed classes where girls were more likely to rate themselves as very clever.

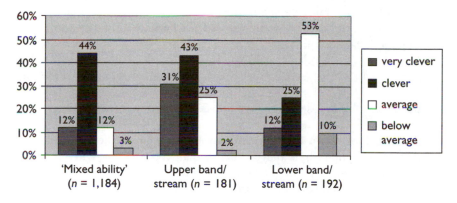

Figure 4.1 Students' rating of their cleverness across academic ability groups (*n* = 1,557)

Students were also invited to rate themselves on a seven–point scale in terms of their ability at school. There were clear differences between those located in higher and mixed ability groups, and their peers in lower ability classes in terms of their self-rating. Students in higher track and 'mixed ability' groups were significantly more likely to rate their school ability positively than were their lower tracked peers. At the other extreme, almost one–fifth of the lower streamed or banded students placed themselves in the 'weak at school' range compared with 10 per cent of those in mixed ability classes and 6 per cent of those grouped in higher streamed or banded classes.

Impact on relationships and learning environments

Student–teacher relationships

Both students and teachers expressed concerns about the ways in which stratified ability grouping impacted on the quality of classroom relationships. There was a widespread belief that teacher interest was based on one's academic abilities regardless of what type of grouping was in operation. Students claimed that teachers preferred either those students in the higher stream classes, or individuals who were regarded as high achievers.

> To make it more fair in school I think the teachers should not keep on pestering pupils and they should not judge some people like saying she is stupid and not giving her another chance. Or saying she is brainy and expect her to get an 'A' on every test.
>
> (A first year student in a higher band class in St Patrick's [ssg fr])

> [What would make school fair would be] All the classes getting treated fairly and not all the brainy people in one class. All [the top stream class] think they're so brainy and everyone else and teachers are always comparing us to [them] and it's unfair.
>
> (A first year female student in a low stream class in Ollan [co-ed Com Col])

Students in mixed classes also raised concerns about the stratification:

> Teachers look down their noses at some pupils and make remarks about them. Some pupils think they are better than everyone else and make little of the people who are not as clever as themselves.
>
> (A second year student in a mixed ability class, Our Lady's [ssg fr])

Students who found particular subjects difficult, or who were not high academic achievers, believed teachers held them in low regard because of this:

> The Maths teacher never really takes any notice of me in class mainly because I find [it] hard and I have the lowest score in the class. I think I will not progress anywhere.
>
> (A second year lower stream student in Dunely [ssb fr])

> I think all students should be treated equally by teachers. If you're not very clever, the teachers shouldn't embarrass you in front of your classmates; they should help you with your problem and not make you feel stupid in class.
>
> (A sixth year female student in Ballycorish [co-ed Com Sch])

High achieving students, on the other hand, were regarded as receiving preferential treatment from the teachers:

> My English teacher can be nice to me but there's a girl in my class who is very clever. He is always praising her and the rest of the class he thinks aren't any good. He is always comparing us to this clever girl.
>
> (A second year student, St Cecilia's [ssg fp])

Some teachers shared the student views about teacher disinterest in students who were not achieving good grades:

> Some teachers have difficulties dealing with 'weak' or troublesome students – [there is] very little encouragement given to weaker students.
>
> (Female teacher in Ballycorish [co-ed Com Sch])

The learning environment across ability groups

Although the classes observed were only those volunteered by teachers in consultation with the researchers, and in that sense biased in favour of manageable or 'good classes' in teachers' terms, nevertheless there were important differences between them in terms of learning climate.

Classes were grouped into four different categories according to the proportion of their total recorded interactions that were on-task. Lower track groups were least likely to have a high proportion of class time on-task: less than half of lower stream or band classes (48 per cent) had a high proportion of class time on-task compared with 65 per cent of high streams or bands. 'Mixed ability' classes were closer to higher rather than lower bands or streams in their time-on-task profile (Figure 4.2).

Students in lower track groups were also more likely to experience classroom environments characterised by a higher level of negative teacher–student interaction as measured in terms of the use of ridicule or sarcasm and other regulatory remarks regarding their behaviour, demeanour or appearance (Figure 4.3). Teacher use of ridicule was recorded in 30 per cent of all lower track classes compared with 16 per cent of mixed groups and only 10 per cent of higher groups. There was also a higher level of incidences of surveillance in the lower band or stream classes.

There were some differences across class types in the incidences of ridicule and surveillance recorded. We did not record any instances where teachers used ridicule in single-sex girls' classes, regardless of attainment level. However, female and male students in single-sex classes were subjected to surveillance, even in higher track classes, albeit less frequently than their lower banded or streamed

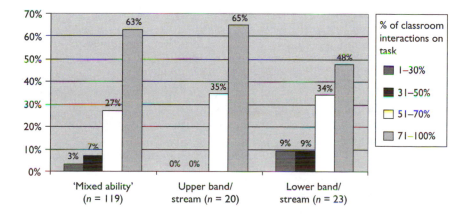

Figure 4.2 Differences across ability groups in classroom interactions that were 'on-task' (*n* = 162)

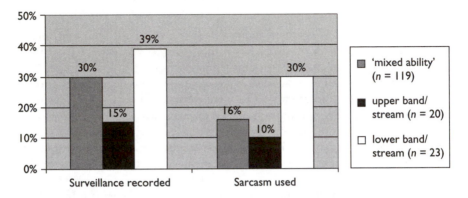

Figure 4.3 Proportions of classrooms where teachers used surveillance[a] and sarcasm in their interactions with students across ability groups (n = 162)

Note
[a] We have defined *surveillance* in this context as teacher criticism or correction of the student's person (appearance, demeanour, posture, expression) rather than of any specific misbehaviour, such as lack of attention or active disruption.

peers. There were no recorded incidences of surveillance by teachers in higher banded or streamed classes in co-educational schools.

Differentiation within mixed classes

A number of students in mixed classes claimed that there was greater attention given to students taking the higher papers:

> When I was doing my junior cert, I was in an honours [higher level] Irish class but I was doing pass. My teacher never spent any time with me doing work. There were five pass pupils and we were all intelligent because we were in the top 60 out of 120 in our year. But the highest anyone got was a B in pass. I got a C. I struggled through my work because 5 minutes out of every 40 minutes was spent on us. This has almost ruined my career ambitions of being a teacher.
>
> (A fourth year student in Ballinroe [ssb fr])

Within-class streaming

Of the 162 classes we observed, just three were internally streamed into higher and ordinary level groups. Two of these were Business Studies examination (Junior and Leaving Certificate) classes, one in a boys' school and the other in a girls' class in a co-educational school. There were eighteen students in one class and nineteen in the other; higher level students comprised 39 per cent of the girls' class and 47 per cent of the boys' class. The third class was a senior cycle Biology class. Due to the nature of the work taking place (individual revision) it was not possible to compare this class with the other two as there was too little student–teacher interaction the day we observed it.

We analysed the two Business Studies classes in detail to determine if students' claims about differential treatment in mixed groups were tenable. We found that teachers did differentiate between pupils to the advantage of the higher course students in both of these classes. In both cases those taking higher level papers received a disproportionately higher amount of teacher time and attention (Figure 4.4). In the girls' class half of all recorded teacher assistance was given to students taking the higher level paper although they comprised 39 per cent of the class. All work-related praise given by the teacher went to individuals in this group; in addition, almost all public engagement about the comprehension of the work at hand was with these students. They also received a disproportionately low level of criticism from the teachers for their behaviour.

In the single-sex boys' class, 75 per cent of all work-related praise was given to those doing the higher level course although they comprised just 47 per cent of the group (Figure 4.5). In contrast, all public criticism in the class was directed towards the students taking the subject at ordinary level. In this class, however, most public engagements with students about the comprehension of the material and related issues (87.5 per cent) were with students taking the paper at ordinary level. The teacher was involved in social interaction (jokes) with two students in the class, both of whom were taking the paper at higher level.

What these two cases indicate is that stratification can and does occur within mixed classes. In each of the classes, students taking the subject at ordinary level were subjected to far more criticism for their behaviour, yet they were not

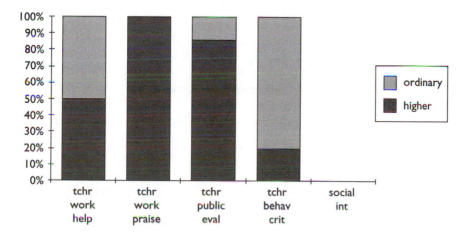

Figure 4.4 Differences in teacher–student interactions in a mixed group (single-sex girls' business studies class, 6th year, Ollan [co-ed Com Col])

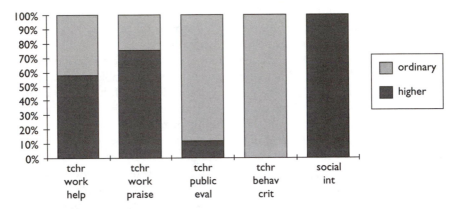

Figure 4.5 Differences in teacher–student interactions in a mixed group (single-sex boys' business studies class, 3rd year, Dunely [ssb fr])

evidently more disruptive or inattentive than students taking the subject at higher level. The tone of the teacher's interaction also differed across the groups, with teachers being more supportive in both classes of those taking the higher level course. Both teachers gave these students 'tips' for the forthcoming examinations but did not give similar advice to the students taking the ordinary level course. The teacher in the boys' class clearly disliked one of the students taking the ordinary course, calling him by his surname throughout and asking him to 'shut up' when he asked a question at one time.

Academic ability and peer relationships

Regardless of the type of grouping in operation, students were keenly aware of their lower status if they were not academically successful in school. They felt that other students did not respect them:

> Some pupils think they are better than everyone else and make little of people who are not as clever as themselves.
> (Second year student in a mixed class in Our Lady's [ssg fr])

> People don't treat me right because I'm not as intelligent as the other pupils in the year.
> (Second year student in a mixed class who was in lower sets for core subjects, in St David's [ssb fp])

Teachers in a number of different schools also expressed concerns about the level of emphasis on high academic attainment generally. They expressed particular concern about the awarding of prizes for examination achievement and academic excellence to the exclusion of all else. They noted how such a system served a privileged few:

> The sixth year awards are very exclusive. The majority of students are made to watch a small select minority for academic achievement. It excludes the student who had achieved her own capability but will not get the 'A's.
>
> (Female teacher in St Peter's [ssg fr])

Being labelled as academically clever was not always a bonus however. In St Dominic's (ssb fr) (a designated disadvantaged school with a high working-class intake) a number of boys commented on the problems of teasing if they received too much praise from teachers for their work.

> [It's a problem when] . . . the teachers respect me like I'm a brainbox.
>
> (First year student in St Dominic's [ssb fr])

> Students call you a lick because you are in a high class but I don't know how I got there. And if there was a person more clever than you the teachers will treat him better than you, and they [other boys] will pick on you.
>
> (First year student in St Dominic's [ssb fr])

Similarly, in Ballydara (co-ed Com Col) those students who were higher academic achievers could be singled out as 'snobs' by their peers. In one case, a senior male student who was very academically successful in school and state examinations was the target of rumours regarding his sexual orientation and suffered teasing and exclusion by peers.

Sense of place within the school community

Despite the reservations expressed by a minority of students about being teased for being high achievers, this was not a major issue in student essays or focus group interviews. Overall the data suggest that the high academic achievers, be these in mixed or banded classes, are high status individuals in schools. The high status accorded to them for their school work was replicated in other stratification systems within the school including the exercise of authority:

> There are people in this school who would make very good prefects but are not academically inclined therefore do not receive badges!! It is usually bright students who become prefects.
>
> (Sixth year student in St Cecilia's [ssg fp])

> I would like to see equal responsibility to each student, not just to good students. Stupid students don't have as much say.
>
> (Second year student in Ballinroe [ssb fr])

One of the questions presented to students was whether they felt at the centre of their class or located at some distance from the centre on a scale of one to five, with one representing the centre.

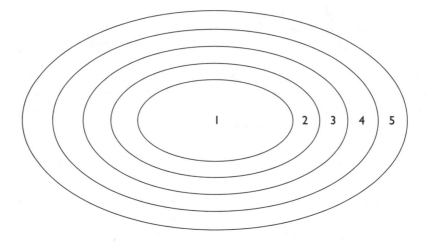

Those in higher bands or streams were more likely to rate themselves as belonging to the centre of their class, while those in the lower bands were more likely to consider themselves outsiders (Figure 4.6). Almost one-third of all students in higher stream or band classes (31 per cent) saw themselves as being at the centre in comparison with less than one-fifth (19 per cent) of their peers in lower or mixed bands.

The ability group in which students were placed also appeared to influence their rating of school climate. Those in lower bands or streams were again somewhat more likely to rate the school's atmosphere negatively across a range of descriptors than were their peers in either mixed or higher bands (Figure 4.7). It is interesting that with the exception of 'strictness' students in mixed classes had the most positive perception of their school's overall social climate. There were interesting differences across school type in the ratings given to school climate, depending on gender intake. Students in single-sex girls' schools were less likely to regard their school as gloomy, unfriendly or unwelcoming regardless of the type of group in which they were taught; however, they gave their schools more negative ratings when it came to strictness and tension. Students in single-sex boys' schools (and, to a lesser extent, co-educational schools) were more likely to describe their school climate as gloomy, unfriendly and unwelcoming. This was true of those in lower as well as higher attainment groups, although those in lower tracks were more likely to regard school negatively.

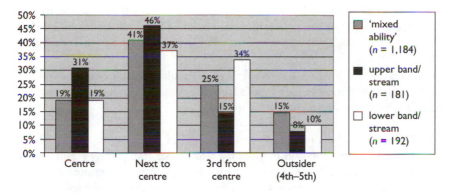

Figure 4.6 Differences between students in different grouping systems in terms of their sense of place within their class group (n = 1,557)

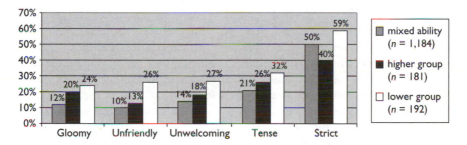

Figure 4.7 Students' rating of school climate across groups (n = 1,557)

Streaming teachers

The impact of stratified ability grouping on status and esteem occasionally extended to teachers' experiences also. Teachers in St Patrick's (ssg fr) claimed that 'staff streaming' occurred in their school. Those who taught the lower bands and sets believed that they had lower status than those teaching high achieving classes. Teachers believed that teaching subjects associated with lower academic achievers (especially practical subjects such as Home Economics) led to labelling by association:

> Teachers of less academic subjects are seldom asked opinions on important issues. General Home Economics was dropped because numbers were too small (10) while Physics and Chemistry each with six students were retained. This certainly is to the disadvantage of the less able pupil.
>
> (Female teacher in St Patrick's [ssg fr])

Overheard conversations in my classes have indicated to me that my subject (a practical subject) has been denigrated by a few other teachers to their classes. . . . [They see it] as being only suitable for weak underachievers.

(Female teacher in St Patrick's [ssg fr])

While teachers in St Patrick's school were particularly aware of how a teacher's status was determined in part by the students they taught, it was not the only school where this sentiment was expressed:

There should be a much more obvious policy in existence within departments regarding rotation of ordinary and higher level classes – and syllabus 'C' where applicable. There may be some exploitation of people who have genuine good will and are co-operative [and agree to teach the less academic classes] – which eventuallly will lead to unfair treatment.

(Female teacher in St Peter's [ssg fr])

Teachers' views

The teaching staff in each school were invited to complete short questionnaires detailing equality concerns regarding their own experiences and those of their students as part of the final visit feedback session. Several teachers indicated that they had concerns regarding ability differentiation in the schools. They focused both on how grouping impacted on their students and also, in some cases, on themselves. Ten per cent of respondents described the use of streaming as unfair to all but those in the highest ability group.

For teachers, the equality concerns surrounding ability differentiation were part of a wider educational problem – the over-emphasis on a very narrow, pressured definition of academic attainment. This was not merely a negative dimension of life in their particular school, but was a social and systemic issue.

The emphasis on academic achievement is still too prevalent. [There is a] need for higher profile to be given to career-orientated education that may not always be of an academic thrust.

(Female teacher, St Peter's [ssg fr])

I think some students are being moulded to suit the exam system.

(Female teacher, St Patrick's [ssg fr])

[There is a] lack of teaching for leisure time especially arts, music, drama. [There is] too much emphasis on 'points'[4] in our society.

(Male teacher, Ballinroe [ssb fr])

We are too pre-occupied with exam results and less about an holistic, life-preparation education.

(Male teacher, St Cecilia's [ssg fp])

Concerns about the overall pressurised nature of second-level education were not confined to teachers. The selection and grading of students on the basis of their grade point average on the Leaving Certificate Examination was a particular source of anxiety to several students. Even students in the early years of second-level education were conscious of the pressure of later examinations:

> [To make school more fair and equal there should be] less pressure on students about exams, about passing and failing. Making a fairer points system for the Leaving Certificate would help.
>
> (First year student, St David's [ssb fp])

> I think there shouldn't be as much emphasis on Junior Cert and Leaving Cert as there is. I think they should rule out the Junior cert and Leaving if in any way possible. I think there is too much stress put on the students due to these tests.
>
> (Third year student, St Peter's [ssg fr])

Conclusion

Our data suggest that stratification on the basis of academic achievement operates in two distinct ways across schools. It operates at an institutional level in terms of so-called 'ability grouping' across classes, and at an interpersonal level within classes in terms of the scope and nature of the time and attention given to different types of students. Even when students are not formally grouped by their academic achievements, teachers can and do stream students mentally (Barker Lunn 1970). The persistent use of the language of 'weakness' throughout teachers' accounts of low track classes and students who are not high academic achievers certainly suggests that there is a culture of stratification in the mindset of teachers (and indeed of students themselves) that will not be undone by eliminating streaming or banding. In analysing the issue of stratification in education, therefore, we need to take account of both between-class and within-class systems of stratification. While mixing students for most subjects does seem to create more positive learning climates in terms of time on-task, the quality of teacher–student interaction, and attitudes to schooling generally, it does not entirely eliminate processes of preferential treatment. Even in schools where 'mixed ability' is the prevailing policy, students reported how stratification and exclusions occur.

Notwithstanding the above, the data provide strong evidence that tracking by academic achievement has negative effects on students in terms of self-esteem, sense of belonging to one's school and class, relationships with teachers and relationships with peers. It is also evident that lower streams or bands have a somewhat more negative learning environment and that the time on-task within their classes is lower than in either mixed or high stream classes. Given what we know already about the importance of positive and focused education environments (Oakes 1991; Hacker *et al.* 1991; Gamoran *et al.* 1995; Boaler 1997a), and of positive teacher–student relations (Charles 1996; Pollard and Tann 1993; Slee 1995) for learning, it seems increasingly clear that students in higher tracks are relatively advantaged in a tracked system. The fact that students themselves expressed envy of the differential treatment meted out to high stream students (and of students who are highly regarded academically), and that students most often want to move to high tracks if given the choice, strongly suggests that students are also aware of the privilege of being in a high track.

Part 3

Issues of recognition and multivalent identities

In Chapters 3 and 4 we have outlined the unique ways in which schools work to promote inequality in social class and so-called 'ability' terms. We outlined the complex and multifarious ways in which schools create important distinctions of class and 'ability' between students, distinctions that ultimately translate into significant inequalities in the distributive outcomes of schooling.

Inequality in education, or in society generally, is not simply an issue of distributive justice, important though the latter may be. It is also a question of how gender, ethnic, sexual, religious and other differences are managed, and how power relations are arranged; it is a problem of culture and power as well as a problem of opportunity and material gain.

In Part 3 the focus is on how schools work in the management and recognition of differences, especially gender differences. Chapter 5 focuses on the life inside girls' schools, Chapter 6 on boys' schools, and Chapter 7 on the co-educational sector. The strong focus on gender arises from its significance in the development of deep structural divisions within schooling in Ireland. Gender is not treated however as a singular undifferentiated status. Inspired by the work of Fraser (1995, 1997) in particular, we examine gender as a multivalent status, deeply interfaced with social class, age and other differences.

While the strong focus on gender undoubtedly reflects the limitations of our own paradigmatic and domain assumptions as well, it must also be said that it reflects the ways in which differences are managed, or, more accurately, ignored, in education policy and practice. There are assumptions of homogeneity around sexuality, ethnicity and ability, that make it difficult for students to either attend certain schools or to 'come out' about their differences if they do attend, be those relating to abilities, religion, sexuality or ethnicity. Thus, while inequalities experienced by ethnic, racial, ability, religious and sexual minorities are profound, they were difficult to analyse in depth in a study of this kind. The broad macroscopic approach of the study did not allow us to focus in depth on particular differences. More importantly, as there were only a small number of identifiable minority students in any given school in terms of ethnicity, religion and disability, research on minorities was not easy. This was compounded in the case of lesbian and gay students, by the silence and denial about sexual differences that pervades education policy. A more detailed and in-depth study focused on minority questions alone would be required to do justice to understanding the breadth and depth of inequalities that arise for religious and ethnic minorities, including Travellers, and those who are disabled, or those who are lesbian or gay in schools.

Differences of race, sexuality, disability and religion are examined in Chapter 8, however, though we are constrained in the analysis by the denial and silence around sexual differences in particular, and by the segregation of schooling for disabled children and Travellers at second level.

The gendering of identity in single-sex and co-educational schools

Gender as a multivalent collectivity

In social class terms, the roots of the social injustice are in the politico-economic relations of society. Although working class students can and do experience cultural injustices that are related to their class, their generative source is socio-economic rather than cultural (Fraser 1995). Equally, although subordinated social classes may experience power-related deprivations in terms of their ability to control decision-making or influence events, their powerlessness is primarily economic in its generation. It is derived from their subordinated position in the economic realm, just as the disproportionate political influence of the wealthy is tied to their capacity to determine the ordering of economic relations within a given society (Phillips 1999).

Gender-related injustices however are not singular in origin. Although they can and are often construed as a status-related problem, deriving from the subordination of the feminine to the masculine in society, they are not simply generated in the cultural realm (Fraser 1997). The structuring of relations between women and men is not just a set of status relations, it is also a set of relations that are deeply economic and political in character.

At its most basic, the paid productive work of the 'public sphere' has been separated from the unpaid reproductive work of the 'private sphere' in a manner that is almost entirely gendered. The sexual division of labour is therefore a deeply economic set of human relations. It is premised on a horizontal segregation of types of work that are high and low status, and high and low paid, both inside and outside the household, on the one hand, and a vertical segregation between women and men in terms of income and power within occupations on the other (Beechey 1987; Delphy and Leonard 1992). The separation of spheres has also institutionalised a deep set of power inequalities between men and women, whereby women's unwaged domestic and care labour frees men to hold public power, a power that they may use again to further control women in the family and in the wider cultural and political realms.

Gender is therefore not simply a bivalent collectivity as Fraser (1995) has suggested, it is a multivalent collectivity in the sense that the roots of gender injustices cannot be pinned to either the economic, the cultural or the political realms alone. Inequalities between men and women are endemic to the fabric of our economic, cultural and political lives. They are constitutive of politics, economics and culture itself.

The question here then is, what role does schooling play in the gender process? Does it work towards reproducing the gender order, or does it challenge these gendered assumptions? Is the experience the same for girls and boys regardless of school type, or social class, age, stream, etc.?

Because of the gender segregation of so many second-level schools in Ireland, we chose to analyse gender experiences by examining life inside single-sex girls' schools, single-sex boys' schools and co-educational schools separately. We explore the complex ways in which school cultures promote differences between boys and girls, differences that anticipate different and, at times, stratified roles within the gender order.

Setting the context

Ireland is unusual in a European context in that a large number of schools are still single-sex institutions at both primary and second level: 42 per cent of second-level students attend single-sex schools, and the majority of these are girls (Table A9).

The gender divide between schools can only be understood in terms of the differences in school type. As noted in Chapter 2 above there are four different types of second-level schools in operation, secondary, vocational, community and comprehensive. Although all types of schools prepare students for the two major public examinations, they differ in both their gender and their social class trajectory, largely for historical reasons.

Currently 61 per cent of students attend secondary schools; these are almost entirely denominational, mostly Catholic, and 65 per cent of them are single-sex (see Table A1). A majority of single-sex schools are also girls' school and almost half of girls (48 per cent) in second-level education attend these. While secondary schools are more middle-class in intake than other school types, they vary greatly in social class composition depending on history and location.

The gender-segregated nature of many Irish schools is part of the legacy of the denominational origin and control of education since the nineteenth century (Akenson 1975). As noted by Hannan and Boyle (1987: 31): 'The current role of schools can only be understood in terms of the historical origins and circumstances from which the different congregations developed their traditional apostolate.'

Throughout the nineteenth century, a large number of Catholic religious orders were either founded in Ireland or invited in from abroad by bishops. Many of these orders established schools across the country (Fahey 1987; Clear 1990). The distinctive educational traditions associated with older religious orders provided models for the new orders as they established schools throughout

Table 5.1 Breakdown of all secondary schools in the Republic of Ireland by gender intake and school type (*n* = 445)

School gender intake	Free-scheme	Fee-paying	Total
Single-sex girls	142	17	159
Single-sex boys	109	17	126
Co-ed	137	23	160
Total *n*	388	57	445

Source: Figures compiled from full database of pupil and school numbers for the academic year 1995/96 provided by the Statistical Section, Department of Education and Science.

Ireland in the nineteenth century. Segregation of school populations by gender, following traditional Roman Catholic thinking (Drudy and Lynch 1993), was one of the distinctive aspects of the structure and culture of religious-run second-level schools from that time.

The second major educational sector is the vocational sector with 32 per cent of all schools and 26 per cent of all students. Most of these schools are co-educational; they differ significantly from secondary schools in their culture and ethos, not least because they are under the management of local authority-style bodies, namely vocational educational committees. All were established after 1930. Vocational schools were originally founded to provide vocational training for apprenticeships. They had a long tradition of serving working class, low income and small farm families. Given their traditional profile in the more technical subjects, they have traditionally attracted more boys than girls and this is still true today. In recent years, some vocational schools have been reconstituted as community colleges, while others have been involved in amalgamations with local secondary schools resulting in the foundation of community schools. community schools and comprehensive schools form the third category of school, serving 13 per cent of all second-level students. These are co-educational schools, established since the late 1960s, many of them in areas of urban expansion. While community schools operate under a joint agreement between a given vocational education committee and a Catholic religious order, comprehensives are under one governing authority, either Catholic or Protestant.

The various traditions associated with different types of second-level schools have impacted on the gender-differentiated nature of students' experiences within them. Curricular and extra-curricular provision varied traditionally, between girls' and boys' single-sex secondary schools, and also between secondary schools and those in the vocational sector (Hannan *et al.* 1983; Hannan *et al.* 1996). In terms of extra-curricular experiences, music and the arts have traditionally been promoted mostly in single-sex girls' schools, while sports (particularly field and contact sports) continued to be of greater importance in boys' secondary schools (Lynch 1989). School climates, measured in terms of levels of social control, the type of discipline in operation, levels of student-participation in the life of the school (especially in any type of leadership and caretaking, nurturing roles), have also been found to be strongly gender-differentiated across single-sex schools (ibid.).

While previous studies of schools had relied strongly on questionnaire-type data to assess the culture of schools in Ireland, this study set out to understand it by spending time in schools and classrooms. It explored the cultural life of schools by observing and listening, as well as by using more formalised research instruments, including documentary evidence, interviews and questionnaires. It sought to go deep inside schools to understand their role in promoting particular gendered identities.

Gender questions

Gender is now one of the most heavily researched subjects in education (Arnot *et al.* 1999). The difficulty with studying gender therefore is that there are numerous questions to be answered, numerous avenues to be explored. The questions vary from those about the relative attainment of boys and girls, to those about modes of assessment, curriculum content, pedagogical styles and peer relations. It is clearly not possible to examine each and every gender question in depth in a study of this kind. What we have focused on is the question of gender segregated schooling and how this impacts on the gendering of identity for boys and girls. There were a number of reasons for this.

First, there is a dearth of research on single-sex schools in particular. As most schools in Europe, North America, Australia and many other parts of the world are co-educational, there is relatively little known about life inside single-sex schools either for girls or for boys. We focused on the differences between co-educational and single-sex schools therefore because we had a unique opportunity to explore how single-sex schooling works generally. We also had the opportunity to examine how it operated in relatively non-selective schools in particular. In most countries in Europe, and in the USA, where single-sex schools exist, they tend to be socially elite schools. That is not true in Ireland where 42 per cent of all students attend single-sex schools: many of these schools have a working-class or lower middle-class intake, while only a small minority, 12 per cent, are selective, upper middle-class schools charging fees (see Table 5.1).

The study was also encouraged by our interest in exploring some of the issues arising from the debate within feminism about the potential of single-sex schools to counteract the impact of patriarchal structures and practices for girls (Spender 1982; Weiner 1994). We wanted to examine the extent to which single-sex schools were safe havens for girls: were they spaces in which girls could be educated outside of patriarchal assumptions and practices?

A further reason for undertaking the analysis of differences between school types is the ongoing debate, both internationally and in Ireland, as to the merits and demerits of single-sex and co-education (Goldstein *et al.* 1993; Grant and Sleeter 1996; Hannan *et al.* 1996; Lee and Bryck 1986; Lee, Marks and Byrd 1994; Marsh 1989a, 1989b; Riordan 1990; Steedman 1983). As the focus of much of the debate has been on the relative impact of co-education and single-sex schooling on student attainment, and as there is now a sizeable body of recent work suggesting that, when one controls for all the relevant background variables, single-sex or co-educational schooling may have little independent effect on measured academic performance (Thomas *et al.* 1994; Daly 1996, Hannan *et al.* 1996; Harker 2000; LePore and Warren 1997), it seemed important to explore aspects of single-sex and co-educational schooling that had received less attention, particularly the differences in the social climates across school types.

A related consideration was the growing recognition that an almost exclusive focus on cognitive processes and outcomes has been a serious limitation of much of the research on school effects. Even within the mainstream school effectiveness literature there has been a realisation of the need to assess the non-cognitive outcomes and processes of schooling (Creemers and Scheerens 1994; Gray 1995; Reynolds 1994; Smyth 1999).

Finally, recent policy developments in the Republic of Ireland, where co-educational schooling is being actively promoted by the Department of Education and Science, also encouraged us to explore differences across school types. If co-education is being promoted, then we need to understand how it works in gender terms, and how and if the gender experience of girls and boys differs across schools.

An inclusive perspective on gender

For many years gender analysis was synonymous with the analysis of women's issues. Women were defined as the oppressed and marginalised and the problem was set in terms of, either changing women to compete more effectively in the male terrain (represented by the liberal agenda and dominant discourse); or changing education to make it less patriarchal so that women's interests, knowledge and lifestyles could be accommodated and recognised (argued in the more radical and minority feminist agenda) (e.g. Weiner 1994). While some feminists (e.g. Mahony 1985) had been calling for the opening up of masculinity and masculine identity within education to debate since the 1980s, the past decade in particular has seen the growth of just such a debate (Askew and Ross 1988; Connell 1989; Edley and Wetherell 1997; Gilbert and Gilbert 1998; Head 1999; Mac an Ghaill 1994; Skelton 1997; Swain 2000). Much of the very recent debate about boys, however, has not been about the patriarchal dividend for men in education and elsewhere, or about problematising the dominant definitions of masculinity (Cohen 1998; Jackson 1998). Rather it has been about making sure that boys are not 'victims' of girls' academic achievements (Mills and Lingard 1997; Mahony 1996, 1998). What Kimmel (1996) calls the mythopoetic men's movement (that which defines men as the new victims in society, especially victims of feminism, e.g. Biddulph 1994; Bly 1991; Nordahl 1994 cited in Kruse 1996) has been especially strong in recent public debates in the UK, Australia and Scandinavia. Claims are increasingly made that schools are 'failing' boys (Kenway 1996; Kruse 1996; Epstein *et al.* 1998; Mahony 1998). These issues have also become the focus of media attention in Ireland, although they have not dominated the discourse and debates in academic research in a way that has happened elsewhere (Tovey and Share 2000).

This study was not concerned therefore with prioritising one gender group, and their equality concerns, above another. Rather our interests were in understanding the micropolitics of school life in equality terms. We wanted to explore the ways in which different types of schools promote particular gendered identities for different types of pupils, and the nuances in the cultures within particular schools themselves. A secondary goal was to understand students' definitions of equality and their preoccupations, or lack of same, with the wider equality agenda.

In trying to understand the gendered experiences of students across school types, it is evident that the gender composition of the staff and student population is by no means the only, or even the dominant, factor in determining the nature of particular social experiences within a school. Gender is not a 'pure' attribute operating independently of other characteristics. The social class, racial, religious or ethnic identity of students, as well as factors such as school traditions, can all play a key role in determining the culture within the organisation and the experience of pupils and their parents (Lareau 1987; Sammons *et al.* 1997; Smith and Tomlinson 1989; Reay 1996). Moreover, the way in which parents, pupils or teachers may perceive social climate can be very different, depending on where they are placed individually and collectively within the organisation. As noted in Chapter 4, research on 'ability' grouping indicates that pupils' experience of the school is mediated by stream or track position (Bryck *et al.* 1993; Hallinan 1994; Oakes 1985; Rutter *et al.* 1979; Smyth 1999; Sukhandan and Lee 1998); other research indicates that age, disability and sexual orientation also define the social climate of the school from the pupils' perspective (Barton 1995; Epstein 1994; Harris 1997; Watkinson 1996). The way in which the gender composition of a school impacts on pupils' experience cannot be understood, therefore, purely according to universalistic principles; it takes both universalistic and particularistic forms.

When we set out to study the impact on gender of schooling experience, we were mindful of the great differences that existed across the single-sex and co-educational sectors traditionally, and of the intra-gender differences within a given school type. In the three chapters included in this section, we examine the differing ways in which gender identities were developed across different school types. Chapter 5 examines students' experiences across the four single-sex girls' schools, documenting the unique cultural practices in gender climate across these schools, including the focus on the often contradictory values of high academic attainment and control of physical appearance and personal demeanour. It also documents the extent to which girls resisted the gender order of the school at different times. Chapter 6 explores the ethos and culture of the four single-sex boys' schools, examining similarities as well as differences in the level of emphasis on sporting achievement and physical prowess. It appraises the significance of peer policing of the body and of behaviour in the gendering of identity. Chapter 7 examines the climates of the four co-educational schools, looking first at the low level of awareness expressed by students of gender as an equality issue, and documenting observed instances of gender differentiation across these schools. It then focuses on the operation of gender differences within the co-educational classrooms, and the higher profile of a small proportion of male students.

Chapter 5

Girls' schools: diligence, surveillance and resistance

Introduction

The debate about the appropriateness of single-sex education for girls is part of a wider feminist discussion on co-education (Spender 1982; Weiner 1994). Many feminist educationalists have expressed concerns about the negative impact of co-education on girls' educational participation and attainment (e.g. Clarricoates 1983, Deem 1978; Delamont 1980; Lee and Bryck 1986; Mahony 1985; Spender 1982; Stanworth 1983; Younger and Warrington 1996; Weiner 1994). Such concerns have led to the establishment of some single-sex spaces or classes for girls within co-educational schools (Kruse 1996; Parker and Rennie 1996).

Despite the expressed interest in single-sex education for girls, there is a dearth of research on the ethos of single-sex girls' schools, not least because co-education is the norm in western countries. Indeed, widespread single-sex schooling is associated with historical rather than current educational provision (Gilbert and Taylor 1991). Single-sex schools in most western countries are most often part of the minority private school sector (Signorella *et al.* 1996). Yet single-sex schooling is a cultural phenomenon that needs to be examined in its own right.

The historical context

The origins and traditions of single-sex girls' schools in Ireland impact in no small way on their current culture and climate. During the nineteenth and early twentieth century, a large number of Catholic convent schools were established. The nineteenth-century convent boarding schools for girls were part of a wider European Catholic tradition encouraging, among middle-class girls in particular, the development of 'good taste' and 'appropriate' cultural accomplishments. The importance of politeness, demeanour, good conduct, and order was emphasised; the use of prize-giving and the ongoing public evaluation of work, as well as personal conduct, were common means for achieving the desired end (O'Connor 1987). Religious orders also regarded the inculcation of innocence and docility as important educational objectives for girls, qualities that were traditionally regarded as desirable in female religious life (O'Flynn 1987). Single-sex girls' schools have continued to place emphasis on artistic and social accomplishments rather than sport, in their extra-curricular activities (Lynch 1989). They have also continued to value more highly behaviours and characteristics such as self-control, care and nurture than boys' schools, as well as placing greater emphasis on the control of appearance and demeanour (ibid.). In recent times, however, expectations about self-control and nurturance have been increasingly complemented by strong expectations of high achievement (Drudy and Lynch 1993; Hannan *et al.* 1996). Yet, there has been no serious debate about the conflicts and contradictions these sets of values pose for young women.

The great majority of all single-sex girls' schools are still Catholic convent schools, although they are increasingly under lay management. Very few staff in these schools are now religious, although the religious orders remain the trustees of the school in most cases (Warren and O'Connor 1999). The fact that so many girls' schools in Ireland are Catholic in origin and constitution means that Catholic mores and values regarding femininity exercise considerable influence on their cultures. However, research in the UK and Northern Ireland shows that there can be significant variations between such schools, depending on how the management interpret Catholic ideology (Morris 1997) and the cultural and political context of the school (Donnelly 2000). Moreover, as Inglis (1998) observes, Irish society has changed radically in recent years, especially in relation to attitudes to sexuality. Two contradictory discourses now compete for public legitimacy, one residing in traditional Catholic teaching and the other based on secular, liberal individualism. We live in a time of 'contested ideologies in which there are regular, open challenges to Catholic tradition and common sense. These challenges are strongly felt and highly articulated' (ibid.: 148). Thus, although 48 per cent of Irish girls attend single-sex girls' schools that are predominantly Catholic in ethos, there are numerous challenges emerging to their traditions, ethos and values.

Single-sex schools are more middle class on average in their intake, than are co-educational schools, although such averages conceal significant variations within and between school types (Hannan *et al.* 1996). Social class differences do exist in the intake of different girls' schools, depending on where the school is located, or in a small number of cases (approximately 11 per cent) if the school is fee-paying (it being predominantly upper middle-class in the latter case). However, about 90 per cent of single-sex schools are 'free', that is to say they do not charge fees, although many do ask for a voluntary contribution from parents (see Chapter 3 for a discussion of this).

In setting out to explore the gendering of identity in girls' schools, therefore, it is necessary to avoid stereotypical notions of religious, class and cultural homogeneity. On the one hand, gender ideologies are increasingly complex and contested in Ireland (Tovey and Share 2000); on the other, school climates are far too complex and contradictory to be represented as singular in focus (Ball 1997).

A universal principle

There is one universal practice that has an over-riding influence on the culture of second-level schools in Ireland, namely, the Leaving Certificate Examination (Report of the Points Commission 1999). All students who complete second-level education are selected for higher education on the basis of their Leaving Certificate Grade Point Average (LCGPA). As higher grades give access to the most prestigious colleges and courses, there is intense competition for top grades in this final examination. Even for students who do not progress to higher education, the Leaving Certificate is an important passport to employment. Both employers and training agencies also recruit on the basis of Leaving Certificate performance.

Examination success is therefore the yardstick by which schools are most often evaluated in the public eye. This holds true for all schools, regardless of their gender composition. Notwithstanding the above, schools do vary in terms of how they interpret the pressures and demands of the Leaving Certificate. They mediate the message of success in particularistic ways, and these ways are both gender and social class specific.

Particularistic practices

The social climates of the four single-sex girls' schools were unique in several respects. This was evident from the essays students wrote, from focus group interviews, and from both classroom and general observation, as well as from discussions with, and observations of, teachers. Notwithstanding differences between the schools in terms of their history and traditions, overall the single-sex girls' schools were characterised on the one hand by relatively high levels of surveillance and control of demeanour and behaviour, and on the other, by a strong academic orientation. Interwoven within these was an expectation that girls were likely to be nurturers and carers; caring was, however, an increasingly subordinate value. The data suggest that young women had three goals or objectives presented to them: they were expected to be educationally (and occupationally) active and successful, to be modest in their attire, demeanour and achievements, and to be a carer and nurturer in their social roles. The data also suggest, however, that girls did not always accept or co-operate with these cultural expectations. There was strong resistance in particular to the control and regulation of dress and demeanour.

Surveillance and control

One of the most visible forms of control exercised over girls in single-sex schools was control over dress. In each of the four schools, girls had to wear a uniform (comprising, in all cases, a custom-made top and skirt, tie, specified blouse and specific shoes). Knee-high socks were part of the specified uniform in all four schools although girls could wear tights as an option in three of the four schools. In addition, all four schools had specific rules about jewellery, which was strictly curtailed; it was meant to be discreet and 'tasteful' if worn at all. In St Peter's (ssg fr), for example, the school rules stated: 'Pupils are advised not to wear jewellery into school. They may wear one ring and/or one pair of stud earrings if ears are pierced.'

The wearing of makeup was expressly forbidden in each of the schools. There were also rules with regard to expected student demeanour. The school rules in St Patrick's (ssg fr) reminded students that 'insolent behaviour or language' was unacceptable, and that the school would not tolerate those engaging in 'rowdy or rough behaviour'.

Concerns about surveillance and control were an important theme in the essays written by girls in single-sex schools. Girls expressed resistance to the controls exercised over their dress, demeanour and behaviour. Uniform regulations were regarded as particularly intrusive and fastidious.

> And girls shouldn't have to wear a skirt. It's sexist, in school especially where we should be learning that we are equal to fellows. . . . It's also unfair how girls' schools have to do choir and singing. . . . And I hate when we hear how we should act like young ladies and tie back our hair.
>
> (A third year student in Our Lady's [ssg fr])

> Two of the rules should be changed, that we can only wear one ring and we should only wear our school coats. (1) Our school coats are too cold and don't keep you warm. (2) We are not going to wear about five rings on each finger – about three small ones [all together] would do.
>
> (A second year student in St Cecilia's [ssg fp])

Students regarded the attempts by schools to police their dress and their bodies as an invasion of their privacy and their rights to control the appearance of their own bodies.

> We should be allowed to wear jewellery and make-up and nail varnish and we should be allowed to roll our skirts up and wear our hair the way we want to.
>
> (A second year student in St Peter's [ssg fr])

> It's not fair the way the teachers say your tie is getting *dangerously* low.
>
> (A second year student in St Patrick's [ssg fr])

Control of appearance and individuality was not limited solely to rules and regulations about uniform. Girls also reported that teachers commented critically upon their appearances and mode of dress, even outside of normal rules time:

> Today one of the classes had a non-uniform day and she [a teacher] gave out to a girl for wearing a belly-top!
>
> (A second year student in Our Lady's [ssg fr])

Not only did students perceive that their appearances and bodies were being policed in school, they also claimed that school was attempting to monitor their outer world:

> They [teachers] should let you do what you want at lunch and home time, instead of watching what you do in your own time.
>
> (A second year student in St Patrick's [ssg fr])

> I was unfairly treated when my principal called me up to the office, telling me that the crowd I am hanging around with outside of school are taking drugs. She also told me that I shouldn't be hanging around with them, even outside of school.
>
> (A third year student in St Cecilia's [ssg fp])

In one school, rumours circulated among pupils about attempts by the school principal to control girls' social lives. Whether these claims were valid or not is another matter; none the less they were widely believed by the students:

> She [the principal] tells our parents that we shouldn't be allowed out to discos and she said that when the disco is on she will drive around town and pick up any girls from this school and bring them home.
>
> (A second year student in Our Lady's [ssg fr])

It would be wrong to suggest that all girls resisted the controls imposed on them within their schools. Some internalised the rules and approved of the controls:

> I think that this school is fair and equal. If you work well and put effort in and abide by the rules, life is easy. You are treated by the way you behave which I think is fair.
>
> (A sixth year student in St Peter's [ssg fr])

> I think everyone in this school is given the same opportunities. It is whether or not they avail of them. It could not be made more fair and equal in my opinion.
>
> (A sixth year student in St Cecilia's [ssg fp])

Teachers in each of the four single-sex girls' schools were conscious of students' resistance to surveillance and control of their appearance especially. Teachers varied, however, in how they interpreted student resistance. At the research feedback meeting in St Peter's (ssg fr) some teachers expressed amusement at the level of interest that their students had in matters of appearance and individuality. They did not regard such concerns as matters that had to be taken too seriously; when this aspect of student concern was brought up at the feedback session, teachers laughed. Indeed, in response to this issue, a number of teachers at this meeting expressed a view that clearly reflected their age and social-class assumptions about dress; they 'feared' that if girls had more freedom in their dress, 'they would cultivate a cheap and gaudy image of the school'. Other teachers judged student resistance to uniform controls in moral terms, 'as sneaky' (wearing rings, rolling up their skirts at times and then letting them down for 'strict teachers'). Teachers in St Cecilia's (fee-paying school) had a somewhat different response to the findings regarding student resistance to levels of control and surveillance. The issue was treated with a little more seriousness although the concessions proposed were minor.

Although a certain amount of empathy was expressed with students regarding the tight monitoring of their dress in each of the schools, the uniform was regarded as both desirable and inevitable. At no time, in our discussions with teachers, was there any reference to the human rights issues which arise from policing and controlling students' bodies in this way (Watkinson 1996).

Work and surveillance in single-sex girls' classrooms

The gender composition of the school also had a bearing on the culture of classrooms. Single-sex girls' classrooms were the least likely to feature any disruption or deviation from work tasks. The proportion of total classroom interactions which were 'on-task' compared with those which were disruptive of learning, or 'off-task social interactions' (such as joking, banter, exchange of news), was higher in single-sex girls' classes than in others (Figure 5.1). Three-quarters of all classes observed in single-sex girls' schools had the highest proportion (71 per cent to 100 per cent) of all their recorded classroom interactions categorised as work-focused or on-task, compared with 59 per cent of single-sex boys' classes and 49 per cent of co-educational classes.

Negative sanctioning by teachers (such as telling-off, exclusion from the class or from participation in work) was recorded less frequently in single-sex girls' classes than in either single-sex boys' or co-educational schools. This was not surprising, given the greater on-task focus of single-sex girls' classrooms.

Although surveillance[1] procedures were only recorded as a control mechanism in a small minority of classes (18 per cent; $n = 29$), a disproportionately high number of all such incidences occurred in single-sex girls' classes (Figure 5.2). The teacher of a junior class in St Peter's (ssg fr) publicly corrected a student for the way in which the girl was looking at her while she helped her with an individual written exercise. She asked 'why are you getting so defensive with me?' She corrected the manner in which the student was watching her, saying 'don't look at me like that!' Individual students in other single-sex girls' classes were called upon by name and told to 'sit up straight/properly' during the course of lessons.

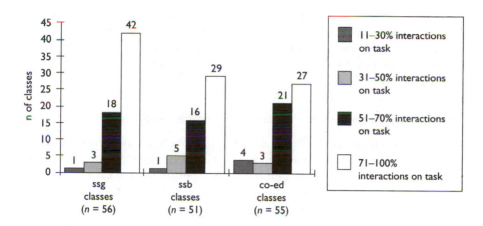

Figure 5.1 Proportions of total recorded classroom interactions which were on-task by school gender type (n = 162 classes)

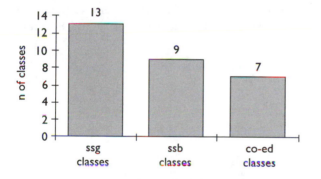

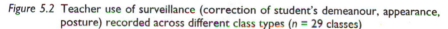

Figure 5.2 Teacher use of surveillance (correction of student's demeanour, appearance, posture) recorded across different class types (n = 29 classes)

Note
Two of the classes in co-educational schools in which surveillance was recorded only had female students, so were de facto single-sex girls' classes located in co-educational schools.

Strong surveillance practices were generally part of a more general system of hierarchical control. A teacher who exercised surveillance over individual students during a senior class in St Peter's (ssg fr) also operated a regimented system of lining up in silence to leave the room once the bell sounded. A very similar control-focused style was observed in other classes of which surveillance was one element. An example of one such class was observed in St Patrick's (ssg fr). It was strongly teacher-led and characterised by a series of controlling devices. These included having a prayer at the outset; students standing up once the teacher entered the room and only sitting when told to do so; use by the teacher of unfinished sentences during the course of instruction to which the whole class responded; and no movement to depart by students after the bell had sounded until the teacher formally dismissed the class. During the course of this lesson, different students were corrected by the teacher for slouching and told to sit properly.

Academic achievement, stress and resistance

While academic achievement was valued in all schools, it was not prioritised to the same degree in either single-sex boys' or co-educational schools compared with girls' schools. Concerns about academic pressures were expressed more frequently by both students (in essays as well as focus-group interviews) and teachers in girls' schools than in either of the other types of schools (Figure 5.3).

In all, 60 per cent of all complaints relating to academic pressure emerged from single-sex girls' schools although these comprised just one-third of all the schools. Interestingly, proportionately fewer girls in co-educational schools wrote essays indicating concern about academic pressure. Essays written on this subject in co-educational schools were almost evenly divided between female and male students. Our data suggest therefore that pressure to achieve, and stress relating to examinations, were more related to school gender type than to student gender per se.[2]

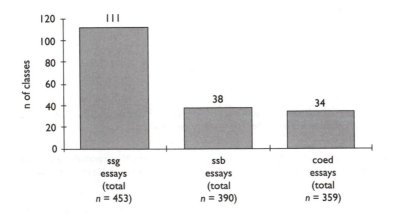

Figure 5.3 Concerns about academic stress and examination pressure by school gender type (*n* = 183 essays)

Note
Student essays concerned with academic or examination pressure accounted for 15.2 per cent of all essays written.

The pressure to achieve sometimes came from individual teachers and in other cases was part of a generalised achievement ethos throughout the school.

> One of our teachers is always making you feel small. Anything you get wrong she shouts at you and tells everyone what you did wrong. She always tells everyone what you did wrong. She always tells me how I am not going to pass my J.C. [Junior Certificate].
>
> (A third year student in St Cecilia's [ssg fp])

> They [the teachers] are saying we are not living up to the standards they have for us. They don't care about us they only care about the results.
>
> (A fifth year student in Our Lady's [ssg fr])

Academic ambitions were not always internalised by the pupils, although in such cases girls reported being disliked by teachers for their lack of interest. In Our Lady's (ssg fr), photocopies of articles from the *Irish Times* about points necessary to gain access to third level courses and national Leaving Certificate grades were pinned to a noticeboard in a classroom frequently used by fifth year students. A handwritten notice was pinned up beside the career advice pages, which read '76 per cent of 1995 Leaving Certificate girls from this school got college or RTC[3] places. Lets hope that 1997 Leaving Certificates can keep up the standard.' During focus group discussions, fifth year students from this school stated that their year group was a disappointment to the school because of their lack of ambition. Some students in single-sex girls' schools (including this senior group in Our Lady's [ssg fr]) expressed a sense of alienation from their school due to the preoccupation with the school's academic image.

> They have compared this year's leaving cert. grades to last year's. They put a lot of pressure on us. The principal doesn't care about us, she just cares about the school's name.
>
> (A fifth year student in Our Lady's [ssg fr])

These concerns did not emerge to any great extent in the boys' or co-educational schools. As was seen from Figure 5.3, there were some complaints expressed regarding examination pressure in these schools. However, these were less focused on the school institution than was the case in the single-sex girls' schools. A number of them related to parental pressures to achieve.

Achieving good examination results, points, and attaining college places were of great significance for girls in single-sex schools. Several students in both junior and senior cycles expressed concern and fear about the Leaving Certificate Examination, being particularly anxious about low 'points' or grades. They had internalised a strong sense of the importance of the Leaving Certificate for both their educational and occupational futures.

> I think exams would be a better experience if you didn't have to worry
> about hundreds and hundreds of points to live up to.
>
> (A fifth year student in Our Lady's [ssg fr])

In preparation for both the Junior and Leaving Certificate Examinations
'covering the syllabus' was the over-riding preoccupation of classroom work,
and this applied to all subject areas. Evidence of this emerged in terms of
references to examinations, tips by the teacher on ways to maximise marks, and
comments on, or evaluations of, a student answer in terms of examination
performance.

The strong examination and achievement ethos of girls' schools was also
evident from the way in which students were evaluated in class. Strong public
evaluations[4] reinforced the feeling of being under the public gaze in terms of
performance. While public evaluations occurred in all classroom types, they
were most common in girls' schools (Figure 5.4) with almost 43 per cent of all
such public evaluations recorded in these although they comprised just one-
third of all classes.

Nurturance and caring

In a study undertaken of schools in the 1980s (Lynch 1989: 65–66) one of the
clear differences between girls' and other schools was the strong emphasis on
the values of caring and nurturance in the former. Not only did girls' schools
implement more personal development programmes for their students than boys'
schools; school principals, extra-curricular activities and prospectuses in girls'
schools placed a strong emphasis on the role of girls as carers in society.

In our present study, while it was clear from the prizes given, the extra-
curricular activities undertaken and staff–student exchanges in classrooms and

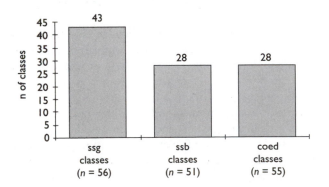

Figure 5.4 Breakdown of classes in which public evaluation is used by school gender type
(n = 99 classes); 162 = total number of classes observed

elsewhere, that care for others was still an important value for girls especially, it did not seem to hold the same status as in the earlier study.

In St Cecilia's, for example, while the year book named caring/social justice as a value promoted through their work for Amnesty and Vincent de Paul (a charity organisation), eleven pages of the eighty-eight page year book were devoted to listing girls' academic achievements (mostly) and some sporting achievements. St Peter's also had a year book. Most of the articles in it listed academic achievements or achievements in the arts and sport. There were some references to caring-type work undertaken by members of the religious order, but only two references to such work by students, a fund-raising event for the Simon community (for homeless persons) and work done by a small group of students for Amnesty. The extra-curricular activities of the other two girls' schools did have a caring dimension (for example, there was an Amnesty society involved in letter writing in St Patrick's) and Transition year students were required to do some visiting of old people in a nearby home; these were not popular activities in either school however.

In both Our Lady's and St Peter's, there was a perception, articulated by home economics teachers in particular, that their subject had become a 'weak link subject' in recent years and that it was declining in status. They claimed it was timetabled in such a way that academically capable students were not encouraged to do it. Given that home economics is the only subject which is on the school timetable which is specifically concerned with issues of care and the home (even though one may not agree with the interpretations of the same that are presented in the subject), the openly articulated sense of exclusion which the teachers of this subject expressed in two of the four girls' schools, indicates a cultural shift in attitudes to an area of knowledge and understanding which traditionally had reasonably high status in girls' schools. Interestingly, teachers of this subject in co-educational schools did not express this type of concern.

Our classroom data and other research evidence from school events such as prize giving would confirm findings from the more formal records of the school regarding the declining status of care as a value in girls' schools. The culture of academic achievement was far more pervasive than that of care or nurture. While a strong emphasis on academic achievement has been documented primarily in girls' schools (Lynch 1989), what was noticeable in this research was the declining status of nurturance and caring relative to academic achievement.

Conclusion

Girls' schools were characterised by a strong academic climate and relatively low levels of disruption in class. A strong work culture was promoted by institutionalised systems of public academic appraisal, both inside and outside classrooms, and by a pervasive work ethic within classrooms. The findings concur with those of Hill *et al.* (1993) in Australia. In a large study across ninety schools involving 14,000 students they found that teachers rated girls as more attentive in class than boys; girls' higher levels of attentiveness were positively correlated with their higher rates of academic attainment.

The work ethic was complemented by systematic procedures for controlling and monitoring behaviour, dress and demeanour. Control of dress was especially strictly enforced both inside and outside classrooms. Although nurturing and caring were also promoted as desirable feminine qualities in girls' schools, they were subordinated values. They were articulated in some official school literature but not invoked in public fora as guiding principles for girls.

The dominant definition of femininity in girls' schools therefore was one that promoted diligence, deference and self-monitoring. Girls were expected to work hard, but in so doing to defer to the systems of control exercised over them, especially in their dress and demeanour. They were being educated to assess their worth not just in terms of school success, but also in terms of their appearance, self-presentation and levels of conformity to rules and regulations. A culture that promoted hard work and diligence, in terms of career and ambition, prevailed in the girls' schools. This was complemented by a strong culture of conformity to norms regarding dress, demeanour and socio-sexual behaviour. Although there were few references to the norms schools promoted in terms of sexual behaviour, it was clear from remarks by students in their essays and focus groups that hetero-sexuality was assumed, as was adherence to basic Catholic moral teaching on matters sexual.

Girls did not accept all the values that the school promoted however. While few rejected the work ethic of the school, there were several examples of girls challenging regulations of dress, manners and speech, in particular. The essays the girls wrote about their schools also indicated how much they challenged and subverted some of the traditional feminine ideologies promoted. Traditional conceptions of femininity were being contested albeit often in a covert, timid manner.

Although the four girls' schools in the study were chosen because they were under the management of different religious orders, and because they served different social classes of students (St Cecilia's and St Patrick's were the most middle class), the cultural climate across these schools did not vary greatly in terms of the core values promoted. While there were clear class differences between the students in St Cecilia's and St Peter's (which found expression in the extra-curricular activities schools promoted, and the types of careers girls were encouraged to pursue in each school), the focus on hard work and the regulation of dress and appearance were equally strong in both.

Chapter 6

Boys' schools

Peer regulation and sporting prowess

Masculine identity and the culture of boys' spaces

The focus on boys' experiences of school is not new; in fact, boys have figured centrally in studies on students' life in school, and on youth culture (e.g. Corrigan 1979; Jenkins 1982; Walker 1988; Willis 1977). However, the focus in these studies was not on masculinity per se; it was on social class relations. It was through the problematising of gendered power relations, and the domination of girls by their male peers in educational settings, by feminist researchers that masculinity in and of itself began to be questioned across a range of social contexts. It was examined not only in terms of the power relations between females and males, but also in terms of the hierarchical relations among males themselves.

Masculine identities are constantly produced and recreated through social practices associated with specific institutions, and in relationships between groups and individuals. Masculinity exists in relation to femininity, and within a hierarchical power relationship in which it dominates femininity.

Furthermore, masculinity is internally hierarchical, with hegemonic masculinity dominating various other masculine identities, particularly that of gay masculinity (Connell 1995; Kaufmann 1994). Indeed, hegemonic masculinity is characterised by the exercise and control of power (Kaufmann 1994). The school is one of the institutions in which masculinity and patriarchal relations of dominance are practised. School structures may even reward students who embody particular dominant forms of masculinity, such as sporting prowess (Edley and Wetherell 1997). Kenway (1996) suggests that regardless of the particular form of masculinity boys adopt, it tends to be ultimately aimed at the acquisition of power, be it physical, cerebral or through the exercise of authority.

Certain sporting activities embody aspects of physical hegemonic masculinity such as strength, agility, prowess and control over the body (Burstyn 1999). Sport can be seen as the only location in which modern man can take on heroic roles (Dunning 1999). Participation in sport operates as a rite of passage from childhood to adulthood for boys through gaining control over their body, by learning to accept physical pain, and creating a strong, agile physique (Gilbert and Gilbert 1998). Participation and interest in sport for boys therefore represents access to hegemonic masculine identity – those who have no ability at, or interest in, sport risk being labelled as being of subordinate status in school by their peers (Dunning 1999; Edley and Wetherell 1997). Yet, boys across all school types do not have an equal opportunity to participate in sporting activity; those from more privileged backgrounds are more likely to be involved in competitive sport (Fejgin 1994).

Single-sex boys' schools (and classes) represent spaces where internal gender hierarchies and identities can become exaggerated. Kruse (1996) describes how, in single-sex classes in operation in Danish schools, the hierarchies within masculinity became more apparent in the absence of females. Other aspects of social climate associated with masculinity also became more visible, including competitiveness and a tendency to communicate in raw and more aggressive forms (ibid.). The school structures can themselves operate to promote and celebrate certain forms of hegemonic masculinity, thus reinforcing gender hierarchies (Edley and Wetherell 1997). Teachers of particular subjects, such as physical education, which are closely associated with hegemonic masculinity, may adopt styles and personas that help to perpetuate existing relations of dominance within masculinity (Brown 1999). The use by teachers of threatening or violent styles of control with male students institutionalises a physically hard and macho form of masculinity, a masculinity associated directly with the ability to give, and take, physical punishment (Beynon 1989).

Gendered identity in single-sex boys' schools

The single-sex boys' schools in the study differed in their culture and climate from other school types in a number of ways. While the dominant conception of femininity in girls' schools was one which emphasised academic achievement, and internal and external surveillance, asserting one's masculinity through physical size, strength or sporting prowess was a pervasive feature of boys' schools. Even though this form of masculinity was not always supported or encouraged by the school authorities, it was accepted complicitly in each of them. Moreover, the peer group in boys' schools appeared to exercise more control in determining the culture of their schools, a finding that concurs with recent research by Warrington et al. (2000).

Masculinity and sport

Sport featured strongly in only one girls' school (St Patrick's). Here hockey was the favoured sport and one at which the school excelled. However, sporting prowess did not generate status and recognition in the way that it did in most of the boys' schools.

Physical strength and sporting ability were prized in all four boys' schools, though to notably different degrees. The equation of superior masculinity with physical prowess and sporting success was particularly evident in the schools where sport was central to the school's sense of identity. It was in those schools with an investment in sporting success that physical and sporting prowess were important institutionally as well as among the student peer-group, namely St David's (ssb fp) and Dunely (ssb fr). Both schools specialised in particular team field-sports with rugby dominating in St David's while hurling had pride of place in Dunely. A number of teachers within each of these schools were involved in training junior and senior teams, and both schools participated in open competition with other schools in both provincial and national leagues. Photographs of successful teams and trophy cabinets with labelled cups, medals and other awards were on prominent display in the public areas of each school. Many students in these schools believed that there was an institutional bias in favour of pupils who excelled on the sports field. There was, however, much resistance among boys to the hegemonic definition of masculinity.

> Teachers in this school have got hurling teams on the brain and whoever is on the panel are saints to that teacher. They miss homework and tests because the teacher doesn't want them to do it.
>
> (A fourth year student in Dunely [ssb fr])

> [Mr X] prefers boys who play rugby and takes much more notice of them in class. If a rugby player had done some bad work he wouldn't be punished at all.
>
> (A second year student in St David's [ssb fp])

> I get on well in my school, although when I came here first and to this day, teachers and principals discriminate against students who are not interested in sport, especially, hurling.
>
> (A fifth year student in Dunely [ssb fr])

Senior students taking part in a focus group discussion in St David's (ssb fp) explained how certain teachers showed strong preferences for excellent rugby-playing students. One of the participants described how 'if you were good at rugby, you weren't really reprimanded for anything you did wrong to such a severe degree as anyone else basically'. According to one of the sixth years taking part in a separate focus group discussion, junior rugby players were not given detention but instead got to 'sit in the [dean's] office and have a cup of tea'. Another third year student said of the senior teachers who had responsibility for discipline in the school, 'if you don't play rugby, he [a senior teacher] doesn't want to know you'. Student perception of bias in favour of those who played the school sport was confirmed by similar comments by teachers in their questionnaires.

> Disruptive pupils who happen to be good at hurling are treated far more leniently than others.
>
> (A female teacher, Dunely [ssb fr])

Excellence at the particular sport also meant that individual students had the opportunity to exercise authority over others in the peer group. These students were perceived as having, and exercising, higher status within the peer hierarchy.

> There is one person [a rugby peer] here who thinks he is hard and every-body thinks the sun shines out of his hole. Nobody can touch him even though he is as thick as a brick and unfunny. He beat me up and I couldn't do anything about it.
>
> (A third year student in St David's [ssb fp])

Individual students expressed a sense of alienation from their school, and in some cases, from their peers, because of their lack of involvement with, and success at, the particular sport that was of significance in their school.

> I hate this school. Nobody likes you (adults, teachers, school management) unless you are on the [main rugby team]. The adults think that you haven't got a hope and you're a slacker unless you are a super-clever person or you're on a school rugby team. This is wrong and it should be changed.
>
> (A third year student in St David's [ssb fp])

> [I'm] not really accepted by everyone because I'm not that good at sports.
>
> (A fourth year student in St David's [ssb fp])

> Students feel somewhat isolated if they are not on the A or B rugby teams.
>
> (Female teacher in St David's [ssb fp])

Student participation in or, indeed, excellence at sports other than the particular one with which the school was associated was not regarded as having the same degree of standing either with the school institution itself or within the peer group. As one Transition Year student in St David's (ssb fp) explained about his participation in a hockey team outside of school, 'most people here think hockey is "all skirts"'. This particular student expressed hatred of rugby because 'it's too violent'.

Other individual students perceived their school team sport as taking precedence, not only over other sporting or extra-curricular activities, but also over general education in the school.

> Sport has a massive role in Dunely. At times it has too big an influence and it takes priority over education on occasions.
>
> (A fifth year student in Dunely [ssb fr])

Indeed, one female teacher in Dunely (ssb fr) described hurling as 'the religion of the school'.

In the case of both of these single-sex boys' schools, sporting achievement was central to the institution's identity and collective esteem. Both students and teachers in the schools expressed keen awareness of the centrality of their school's sport to the life of the school – some with a great sense of pride; others regarded the significance of the school sport as more problematic. Teachers and students who were not directly involved in the school sport were more likely to question its centrality in the institution, and to note the negative impact of its importance for many different aspects of life in the school.

Sport did not play as central a role in the life of the school, either among students or teachers, in either St Dominic's (ssb fr) or Ballinroe (ssb fr), albeit for different reasons. As has been outlined in Chapter 3, St Dominic's (a designated disadvantaged school) lacked any sports facilities either on its own premises, or even to rent or use in its immediate locality. Students in St Dominic's expressed concerns about the lack of sporting facilities in their school. They noted that although they had a number of soccer and Gaelic football teams, these had to train in facilities over one mile distant from the school itself. All of the league matches the teams played took place on the grounds of other schools. The students were aware therefore of their comparative disadvantage but they did not articulate this in class analysis terms. Although it would be clear to any outside observer that the absence of sporting facilities was directly related to the low income background of the students, and that of the local community generally, students did not name this as an issue. While they regarded the lack of facilities as 'unfair', they did not analyse the causes of this as a social class-related injustice.

Students in St Dominic's appealed to the close association between sporting activity and normative masculinity in support of their calls for access to improved sporting facilities. They argued that it would enhance their physically defined masculinity, or that it would act as an antidote to negative aspects of macho masculinity:

A gym would occupy people so they will not want to fight with people.
(A second year student in St Dominic's [ssb fr])

I would really like the school to get a gym so I could do some weight lifting because I love it.
(A fifth year student in St Dominic's [ssb fr])

[We need a] PE hall. School boxing [is what is wanted].
(A first year student, St Dominic's [ssb fr])

The fourth boys' school in the study, Ballinroe, did not have a sporting ethos comparable to either Dunely's or St David's. This was a school in which there was a conscious effort being made to create a more culturally diverse definition of masculinity; one which would allow and encourage different masculinities to find expression in the extra-curricular life of the school – the school had a senior student council which had been involved in the running of a number of discos and contests for bands, for example. During the time that the research was taking place, the school was in the course of building an extension, which included a large hall that doubled as a gymnasium and performance space with a stage. The following year, the researchers were invited to the school's musical production.

However, despite the fact that sport, and the associated celebration of physical size and prowess, was not a significant feature of the institutionalised life of that school, the dominant masculinity among the peer-group was one which prized masculinity expressed through physical strength. This was evident from the ways in which boys policed one another's bodies in this school (as was the case in the other participating single-sex boys' schools).

> Because of my thin build, I have been bullied in the past which led to low self-confidence and often being looked down on by other physically bigger students.
>
> (A sixth year student in Ballinroe [ssb fr])

Peer policing of the body

The staff in boys' schools generally gave their students considerable latitude in the management of their appearance. They did not attempt to control and sanction students' appearance or behaviour to the same extent as girls' schools. Students attending single-sex boys' schools were responsible for the lowest proportion of complaints in essays regarding control and surveillance of appearance, accounting for only one-tenth of all such essays. In single-sex boys' schools, it was the peer-group, rather than teachers, which took a strong sanctioning and controlling role in matters of physical appearance. Some male students claimed that they were teased because they were unsuccessful in sport at school and/or because of their physical stature. These students believed that if their appearance or sporting skills did not fit the prescribed view of masculinity, this left them vulnerable to being teased, bullied or excluded by peers.

> [I'm] not really accepted by everyone because I'm not that good at sports. For some reason, people often say derogatory comments to my face. I don't know why. But I still get on with my life.
>
> (A fourth year student in St David's [ssb fp])

> I have been teased since I came to the school about my size. I am generally small for my age and comments such as 'a speck of dust is like a mountain to you' have been made. I have never actually been bullied physically but the teasing has sometimes gotten to me.
>
> (A third year student in Dunely [ssb fr])

> When I came to this school some pupils started calling me fat. But I have got on with some of the pupils but still other pupils are pushing me around and still calling me fat.
>
> (A first year student in St Dominic's [ssb fr])

Toughness was regarded as an accepted and expected part of masculine identity in the boys' schools with a predominantly working class intake especially. Second years in St Dominic's [ssb fr] described toughness as a requirement for survival, explaining during a focus group interview that 'you have to be able to stand your ground like' because many of the boys are 'people who pick fights, people who think they're real tough and all'. Survival in this environment necessitated either acquiring the ability to defend oneself, or else being able to 'get somebody else after him [the attacker]'. Telling authority figures like teachers or other adults (including their mothers) was not an option, because to do so meant being branded a 'rat'. As noted above, some students believed that sporting facilities were necessary so that 'masculine aggressiveness and tendencies to fight' could be channelled in a socially acceptable way.

Physically threatening behaviour as a method of sanctioning: an issue for boys and men?

The use of physically threatening or aggressive behaviour by teachers was reported by a very small minority of students in their essays ($n = 49$, 4.1 per cent). The majority (58 per cent) of these reports emerged from single-sex boys' schools (see Figure 6.1). Most of the remaining incidents were reported in co-educational schools. In the latter case all the incidents involved male students, although female students also reported witnessing some of these occurrences. All of the reported incidents also involved male teachers.

Some of these incidents were more concerned with the public humiliation of students rather than the infliction of pain.

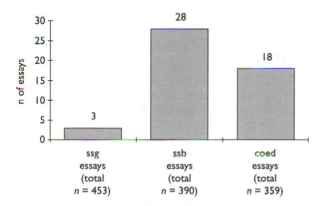

Figure 6.1 Breakdown of threatening or physically aggressive incidents reported in student essays by school gender type ($n = 49$)

> I was unfairly treated when I was in first year. If we did not know something in the class, we would have to beat each other with a tin whistle. Or stand down on our knees for the class period.
>
> (A fourth year student in Dunely [ssb fr])

Other reported incidents involved teachers using aggressive tactics:

> I was just getting a book from my friend during study period and Mr . . . shouted at me to shut the fuck up. He came over and put his hand on my head and started pressing down on my neck saying if I didn't shut up he would break my neck.
>
> (A fifth year student in St David's [ssb fp])

> In first year, Mr . . . winded me with a punch in the chest for being late for PE. A couple of weeks ago I had to write my name down on a page. The teacher thought he was really smart and said mark your x down on there anywhere. I wrote an x down on the page and he came over and started punching me in the back and in the head.
>
> (A fifth year student in Dunely [ssb fr])

During the course of data collection, we observed instances of physically aggressive contact between individual teachers and students in two of the four boys' schools. These two schools had a strong sporting ethos. In focus group discussions, a number of students in St David's (ssb fp) suggested that pride in physical prowess, and success in sport, was a key component of the school's culture. It was their belief that the culture of the sports field infiltrated the classroom culture at times; teachers dominated students by showing them that they were physically more powerful both on and off the field. However, as comments from a third year focus group in St David's indicate, a teacher's role as a sports coach did not, in their opinion, excuse such behaviour towards students, which included shoving them against lockers or into classrooms. These boys regarded the teacher in question as 'bad-tempered' and 'two-faced'. They explained his behaviour in terms of his wish 'to show you he's in authority'. The second year focus group discussed the same teacher, explaining that 'he's a great [sports] coach, but you just do exactly what he says'. They felt that there was a possible link between his disciplinary and sports coaching styles, and expressed fear of his bad temper, saying that he was known as 'a bit of a psycho'.

Not all students in these schools regarded threatening or aggressive behaviour of individual authority figures as problematic or undeserved; one participant in a third year focus group discussion in Dunely explained that such incidents occur 'if the students are being bold and messing . . . they do get it'. During the course of their focus group discussion, sixth years in Dunely explained that other students often laughed when a peer was physically disciplined. However, while they appeared to express some acceptance of this mode of exercising of authority over younger students – these sixth years recalled being 'hammered to death' as juniors – they would not accept it as seniors. Teachers could no longer treat them in this way, they explained, because they were physically bigger than the adults, and would 'hit them back'.

Although the incidents of physically threatening or abusive behaviour were rare occurrences, they did happen among a small number of male students and male teachers. While insignificant in scale, they were significant symbolically as they created a physically threatening climate at certain sporting events and in certain classes.

Modes of social interaction in single-sex boys' classrooms

As noted in the previous chapter, interactions in single-sex boys' classes were, on average, less likely to be on-task than in girls' classes; boys were also less likely to have public evaluation of student work by teachers. Students in single-sex boys' classes were more likely to be addressed solely by their surnames than were students in either co-educational or single-sex girls' schools. While addressing students by surname occurred in a small number of all classes observed (7.6 per cent), it was most frequent in classes in single-sex boys' schools, accounting for over half (58.3 per cent) of all such instances.

There were some interesting differences in patterns of social interaction between boys' and girls' classes also. Students in single-sex boys' classes were slightly more likely to initiate social contact with teachers during the course of a lesson than were girls in single-sex girls' classes, or students generally in co-educational classrooms (see Figure 6.2). Such social interaction included making jokes with the teacher and sharing or seeking general information. What was clear from observing the classes was that boys in single-sex classes made greater attempts to define the parameters of the classroom situation than girls in single-sex classes. Within co-educational classes, it was boys who also were the primary social initiators. In both single-sex and co-educational schools it is notable, however, that only a small number of boys were socially dominant.

Students in single-sex boys' classes were also more likely than their counter-parts in single-sex girls' classrooms to be involved in incidents of ridicule with teachers. (We have defined ridicule as use by students or teachers of sarcasm or mocking remarks at others' expense in the classroom.) Students in these class-rooms were both in receipt of teacher ridicule and authors of such comments directed at the teacher. In all, almost one-quarter (24 per cent) of all observed classes involved incidences of ridicule, with teachers ridiculing students in 17.3 per cent of all observed classes, while students were observed ridiculing their teacher in 7.4 per cent of all classes (in some classes both teachers and students used ridicule).

Use of ridicule by teachers was most common in single-sex boys' classes, where 29 per cent of all observed classes included such incidents, compared with

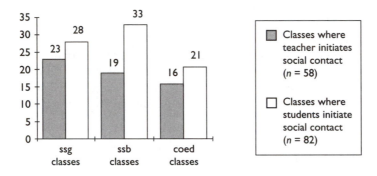

Figure 6.2 A comparison of student- and teacher-initiated social contact during class by school gender type[a]

(In some of the classes both students and teachers initiated contact)
[a] The proportion of classes from each school type is approximately one-third in each case. In total, single-sex girls' classes make up 34.6 per cent; single-sex boys' classes make up 31.5 per cent; co-ed classes make up 34 per cent.

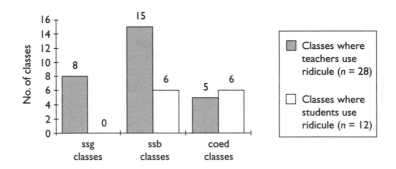

Figure 6.3 Differences in teacher and student use of ridicule/sarcasm in classrooms across school gender types

(In two classes, both teachers and students initiated ridicule)

14 per cent of single-sex girls' classes and 9 per cent of co-educational classes. In co-educational settings, the few teachers in whose classes the use of ridicule was recorded were equally likely to interact in this way with female and male students.

Student ridicule of teachers was not recorded at all in single-sex girls' classes; it was observed in a small number of both single-sex boys' and co-educational classes. It is worth noting that in the latter classrooms, only boys were involved in initiating such interactions.

Conclusion

Our data suggest that the dominant definition of masculinity in boys' schools was distinctive and separate in several ways from the concept of the feminine prized in girls' schools. While academic achievement was a value in all schools, the work ethic associated with it was much stronger in girls' schools. In addition the monitoring and surveillance of dress and demeanour was not as pervasive in the boys' schools, even though each had a uniform. Classroom relations were also different, with boys being more likely to initiate and control both social and academic interactions with teachers. Although they were rare occurrences, boys were more likely, however, to be subjected to ridicule and threatening behaviour by teachers (and on occasion to ridicule teachers themselves). Pressure to conform to a style of masculinity that assumed physical dominance in particular was the most visible and articulated aspect of peer culture in boys' schools. There was plenty of evidence for the type of masculinity that Connell (1995) characterised as being based on dominance and heterosexuality. Although the culture of macho masculinity took social class and gender-specific forms, and was openly contested by some students, prowess in sport and physical height, strength and agility were highly prized among the dominant peer groups in each school; it was especially noticeable in the two schools that accorded high status to those who excelled in hurling and rugby. The powerful influence exercised by the male peer groups on boys in schools has been noted in a number of other studies (Mac an Ghaill 1994; Mills and Lingard 1997; Rout 1992).

One of the four boys' schools in the study (Ballinroe) made a deliberate attempt to counter hegemonic definitions of masculinity based on physical prowess and dominance. It particularly encouraged a wide range of sports and extra-curricular activities and positively engaged students in discussions on masculinity. While the culture of this school differed considerably from the others and especially from the two sports-focused schools, nevertheless the prevailing peer culture was still one that held students who were successful in sports in high regard.

Chapter 7

The complex cultures of co-educational schools

Diversity, silence and hegemony

Introduction

A debate about the merits of co-education over single-sex education has persisted for many years internationally. In the USA, work by Valerie Lee and her associates has documented the merits of single-sex schooling for girls in terms of performance and school experience (Lee and Bryck 1986; Lee *et al.* 1994). Their findings have been strongly challenged, however, not only from within the USA (Marsh 1989b; LePore and Warren 1997) but from research in other countries as well (Byrne 1993). There is a growing realisation that claims regarding the academic merits of single-sex over co-educational schooling are not tenable given the research findings from countries as diverse as New Zealand (Harker 2000), the USA (LePore and Warren 1997) and Ireland (Hannan *et al.* 1996).

As the non-academic outcomes and experiences of education have not been researched extensively, relatively little is known about the social climate of co-educational or single-sex schools. While there is evidence that co-educational schools are places in which both girls (especially) and boys experience sexual harassment (Lee *et al.* 1996) and where girls are exposed to a variety of sexist practices (Hannan *et al.* 1996), there is also evidence that when co-educational schools manage gender differences effectively this can promote improved attitudes to learning among girls in non-traditional subject areas (Jovanovic and Steinback King 1998). Moreover, the reinforcement of gender stereotypes, through formal and informal systems of sexist practices, is not the prerogative of co-educational schools (Ball and Gewirtz 1997; Ball 1997; Hannan *et al.* 1983; Lynch 1989).

One of the objectives of this study was to try to understand more fully how gender relations operate in co-educational schools and classrooms. It is an attempt to explore the cultural climate of these schools; it sets out to examine in particular how co-educational schools may challenge or reinforce inequality by the ways in which they manage gender differences. In this chapter, we explore the ways in which female and male identities are being constructed in co-educational schools.

Classroom interaction: gender differences

The main focus of teacher–student and student–student interactions in the majority of observed classrooms (in the co-educational as well as the single-sex schools) was on work tasks. Although male students were more likely to dominate public work interactions with the teachers than girls on aggregate, one of the most significant findings of the study was that there were also a high proportion of classrooms in which female and male students were equally involved in work-related interactions. In 60 per cent of classes, public work-related interactions[1] were proportional to the gender make-up of the students in the classes (see Table 7.1). That is to say, boys and girls were equally involved in public work-related interactions with teachers and peers. Male students were more likely, however, than female students to be involved in public work interactions in 30 per cent of the remaining classes, while the same applied for girls in only 11 per cent of the observed classes. As has been the finding of studies of gender and classroom interaction over a long period, individuals or small groups of males rather than the entire gender cohort dominate in these situations (e.g. French and French 1984; Garner and Bing 1973; Lodge 1998; Tobin 1993). When boys dominate classroom time, it is not simply a case of all boys dominating all girls; a small minority of boys (and sometimes girls) tends to dominate the airtime of the class. Quieter girls and boys participate in class in a less public, less interventionist way.

While the data do support earlier Irish research, indicating that male students are more engaged in the public life of the classroom (Drudy and Ui Cathain 1999; Dunden 1993; Hanafin 1994), they also suggest that not all classes are the same. There is a large body of classes that may be gender balanced in their work-related interactions.

In examining classes where small groups or individual male, and occasionally female, students dominated on-task interactions, a number of different factors were considered. Class size did not appear to be an important consideration in determining the gendered pattern of interaction, although the pedagogical style of the teacher, the age/seniority of students, the gender balance of the class and the nature of the subject taught did appear to have some impact.

Table 7.1 Gender differences across co-educational classes in patterns of public work-related interactions (*n* = 47)

	%	*n*
Evenly distributed public on-task interactions by gender composition of co-ed class	59.6	28
Co-ed classes with female dominated public on-task interactions	10.6	5
Co-ed classes with male dominated public on-task interactions	29.8	14
Total	100	47

Figure 7.1 indicates how male students were more likely to dominate in classes that were student- rather than teacher-led. Student-led classes were those in which students played a central role in initiating work and other exchanges.

Male students were also slightly more likely to dominate junior rather than senior cycle classes (see Figure A1) and to dominate in some subject areas rather than others (Figure A2). The only subject in which girls were involved in a disproportionately high level of interactions was Art, a subject in which girls also tended to be in a clear majority. Home Economics and Mathematics were the two subjects in which boys were most likely to dominate, although dominance occurred for very different reasons in both. In Home Economics, boys were in the minority and the teachers seemed to be anxious to include them. In so doing they gave them extra time and attention (this also happened for girls in Woodwork and Metalwork, albeit to a lesser degree). In Mathematics, teachers tended to use a lecture and demonstration method and often called out for answers to problems; boys were more likely than girls to respond. Although Mathematics classes were evenly balanced in gender terms, boys dominated public work interactions in three of the seven classes. Language and Science classes showed the most even patterns of participation in gender terms.

As noted above, one of the most noticeable features of classrooms was the way in which a minority of students dominated public interactions. This could not be explained simply in terms of a teacher's pedagogical style, it was also an outcome of a student's public learning style.

There were a number of different ways in which students maintained a highly visible or dominant position in the classroom. The most frequently observed style was that of the assertive learner. It involved taking initiative on work issues

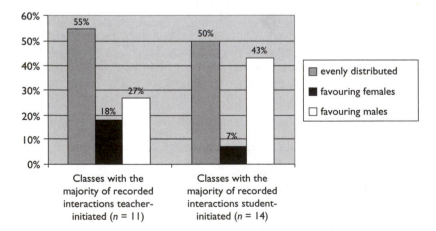

Figure 7.1 The relationship between teacher and student styles and gender in public work interactions in co-educational classes (*n* = 47)

in the class, asking questions and making comments, etc. This student style was observed in a range of co-educational classes (and in single-sex classes as well) and most clusters of assertive learners tended to be male. A female cluster of such students was observed in only one co-educational class, a personal development subject with senior cycle students. Assertive learners tended to dominate discussion or lecture-style classes particularly, where they asked questions, made work comments, and responded to teacher questions before other students.

In a small number of co-educational classes, the most visible students were those who were disruptive learners. Classes where such severe disruption formed a high proportion of ongoing interactions were relatively rare, occurring in only seven[2] of the forty-seven co-educational classes observed. As was the case with the assertive learners, those engaged in visible disruption were more likely to be male than female. Notwithstanding this, one cannot always draw a neat dichotomy between disruptive and assertive learners. Some of those who were most actively engaged in disruptive behaviour were also actively engaged in on-task public interactions. Others were almost solely engaged in disruptive interactions. Of the seven classes where severe disruption was a significant element overall, three involved mixed gender groups, three involved mainly male public disruption, and one involved a highly disruptive female student.

When one dissects the gendered patterns of interaction in co-educational classes, it is clear that they are not of a piece. Even though most classes we observed were gender-balanced in terms of public work-related interactions, aggregate measures of interaction indicate that boys control public discourse more than girls do. A small minority of boys accounts for this gender disparity however. When dominance occurs, it is a minority of boys who control the airwaves of the classroom; these boys dominate girls and quieter boys. Boys who exercise the type of controlling behaviour and discourse characterised by Connell (1995) as 'hegemonically masculines' are ones who tend to dominate. Girls who adopt similar styles also dominate occasionally.

The control of the public life of the classroom is not solely influenced by student styles, it is also influenced by the pedagogical style of the teacher, by the nature of the subject taught, by the age profile of students and the gender balance of the class.

Classrooms: sanctioning boys

Although boys are more likely to get teacher attention and to dominate the public discourse of the class than girls in some classes, their public engagement is by no means always positive. Students' claims in essays that boys received a disproportionately high level of negative sanctioning in class were borne out in classroom observation. Data from the observed classrooms showed that there was a tendency for male students to receive harsher teacher criticism or sanction. Negative sanctioning of students by the teacher relating to some aspect of student behaviour was recorded in nineteen (40 per cent) of the forty-seven co-educational classes observed. In more than half of these (58 per cent), all sanctioning recorded was directed at male students. In only 11 per cent of cases were girls in co-educational classrooms the sole focus of negative attention (Table 7.2).

The reasons for the higher level of negative sanctioning of male students varied. In some instances, there was an obvious correlation between level of student disruption of the class or the teacher (by individual male students) and sanctioning by the teacher in response.

In others, female and male students were equally disruptive of class learning, but male students were more severely sanctioned. This happened in two second year classes in Ballydara (co-ed Com Col) and in a fifth year class in Ballycorish (co-ed Com Sch). In Ollan (co-ed Com Col), two second year male students were rebuked in one particular class although they were not disruptive.

Not all disruptive behaviour was negatively sanctioned however. In two separate classrooms in Ballycorish (co-ed Com Sch), a small number of highly disruptive male students received minimal comment and no sanctioning from the teacher.

The most severe form of sanction used in any of the observed classes was exclusion or removal of a student from the room. This only happened in two of the forty-seven co-educational classes observed; on both occasions it was boys who were required to leave the class. The incidents involved senior classes and both of these incidents were observed in Ollan (co-ed Com Col). In neither case was this sanction connected directly with disruptive behaviour; it arose because of student failure to complete school work.

Social interaction in class

Social interactions between teacher and students were recorded in most (57.4 per cent) co-educational classes, although they accounted for a small proportion of the overall interactions recorded.[3] The majority (76 per cent) of such interactions involved male students and their teacher, and on a few occasions they involved ridicule of the teacher.

Table 7.2 Gender differences in the use of negative sanctions in co-educational classes (n = 19)

Proportions of all recorded negative corrections	Classes with recorded negative correction (%)
100% corrections to girls; 0% to boys	10.5
60–79% corrections to girls; 21–40% to boys	5.3
50–59% corrections to girls; 41–50% to boys	10.5
41–49% corrections to girls; 50–59% to boys	5.3
1–19% corrections to girls; 60–79% to boys	10.5
0% corrections to girls; 100% to boys	57.9
Total co-ed classes with negative correction	100.0
n	19

There was little evidence of peer teasing or bullying within classes in either co-educational or single-sex schools as classrooms tended to be strongly teacher centred, and taught as a whole group. As they were constantly under observation by the teacher, students could rarely harass other students in any open way. However, we did observe a few incidences of teasing and taunting in nineteen of the forty-seven co-educational classes. Of the incidences recorded of peer teasing, bullying and, in a few cases, fighting between students, almost two-thirds (64 per cent) involved only male students.

While it is clear that boys are more visible in class through both their assertive and disruptive learning styles, and through their social interactions with teachers, they also seem to be the students who are known best by teachers in terms of their first names. Boys were more likely than girls to have their names used publicly in class by the teacher, while girls were more likely to go unnamed when addressed by teachers in the lessons we observed (see Figure 7.2).

Gender awareness in co-educational schools

There were a number of ways in which students' attitudes to gender issues were explored in the schools taking part in the study – through the use of a questionnaire, through student essays and in focus group discussions. While the questionnaire presented students with questions about school climate, the student essays allowed students the freedom to write about whatever inequality they thought was most pressing in their schools.

Although girls did express more reservations about gender inequality in both the questionnaires and the essays, gender differences were not statistically significant in the questionnaire items. Responses to the statement 'Boys and girls are treated equally well in this school', showed that 65 per cent of girls and 70

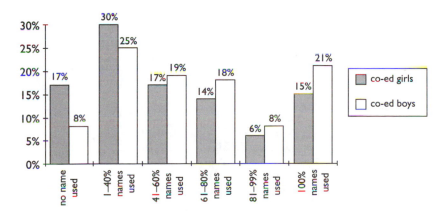

Figure 7.2 Gender differences in the use of first names by teachers in all interactions in co-educational classrooms (*n* = 47)

per cent of boys agreed with the statement. The aggregate scores for each gender across schools conceal differences between schools however (Table A10). Almost all girls (96 per cent) and over 82 per cent of boys in Ballydara (co-ed Com Col)[4] claimed that girls and boys were not treated equally in gender terms in their school, as did 78 per cent of girls and 80 per cent of boys in St Ita's (co-ed fp). Yet in Ollan (co-ed Com Col) less than half of the girls (42 per cent) and 51 per cent of boys claimed there was gender inequality. What is important about these findings is that the schools which reported greatest gender inequality were not the schools where it was always most visible. In both St Ita's (co-ed fp) and Ballydara (co-ed Com Col) there was a debate about gender issues going on at staff level: the principal in Ballydara (co-ed Com Col) was making a concerted effort to promote gender equality in the school, by ensuring that girls and boys were equally represented on various student councils in the school, and by maintaining a gender-balanced review of promotions. The ability to name inequality appeared to differ across schools; it was most developed where a gender discourse was already in place.

The differences in the ability to name gender inequalities were especially notable in student essays. Only a small minority (14 per cent) of all essays written by co-educational students about their experience of inequality in their schools made specific reference to gender injustices.[5] However, of those that did, the majority were written by girls: 21 per cent of girls in co-educational schools listed ways in which they experienced gender inequality in their schools compared with 5 per cent of boys.

The four co-educational schools were more diverse in character and intake than the single-sex schools,[6] and the response to gender issues reflected this diversity, especially in terms of gender awareness. Direct references to incidences of gender inequality in the school emerged most strongly in St Ita's, (co-ed fp) a school with a predominantly urban, middle- and upper middle-class intake (Figure 7.3).

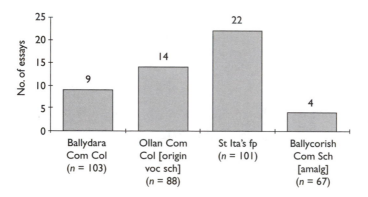

Figure 7.3 Number of student essays naming gender as an equality concern within co-educational schools (*n* = 359)

Thirty-eight per cent of the essays from girls in this school had some comments about gender inequality compared with 7 per cent of boys' essays (Table A11). The students in St Ita's, particularly the girls, displayed an awareness of their rights relating to gender issues, and an ability to name gender inequality that was not evident to the same degree in the other three co-educational schools.

For girls attending St Ita's, a major gender concern centred on sport. Many female students were indignant at the perceived institutional bias in favour of traditional male sports.

> Girls are treated as less important in this school, and the principal here doesn't seem to care, because the girls' hockey team won the whole tournament, and a huge big trophy and all, but the principal just said one small thing about that [at assembly] but when the boys' rugby team win one match it's headline news for weeks.
>
> (A first year female student in St Ita's [co-ed fp])

Physical education was gender segregated in St Ita's. Female students viewed the activities provided for the girls as boring and inferior.

> Girls and boys should have PE together maybe every 2 weeks. This is a co-ed school. The boys always play [rugby/football] while the girls do gymnastics, which isn't fair.
>
> (A second year female student in St Ita's [co-ed fp])

Gender inequalities in relation to sport were also noted by two students in Ballydara:

> The principal never announces when camogie or hockey is on. We have to find out from the trainer, but Gaelic football and rugby [for boys] are announced every week. When the camogie team get to the final, only the other camogie players are allowed to go, but when the hurling team [boys] got to the final, he hired a CIE bus and brought everyone who wanted to go.
>
> (A fifth year female student in Ballydara [co-ed, Com Col])

Although only a small proportion of all essays written in Ballycorish (Com Sch), Ollan (Com Col) or Ballydara (co-ed Com Col) made any reference to gender inequality, these were written mostly by young women (Table A11). In a number of these, girls expressed concerns about the gender-stereotyped views of teachers:

> The principal only asks the boys to help in carrying chairs for example. What really gets me fuming is when we're having a debate or a quiz, the teacher usually asks the boys all the sports questions and the girls the gossip questions.
>
> (A fifth year female student in Ballydara [co-ed Com Col])

We have a male teacher who is very sexist towards girls in the class. He told us we were useless and that the boys should have more chance to develop their skills than us (even though we've never done that subject before). He hardly ever calls us by our names (he says 'Girl' or 'Woman'). He says he is only messing with us and he probably is but I still find it very downgrading.
(A fourth year female student in Ollan [co-ed Com Col])

While picking subjects to take at junior cert level, I wanted to do Mechanical Drawing. However, some boys decided they also wanted to do this but there wasn't enough places in the class. Myself and three other girls were then discouraged from doing the subject by our guidance counsellor. We then had to pick another subject. I had to do Art which I wasn't very interested in and the boys got to do Mechanical Drawing.
(A sixth year female student in Ballycorish [co-ed Com Sch])

Institutionalised gender stereotyping in timetabling was also noted:

In first year, girls had to do PE while boys did computers – this year we [girls] do typing while the boys have a free class. This is discrimination as it is just as important for girls to do computers as well as it's just as important for boys to do PE.
(A second year female student in Ollan [co-ed Com Col])

Boys in St Ita's (co-ed fp) were more likely than all other students in co-educational schools to comment negatively on the level of control and regulation of their behaviour within school: 37 per cent of essays had comments on attempts to control personal expression, in particular the expression of feelings, or behaviour that was seen as feminine. They were challenging the way in which stereotypical gender roles were promoted in the school:

Girls are often seen as having to play a very feminine role, boys are often seen as having to play a very masculine role. I don't like this.
(A second year male student in St Ita's [co-ed fp])

[Following a row with a teacher] I felt like crying so I stormed out of the classroom and tried to get up to the principal's office. But I was told by Mr . . . to be a man and not to cry.
(A second year male student in St Ita's [co-ed fp])

Boys in other co-educational schools expressed little concern about gender inequality in their essays. There were just two issues that emerged, however, the most notable being the perceived harsher punishments meted out to male students.

I came in about two minutes late for [Mr X's]'s class and he gave out to me and he made me stand up for the whole class. Then two girls came in about five minutes after me and he said to them to 'hurry up'.

(A first year male student in Ollan [co-ed Com Col])

The other issue mentioned was that of gender inequality in the provision of Physical Education. Boys in Ollan had no PE classes in the year our study was undertaken and this was a cause of considerable annoyance to the boys in that school.

Silences

One of the salient findings from the essays as well as the focus groups was the way in which sexist practices and procedures went largely unnoticed or disregarded by students. Gender inequality was not part of most students' daily vocabulary-of-analysis. Students often seemed to lack both the language and the general awareness to articulate concerns about gender issues. There was also a sense in which sexist behaviour was considered 'normal'.

Although Ollan (co-ed Com Col) was the co-educational school in which sexist practices were most visible, in terms of the overwhelmingly male profile of senior staff, the lack of discussion of gender issues, and the reluctance to challenge visible sexist practices among teachers and male students, it was also the school in which girls were least likely to claim there was gender inequality. An example of how pervasive this silence was is evident from the following practice witnessed (and experienced by one researcher) on visits to the school. In Ollan senior boys occasionally lined narrow school corridors while waiting for their next class and tried to touch and grope passing female students and younger female teachers. What was evidently a form of harassment for both female students and teachers was not challenged by teachers or management. Neither did any of the female students at this school raise the issue in their essays. When the researcher brought up the issue with senior students at focus group interviews, the girls did not make any comment about it. Senior male students said it was a 'bit of fun', something 'harmless'. However, for both less established female teachers and female and junior students, the experience was not fun. It was described by one female teacher as 'running the gauntlet'.

In Ballycorish Community School we attended the school prize-giving. As certain prizes in the school, such as 'best all-round student of the year', were largely based on popular vote, it was clear from the voting practices that girls were voting for boys for this prize ahead of other girls. The reverse was, evidently, not true of the boys; the boys' vote was going mostly to boys. In subsequent discussions with the staff we raised this matter with teachers. We were told that this was a pattern over a number of years; staff were concerned about it but had not yet found a way of addressing it. Students did not comment on this matter at all, however, either in essays or interviews.

Equalising access to subject provision for male and female students would be regarded as standard educational practice in a co-educational school, yet it was seen by some students as something of a breakthrough in gender relations. It was clear that students held quite traditional views of gender roles, and saw any change in these as something worthy of praise and note.

> Students are treated equally in some cases. In this school, it's great that teachers encourage you to do a subject that you like such as a girl doing Metalwork and a boy doing Home Economics, despite their sex!
> (A sixth year female student in Ballycorish [co-ed Com Sch])

The silences that characterised gender-biased incidences and practices in co-educational schools indicated a general lack of awareness among both students and staff on gender issues. While there was some discussion in the schools about the gender implications of co-education, and concerns were expressed by principals in Ballydara (co-ed Comm Col) and in Ballycorish (co-ed Com Sch) in particular about gender inequality in their schools, the subject was not a core part of the educational discourse of most teachers. Informal conversations in staffrooms with teachers indicated that while some female teachers did have concerns about gender inequality in the schools, these were not a priority for staff generally. Gender differences were generally taken for granted, they were not named. The unintended effect of this was that there was no evident safe space where such issues could be raised by students in the ordinary business of the school.

Conclusion

Although we found strong evidence that public on-task interactions between students and teachers in class are more often gender-balanced than not, none the less, of the 40 per cent of classes that were not gender-balanced, males dominated three out of four. Male students were also more likely than their female peers to publicly engage in both the social and work life of the classroom, although a minority of assertive girls were also observed in the co-educational settings. Male dominance of class time does not mean dominance by all males of all females when it occurs. It tends to be a small minority of boys who dominate class time, and on fewer occasions, a small number of girls. There is a large cohort of boys who are relatively quiet in class and an even larger cohort of girls.

Our findings here suggest that gender differences in classroom participation are not as favourable to boys as suggested in other studies (e.g. Drudy and Ui Cathain 1999; Howe 1997; Lee 1993; Sadker and Sadker 1985; Warrington et al. 2000). While boys who exercise hegemonic masculine styles (by shouting out answers, calling for attention, interrupting other students and the teacher) are the ones most likely to dominate classrooms in terms of on-task participation, this happened in a minority (30 per cent) of the observed classrooms, and in a small number of cases (11 per cent) girls actually dominated.

The reasons why students dominate classes are not singular. In some class-rooms, individuals or small groups of students were dominant not through the operation of highly assertive styles but because teachers afforded them extra attention due to their minority presence. Moreover, patterns of dominance by the few are not unique to the co-educational classrooms. In single-sex classes, small numbers of girls and boys dominated in their respective classes, a finding mirrored at primary level by Lodge (1998).

Although Howe (1997) has drawn attention to the fact that there is a lack of evidence linking male dominance in class with superior examination perfor-mance, none the less our findings do raise questions about the overall long-term effects for girls and certain types of boys, of being subordinate in their classroom experiences. While the lack of control may not influence performance, it is most certainly a form of socialisation. Certain young women and subordinate males are practising being relatively silent in the presence of other young men in co-educational classrooms. It is hard to accept that such practised subordination is unproblematic (Lave and Wenger 1991). In addition, the learning implications of such public disengagement are also far from clear. There is an arguable case that public disengagement may well reinforce negative attitudes to non-traditional 'female' subjects (such as Mathematics and Science) even if it does not directly influence examination performance (Jovanovic and King 1998).

Connell (1995) suggests that domination of women and subordinate men is one of the defining features of hegemonic masculinity. In this study, we found that classroom dominance involved the acquisition of traits associated with hegemonic masculinity. The students who operated with assertive classroom styles dominated the verbal space of the groups to which they belonged. These students (male, and occasionally female) had interactional styles that exhibited traits consistent with hegemonic masculinity, including the competitive seeking of power and control within the classroom. Students who were solely learning-assertive in their dominant style did not undermine teacher authority, however; the minority who operated disruptively challenged not only their classmates, but also the position of the teacher, for control of the classroom.

Notwithstanding the above, co-educational schools as a whole were closer in classroom and school climate to boys' than to girls' schools. In-class surveillance of demeanour, dress, posture and self-representation was least evident in co-educational schools, and very similar in frequency to that in boys' schools (see Figure 5.2). The work focus of co-educational classrooms was also at a fairly similar level to that operating in boys' classes (see Figure 5.1). In addition, concerns about academic pressure were cited far less frequently in the essays of both girls and boys in co-educational schools. The rate of occurrence of such incidences was roughly comparable to that in boys' schools.

The classroom data suggest that boys were more likely to receive stronger and more frequent negative sanctions than girls; they were somewhat more likely to be ridiculed by teachers (and to ridicule peers and teachers themselves). The rare incidences of physically aggressive behaviour we observed all involved boys, and on a few occasions male teachers and boys. (This was true in both co-educational and single-sex schools.)

While the cultural climate of co-educational schools differed from that which operated in the all-male schools, it also had several similarities. Hegemonic masculinity, defined in terms of dominance, toughness, physical strength and heterosexuality (Connell 1995), was also highly prized in co-educational schools. Boys who did not 'measure up' were often teased and isolated. Just as dominance was a defining element in masculinity in boys' schools, it also featured in co-educational schools. In co-educational schools the targets of dominance were extended from other boys (smaller, younger, weaker, gay) to girls, and even female teachers.

There is also evidence, from inside and outside classrooms, and from student essays, that girls perceive gender inequality to be a bigger problem in their co-educational schools than do boys. Although concerns about gender inequality were expressed most strongly in the school in which it was least visible, it was a concern in all schools, albeit a minority one. The fact that it was girls in an elite fee-paying co-educational school who were most articulate about gender inequality concurs in some respects with Australian research findings where it was found that the feminist agenda is most strongly supported in elite girls' schools (Abbott-Chapman et al. 1986; Connell et al. 1982).

The failure to name and address overt harassment practices (such as attempted groping on corridors) as equality issues is undoubtedly evidence of the fact that students lack the capacity and the opportunity to name gender injustices. The failure to document and articulate obvious sexist practices as injustice is itself part of the equality problem. Girls often fail to challenge sexism or name harassment for what it is as they have learned that to challenge or retort in kind is the antithesis of being female. Being feminine is equated with being facilitative and non-abusive; to overtly challenge sexism is to break with this code and become 'unfeminine' (Lees 1993; Francis 1997). Ironically, to protect oneself is to undermine the very self one is trying to protect.

The lack of debate within co-educational schools about the dominating practices of relatively small numbers of boys in relation to other boys as well as girls suggests that dominance-driven definitions of masculinity have hegemonic status; boys also lack the capacity and space to challenge them.

Chapter 8

The diversity deficit

Minorities and the recognition
of difference

Equality and the recognition of difference

Although much of the debate about inequality in education has been dominated
by concerns about distributive justice, in which education is viewed primarily as
a 'good' to be distributed more equally or fairly, there is a growing realisation that
this is too narrow a perspective on equality. There have been calls in particular
for the need to focus on how schools generate injustice by their lack of accom-
modation of differences (Connell 1993).

The recognition model of social justice is concerned with respect for different
identities, values and lifestyles. It focuses attention on the way sociocultural and
symbolic injustices are rooted in patterns of representation, interpretation and
communication. It outlines the way socioculturally generated injustices take the
form of cultural domination, symbolic misrepresentation or non-recognition, all
of which lead to a lack of respect (Baker 1987, 1998; Fraser 1995; Young 1990).

All subordinate groups in society experience some forms of non-recognition
or mis-recognition, including working-class groups. It is evident, for example,
that those who are economically destitute in society are very unlikely to be
granted great respect or have high status (Phillips 1999). However, the inequality
experienced by the economically marginalised has its generative roots in the
politico-economic domain. It would be altered if people could move out of
the space of economic marginalisation, into economically advantaged social
classes in society.

The generative source of the inequality experienced by many other
marginalised groups however is in the sociocultural domain. It is expressed as
non-recognition, misrepresentation and lack of respect for cultural differences.
The socioculturally marginal are identified as 'other' by the dominant group in
society. Such oppressed groups are subject to what Young (1990) describes as
cultural imperialism. They are both rendered invisible (non-recognition) and
simultaneously subject to negative stereotyping (mis-recognition). Negative
images marginalise them as deviant, ugly and threatening, thus legitimating acts
of violence that can be used against them. Not only are their values, perspectives
and life rendered invisible by the life worlds of the dominant group which

permeate cultural and institutional norms; this invisibility causes members of oppressed groups to view themselves through the lens of supposed 'normality'. Furthermore, they often internalise the negative stereotypes to which their group is subjected (Bell 1997).

Inequalities of recognition are fundamentally injustices relating to identity and status therefore. These involve institutional practices of denial, denigration and subordination (Fraser 2000). In schools cultural non-recognition or misrepresentation is grounded in the practices and processes of curriculum provision, pedagogical approaches, peer culture and organisational norms and processes.

Fraser (1995) suggests that the failure to respect the sexual orientation of people who are gay, lesbian or bisexual represents, in many respects, the classic case of non-recognition. The principal cause of the injustice gays and lesbians experience is the failure to recognise their sexuality, the unwillingness to name it and facilitate it on equal terms with heterosexuality. Our entire culture is pervaded by a presumption of heterosexuality, a presumption that also underpins education (Epstein and Johnson 1994). Other groups also experience both non-recognition and mis-recognition, including racial and ethnic minorities, people with disabilities or different abilities and religious minorities. Stereotyping and the denigration of difference have, for example, frequently contributed to the exclusion of students with disabilities from full participation in education (Slee 1997). Failure to consult with those students who are differently abled further compounds their non-recognition and experience of exclusion (Mason 1990; Slee 1998). The level of non-recognition experienced by these different groups varies, however, with the unique cultural and historical contexts of societies and institutions, including schools.

Homogeneity and segregation

Irish schools have traditionally been characterised by homogeneity of student intake. There is a long tradition of segregation of students by belief, by different abilities, by racial affiliation as well as by class and gender. Maintenance of separate educational (and subsequently social) worlds is an often unquestioned institutionalised practice. As Young (1990) argues, oppression of minority groups can occur through the unquestioned norms, practices, habits, processes, hierarchies and cultures of institutions. Social inequality is embedded in both institutional and cultural norms as well as in the beliefs, values and practices of individuals (Bell 1997). Segregated educational provision may well be regarded by many as serving the best interests of different groups of students with different needs. However, the tradition of institutionalised segregation has merely served to perpetuate and justify continued non-recongition and mis-recognition of minority groups.

Travellers[1] are Ireland's largest indigenous ethnic minority group. They have experienced discrimination in the way Irish society in general, and the Irish state in particular, has treated them (McVeigh 1995). Initial provision of primary education for Traveller children involved establishing separate classes (Kenny 2000). Frequently, these children not only experienced institutional segregation but also were subject to rejection by other pupils in the schools (McDonagh 2000). Few Traveller young people have tended to go to second-level schools, opting instead for segregated Training Centres (Drudy and Lynch 1993). Prior to the 1990s, few if any Traveller representatives were included in policy review committees or other groups examining, and making recommendations regarding educational provision for Travellers.

The segregation of Travellers from settled children was mirrored in the education of disabled students. Until the 1980s, children and young people were categorised for educational purposes according to whether they were 'normal' or 'disabled' and educated separately (Kenny et al. 2000). As was the case in Britain, segregated special schools were established to meet the particular needs of different groups of young people, including those with sensory impairments and learning difficulties (French and Swain 1997; Rieser 2000). During the 1990s commitment to the inclusion of young people who were differently abled in mainstream schools began to be expressed at policy level (Kenny et al. 2000).

Despite the rhetoric of inclusiveness, the educational experience of students with disabilities in integrated schools was one of inadequate support and lack of understanding of their needs (Daly 1999; P. McDonnell 1995). In their accounts of their schooling, young people with disabilities have documented their experiences of being pitied, of low teacher expectations, and of the lack of institutional supports and facilities. They also noted the hugely positive support of friends (Kenny et al. 2000).

The segregation of schooling in terms of ethnicity (Travellers) and disability is further compounded by religious segregation. State attempts during the nineteenth century to create a pluralist educational system were successfully resisted by denominational interests (Coolahan 1981; Clarke 1998). After independence, the 1937 Irish Constitution gave a legal underpinning to denominational education, while the State underwrote it financially (Glendenning 1999). During the 1970s a movement aimed at establishing multi-denominational primary schools developed. This met with some success (Linehan 1996). However, it also encountered resistance from powerful interest groups including the churches and individuals within the State (Cooke 1997).

The large majority (over 90 per cent) of the population of the Republic of Ireland is formally Roman Catholic. The remaining population belongs to other religious denominations and beliefs, including the various Protestant denominations, the Jewish community, an Islamic community, and a growing number with secular beliefs. At primary level, the religious profile of the schools roughly mirrors that of the population, with 93 per cent being under Catholic management and 6 per cent under Protestant management. The remainder comprises a small number of multi-denominational or other schools. At second level, 57 per cent of schools are under denominational control. At present, multi-denominational (non-segregated) schools still make up less than 1 per cent of all primary schools in the country. The second-level schools (mostly vocational schools and community colleges) that are classified as multi-denominational by the Department of Education and Science also operate under varying levels of denominational influence depending on their traditions, staff, student intake and location.

While religion, ethnicity and disability have been used to classify and divide students in a public way educationally, those who are gay, lesbian or bisexual are confronted instead with a great silence. The silence that surrounds sexual orientation in the education sector reflects a wider discomfort around sexual issues that has characterised Irish society over a lengthy period (Inglis 1999). Gay, lesbian and bisexual identities remain largely invisible within educational contexts both in terms of formal curricular content and the more informal aspects of the life of institutions. While the recently introduced *Relationships and Sexuality Education* programme (RSE) does contain a limited amount of material on sexual orientation, its inclusion in a school's curriculum is optional as the content has to be decided locally and in consultation with the school patrons, teachers and parents. O'Carroll and Szalacha (2000) report that during the course of their research on the RSE programme, it emerged that not one second-level school had in fact completed the sexual orientation component of the *Relationships and Sexuality* programme. The introduction of a programme for single-sex boys' schools, *Exploring Masculinities*, sparked off controversy in the Irish media. One of the key criticisms of this programme was that it allegedly promoted homosexual lifestyles (Waters 2000) because it included a small section examining issues of sexual orientation. The limited research that has been done regarding educational experiences of those who are gay, lesbian or bisexual indicates that schools are lonely and isolating places, contributing to depression, extreme self-criticism, fear of rejection and harassment (Glen/NEXUS 1995). There is also little evidence of support for teachers who are gay or lesbian (Gowran 2000).

The way schools in Ireland have traditionally managed diversity therefore has been through segregation, and in the case of sexual orientation, denial and silence. While there is now a move away from these traditions, in terms of formal policy, practices of segregation, division and silence are still very visible in schools.

The absence of diversity within participating schools

The student intake in each of the twelve schools tended to be strongly homogeneous, reflecting the long history of formal segregation in place within the State. Even where there were small numbers of students from ethnic, religious or disabled groups within the schools, their differences were generally not claimed in any public or formal way by the school as an institution. It would be unfair to the schools, however, to suggest that school management was indifferent to the needs of minorities. There was a reluctance to focus on differences of religion, ethnicity and disability in a public way because of the small numbers of students involved. With very small numbers of minority students, to name differences was to name individuals. The teachers and principals feared that focusing attention on their differences might compound any difficulties they had in living in a highly homogeneous environment.

Traditionally, students with learning disabilities and those with major physical disabilities have attended segregated schools. Not surprisingly, therefore, less than 2 per cent of students in the study defined themselves as disabled, and most of their impairments were relatively minor sensory (hearing, sight, speech) or mobility impairments. Only six students claimed they had learning difficulties (less than 0.5 per cent of all those surveyed).

The participating schools were also quite homogeneous in their ethnic and racial intakes. In over 92 per cent of cases, both parents were Irish. Of those with a non-Irish parent, most were white and either from the UK, the USA or Canada, Europe, or some other 'developed' country (88 per cent). None of the students in the survey, or in the classes we observed, were members of Ireland's largest ethnic minority, the Travelling community. (This is not surprising given that most Travellers do not transfer to mainstream second-level schools but are more likely to attend segregated training centres.) Only one of the participating schools had an identifiable group of ethnic minority students.

Nine of the twelve schools in the study were owned and managed by various denominational bodies. The remainder comprised a community school, in which the Vocational Education Committee and a Catholic religious order were joint trustees, and two community colleges, both managed by the Vocational Education Committee of the relevant local authority. The religious intake of the majority of the schools was also quite homogeneous, reflecting the formal affiliation of the vast majority of the Irish population to the Roman Catholic Church (Central Statistics Office 1991).[2] Of those surveyed in the schools, 85 per cent professed to be Catholic, 6 per cent agnostic, 3 per cent Protestant, 1 per cent 'Christian', and less than 1 per cent other beliefs. The remainder did not answer the question.

As we were unable to ask about the sexual orientation of students for the reasons explained in Chapter 1, we do not know what proportion of students defined themselves as gay, lesbian or bisexual. What we were able to examine however was student attitudes to sexual differences and these are discussed below.

As part of our study, we asked students to write about their most pressing equality concerns and their own experiences of inequality in their school lives.[3] Only a tiny minority of all those who wrote such essays ($n=1,202$) named any minority identity as a factor contributing to their experience of inequality in their school (Figure 8.1).

The lack of awareness of equality and minority identities expressed by young people in schools was mirrored by a similar lack of concern expressed spontaneously by their teachers. While 12 per cent of teachers who answered a question on important equality issues in Irish education named gender, less than 1 per cent of these respondents named disability, sexual orientation, religious

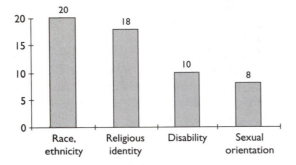

Figure 8.1 Numbers of student essays in which minority identity issues arose as named equality issues in their school (*n* = 1,202)

identity, race or ethnicity as a factor contributing to educational inequality in the school.

Sexual orientation – invisibility and rejection

Those who were gay, lesbian or bisexual were the most invisible and marginalised minority in terms of public discourse. Ten of the twelve schools in the study did not deal with differences in sexual orientation in any systematic way. This was equally true of denominationally controlled and multi-denominational schools. There was no recognised space in the education programmes of these schools where issues of sexual orientation could be discussed in a safe and inclusive way. Sexual orientation was a taboo subject in a number of different respects. Neither school prospectuses nor year books made any explicit reference to sexual difference. While we presented results from our attitudinal data to the staffs in all twelve schools, indicating the high level of homophobia among students, the problems arising from homophobia (or lesbophobia) were only raised by teachers in the public discussions in one all-boys' (Catholic) school.

This institutional invisibility was reinforced by the lack of a vocabulary to name and discuss sexual differences. Students were generally not accustomed to addressing the subject of sexual orientation, so they literally did not know what to say or how to say what they did feel or know. When the subject of sexual orientation emerged either in whole-class contexts or in focus-group discussions, it caused a lot of discomfort and unease among both junior and senior students in general.

The fact that the issue of sexual orientation was only raised spontaneously in eight of the twelve hundred essays as a cause of unequal treatment in schools is itself indicative of the silence that prevails. This is not to suggest that sexual orientation is not a sensitive or important subject in schools, but merely to point out that it was a subject about which people did not speak. The schools participating in our study were by no means unique in terms of their institutional silence and discomfort regarding sexual orientation. A review of Irish educational research on this subject revealed silences not only in schools but also in the research literature (Gay HIV Strategies/NEXUS 2000; O'Carroll and Szelacha 2000).

When the subject of sexual orientation emerged in the focus groups, it caused a lot of discomfort and unease among both junior and senior pupils in general. The subject of sexual differences evoked sentiments of ignorance, fear and hostility, especially among boys. Students made strongly homophobic remarks about gay men in particular:

> Set all fags on fire.
>
> (A second year student in Ballinroe [ssb fr])

> Gays should not be allowed to be educated. They have a perverted problem.
>
> (A third year student in St David's [ssb fp])

> Mr . . . has a problem with me but maybe that's because I have a problem with him, he is GAY! He is always poking me and I think he is bent.
>
> (A third year student in Ballinroe [ssb fr])

Being gay was also perceived as a disorder by some:

> I think this school should be made a co-education [school] for the sake of the students already attending. For I'd say of the students that don't really mix outside they probably end up *gay*.
>
> (A third year student in St David's [ssb fp])

And teasing and bullying among boys sometimes centred on labelling someone as gay.

> Sometimes out in the yard, I don't like it when people call me names or say I'm gay.
>
> (A first year student in St Dominic's [ssb fr])

Students participating in the study were presented with a series of attitude statements regarding minority groups. Their lack of understanding and feelings of negativitiy towards sexual minorities emerged clearly, especially among boys. In response to the statement 'It is not unusual to be gay or lesbian', almost half of all students (48 per cent) disagreed, indicating that they considered such identities as deviant from the dominant cultural norm (Figure 8.2, p. 144). Discovering that a friend was gay or lesbian was considered grounds for termination of friendship by a majority of respondents. In response to the statement 'If I found out my friend was gay or lesbian, that would end our friendship', 55 per cent indicated that it would.

It was notable, however, that where an individual teacher or a specific school programme had addressed the issue, as had occurred in two of the schools, pupils in focus groups were better able to examine their own ambiguous feelings and fears. A proactive approach by their school or teacher was judged by them to have helped to create a space in which this aspect of sexuality could be explored. A few students observed, however, that there was a need for a lot more education on the subject of sexuality.

> [There is a need for] mass education about the normality and acceptability of homosexuality. There is a huge lack in sex education in school [on this subject].
>
> (A sixth year male student in St Ita's [co-ed fp])

Travellers and racial minorities

Although non-recognition (silence) and mis-recognition (negative stereotyping) were most acute in relation to sexual orientation, mis-recognition also operated strongly in relation to ethnicity (Traveller status especially), racial identity (especially as signified by colour and, to a lesser degree, by accent), disability and religious differences. Mis-recognition, in the form of deep-seated prejudice towards Travellers, was encountered across most of the schools in discussions following on from essays. Many students were quite willing to express their dislike and antagonism towards Travellers in public although a minority of students did contest their prejudiced views in the focus groups.

In general, Travellers themselves were regarded as responsible for the discrimination and prejudice they experienced. A sixth year girl in Ollan (co-ed Com Col) explained during a focus group discussion that 'Travellers could fit in like anyone else – if they tried they'd fit in. They only make trouble for themselves.' Students referred to them as 'knackers' during the course of focus group discussions and in their classrooms. In some cases, ridicule of a particular area or location was related to the fact that some of the people who lived there were Travellers.

The historical denigration of Travellers was used by some as an explanation for the continued prejudice against them. In the course of focus group discussions, a third year boy in Ballinroe (ssb fr) explained that 'people act on the reputation they [Travellers] have. People are used to hating them.'

A number of students believed that Travellers would not be accepted by parents or other students in their school.

> I think because this school is quite snobbish there are inequalities, which are a result of students' attitudes. . . . For example, although I myself wouldn't have anything against a Traveller coming to this school, I think she would get a hard time due to a large number of snobs in the school.
>
> (A sixth year student in St Cecilia's [ssg fp])

A fifth year male student in St David's (ssb fp) explained 'my parents pay for me to have privilege and [they] wouldn't like Travellers in this school'.

The hostility and negativity expressed in comments such as those quoted above were reflected in the negative responses to attitude statements regarding Travellers in the student questionnaire. In response to the statement 'Travellers would fit in well at this school', only one-quarter (24 per cent) of all respondents were in agreement. Almost all the respondents (91 per cent) felt that 'Having Travellers in this school would make life difficult for the teachers and the pupils'. Travellers were not seen as potential friends; indeed, students feared that being associated with a Traveller would result in social rejection – over half the students agreed that 'If I made friends with a Traveller, my other friends might not go around with me anymore' (Figure 8.3, p. 144).

Where positive attitudes were expressed, these tended to be held by individuals who had previous or ongoing positive contact with Travellers (as neighbours or as school friends in their primary schools). Some of the students attending both urban and rural schools had been in primary classrooms with Traveller children. These students explained how they had no problems with their Traveller classmates, 'everyone got on fine'. Some of the most noticeably positive attitudes expressed by individuals were in towns or places where a proactive approach had been taken in a locality to increase understanding and acceptance between Travellers and settled people. For example, one male student in a school in one such town argued with the researcher while completing his questionnaire that a Traveller student could be offended at the content of some of the attitude statements, and that it was debatable whether or not they should be used at all as they might fuel prejudice. During the course of a focus group discussion with another class group in the same school, a male student argued with his peers that 'Travellers have the right to have an education'.

The lack of any sizeable ethnic minority in most schools meant that there was no way of exploring students' responses to racial and ethnic minorities, except hypothetically. A fifth year male student in St David's (ssb fp) argued during a focus group discussion that individuals belonging to racial minorities would be tolerated, but that this would change 'if a large number of them came to the school, then people [would be] prejudiced and resentful'. Indeed, this expectation mirrored the situation in the only school where there was any evidence of a clash between different ethnic groups. This school had a sizeable minority of non-national students. As these students were a relatively homogeneous group culturally, they were readily identifiable as 'different'. This is how one of the overseas students described the attitudes in the school:

> Foreigners are treated as though they are not only unintelligent, but also cheaters and wasters by the teachers. . . . Students treat new people who are not from Ireland like dirt and the only people who have made any efforts at nice behaviour after being here 3 months are the other foreign students.
> (A fifth year student in St Ita's [co-ed fp])

While there was some evidence of mis-recognition of individuals or groups belonging to racial minorities in schools, the attitudes expressed by students towards Travellers were noticeably more negative. Student responses to attitude statements clearly demonstrated much higher levels of negative stereotyping and rejection for Travellers than for other ethnic or racial minorities. For example, less than a quarter (23 per cent) of respondents agreed with the statement 'In this school you would get bullied if you were black or coloured' while three-quarters (76 per cent) said that Travellers would not fit into their school.

Comments by the small minority of ethnic minority students in the study do suggest, however, that there is little understanding and appreciation of ethnic and racial differences. One student reported how differences in his appearance and accent posed difficulties for him:

> I am originally English so when I arrived in this country I got some abuse because of my accent. I am also quite dark-skinned, so in this country it pertains to being a 'Nigger'.
>
> (A fifth year student in Ballinroe [ssb fr])

Religious belief

As most Irish schools are relatively homogeneous in religious terms, including those in this study, it is not easy to assess the level of religious prejudice or discrimination that prevails. At focus groups and in informal discussions, students appeared to have little interest in religion per se, a finding that concurs with that of McDonnell (1995).

In most schools, the views expressed indicated a sense of ignorance about religious differences rather than prejudice against any particular set of beliefs. In Ollan (co-ed Com Col), a school situated in an area with a very homogeneous population in terms of belief, junior pupils expressed worry about their ability to understand or be 'close to' a peer with a different religious affiliation. When probed, this appeared to be based on complete lack of contact with members of other religious denominations or beliefs. They simply said they did not know if they could cope with difference as they had no experience of it. A senior male student in St David's (ssb fp) expressed the view that his school's homogeneous religious intake encouraged rather than challenged his own prejudices, explaining 'I know I see Protestants, for example, as different, "not like us"'. He felt that if his school had a more diverse student intake, people could become accustomed to difference.

In one school where there were identifiable religious minorities, there was a widespread belief among these students that the majority were not especially tolerant or respectful of their religious beliefs, particularly where those beliefs impacted on student lifestyle and ability to participate in peer culture.

> The students are very cold to you if you are smart and you don't do drugs or smoke or drink when you go out. They have problems with you if you have ANY morals or religion about your life.
>
> (A fifth year female student in St Ita's [co-ed fp])

Ballycorish (co-ed Com Sch) was a school with a predominantly Roman Catholic student intake, yet it had a sizeable minority of students from a range of Protestant denominations. Students were aware of the family religious affiliation of their peers because it was a close-knit rural area. There were no prejudicial views expressed by any students during focus group discussions, nor were there any complaints regarding this issue in their essays. Senior students taking part in two different focus group discussions in this school expressed the view that the mixed religious intake in their school had a very positive effect: 'people are not bothered [about religious difference], mixing people of different religions in school helps them not to care about difference'. Friendships across religious divides were the norm in their school.

In general, issues for individual students belonging to minority religious beliefs related to non-recognition rather than hostility and rejection. However, there were exceptions. One student from a minority faith in a single-sex boys' school complained:

> I am a Protestant and I am in a Catholic school. The other pupils do not understand me and give me a hard time. My last year's religion teacher nearly had a heart attack when [the teacher] discovered my religion. [The teacher] began to treat me more like I was above the class. I received a lot more attention than other class members and the class naturally assumed I was a lick. They threatened me with threats like I'll send the IRA to your gaff. Now they are only slightly better.
>
> (A third year student [ssb fr])

Comments made by students either during focus group discussions or recorded in more informal situations showed that, for some, Protestant identity was exclusively associated with Northern Ireland and unionist politics. In a single-sex girls' school, students talking informally about a teacher they liked said they assumed that this person was Protestant because of having a Northern Irish accent and background. In St Dominic's (ssb fr), one focus group clearly associated all Protestants with activities and beliefs of the Orange Order, unionism and Glasgow Rangers. One of the boys in this group explained that he would not want any Protestants in his school 'because they think they're English'.

Responses to attitude statements regarding religious affiliation of peers showed a lower level of negativity and hostility than did statements either regarding Travellers or people who are gay. None the less, there was some evidence of distrust around religious differences. One-quarter (25 per cent) of students agreed with the statement 'I would like my close friends to have the same religion as myself'; 14 per cent of respondents agreed that 'Pupils of different religions should not be mixed in the same school'. Almost half (46 per cent) of students disagreed with the statement that 'In this school it does not matter what religion any pupil has'.

The most striking aspect of any discussion regarding religious identity was its apparent lack of any relevance to the lives of young people. During the course of focus group discussions, most young people stated that religious belief was either an entirely private, individual matter, or was of no particular importance in their own lives. In some cases (and this was also evident in some essay comments) students expressed a certain tension regarding the significance afforded to religious expression or identity and the ethos and authority of their school.

> [I would like] less influence of the church on the school. The church inflicts morals and opinions which are sometimes unwanted.
>
> (A sixth year male student Dunely [ssb fr])

> Religion should not be [a] compulsory [subject] but there should be religion classes for those of different religions, not just Catholic.
>
> (A sixth year female student, St Cecilia's [ssg fp])

Disability

The silence around the subject of disability was not underpinned by the same hostility that characterised students' attitudes towards members of the Travelling community or to those who were gay, lesbian or bisexual. Indeed, responses to attitude statements regarding persons with disabilities were generally positive. For example, in response to the statement 'Disabled pupils are treated as well as everyone else in this school' over three-quarters (76 per cent) of all students agreed. There was a greater likelihood of students expressing pity for someone with a disability than dislike or antagonism; they were more often defined in terms of a discourse of charity than a discourse of antagonism or fear.

Students who had little previous contact with disabled students defined them as deserving 'sympathy' and being 'in need of care'. In response to the statement 'Pupils who have disabilities should go to special schools' most did not accept this; however, almost one-third (29 per cent) of all respondents agreed that special schools were the more appropriate place for learners with disabilities. During a second year focus group discussion in St Dominic's (ssb fr) students explained this in terms of the unsuitability of the environment in the school (including behaviour and attitude of students) to cater for the perceived needs and vulnerability of a person with a disability. One of the participants explained 'it's not that you wouldn't want him here – it's for his own safety'. Attitudes to disability therefore reflected assumptions about the dependency of disabled people, combined with a view that having an impairment was some type of tragedy deserving sympathy.

Where students had had some opportunity to mix on equal terms with disabled students in their school, there was some evidence of a 'rights' perspective on disability issues. Students expressed concern about the unsuitability of their school buildings (and in one case of the pushing on crowded corridors and stairs) for a person with a mobility-related impairment.

There could be better facilities for the handicapped pupil such as a lift so he can get upstairs instead of being stuck downstairs all the time.

> (A fourth year student in St David's [ssb fp])

More facilities should be provided for the disabled people and extra time between classes so they can get to class on time.

> (A sixth year student in St Cecilia's [ssg fp])

Where pupils had direct contact with a person with a disability in their class, or as a member of their friendship group, they did not describe that individual in terms of their 'helplessness', or with a sense of pity. Indeed, third year students participating in a focus group discussion in Our Lady's (ssg fr) described how annoyed they felt when others (students or staff) treated their disabled classmate as different or helpless. A second year boy from St David's (ssb fp) spoke about the impact on his own attitudes of having a wheelchair user in his class. 'Before John [not his real name] came to the school if I looked at a person in a wheelchair I really didn't know a lot about them. But when John came I realised he's just another person.'

Overall, disability was a very minor equality theme in essays, with only ten students naming it as an issue spontaneously. This does not suggest that disability-related inequalities are not important in and of themselves; rather it suggests that disability equality issues had not arisen for the very small group of disabled students in the schools we were in.

The dominant attitude to disabled students, expressed in both the discussions and the essays, was one of concern and care. Of those who expressed a view, most felt that disabled students would be dependent, vulnerable and in need of care. There were only a few individual students who were aware of the educational rights of disabled students, and the majority of these were either friends with, or in a class with, a disabled person.

Gender differences

There were noticeable gender differences in the attitudes expressed towards members of minority groups. In all cases, boys were more likely to respond negatively to attitude statements regarding various groups. This was particularly true of their responses to statements about sexual orientation and about Travellers. As can be seen from Figure 8.2, almost half of all male respondents strongly disagreed that it was normal or usual to be gay or lesbian. Far fewer girls expressed such views.

Male students were also more negative about Travellers, and more extreme in their responses. As can be seen from Figure 8.3, almost one-third of all boys strongly agreed that they would be in danger of losing their other friends if they became acquainted with a Traveller. Only 10 per cent of the girls expressed similarly strong negative views.

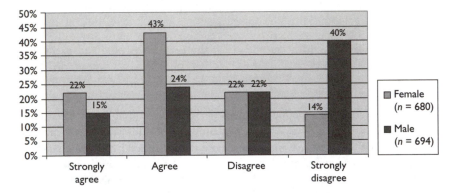

Figure 8.2 Student level of agreement with the statement 'It is not unusual to be gay or lesbian' (*n* = 1,374)

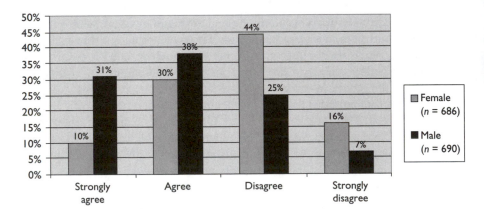

Figure 8.3 Student level of agreement with the statement 'If I made friends with a Traveller my other friends might not go around with me anymore' (*n* = 1,376)

The more negative views of minorities expressed by the boys in the study lend support to claims by Robert Connell (1995) and Michael Kaufman (1994) about how masculinity is defined. If, as Connell suggests, the most glorified form of masculinity is one that is premised on principles of domination, not only of women but of subordinate men, then it is easy to see why boys and young men denigrate groups they believe to be inferior, in particular gay men. Their hostility towards Travellers and gay men involves a distancing from subordinate males, and from subordinated masculinities in society generally. It is a way of identifying with 'hegemonic masculinity', itself a supremacist concept (Connell 1995).

Conclusion

Young people are active contributors to cultural values, norms and practices (Qvortrup 1993). In the way they spoke to each other, and about each other, and in the way they expressed their fears, hostilities and anxieties about minorities, it is evident that young people are actively reproducing hierarchical, oppressive relations in society through their own peer interactions, values, norms and culture (Corsaro 1997; Lodge and Flynn 2001). However, the culture of disrespect for differences is not entirely a product of peer culture. It is played out within an education system which, for a long period of time, has been characterised by segregation, and a lack of recognition for difference and diversity, in its institutional processes and structures.

The data suggest that the groups that experienced the strongest forms of non-recognition (denial of their existence or lifestyle) and mis-recognition (negative representations) were those that were gay or lesbian, and Travellers. The analysis of attitude statements in particular, but also essays and focus groups, indicated that those who were gay or lesbian, and those who were Travellers, were often not seen as suitable friends or even school companions. While there were exceptions, differences were frequently judged as inferior, or as abnormal and deviant. In all cases boys were more negative in their attitudes than girls, significantly so in many cases. While disabled people, religious and racial minorities were also the subject of negative stereotyping, at the time of our study, they did not evoke the same level of hostility or disrespect as gays, lesbians and Travellers[4] (Lynch and Lodge 1999).

It was encouraging to note, however, that there was some resistance in schools to the dominant discourses of prejudice against Travellers and gays and lesbians in particular. Where education initiatives had taken place to promote understanding, they did at least create voices of dissent, voices that recognised and respected differences.

Part 4

Discipline and power

Power relations pose a number of equality problems, problems that are inter-related with, but separate from, distribution and recognition issues. In some respects the analysis of power as an equality issue is one of the least developed perspectives within egalitarian thinking. Boundaries between academic disciplines and areas of specialisation have had a tendency to separate these issues from those relating to the distribution of opportunities and resources. Here again, Young (1990) has usefully reasserted the importance of power relations to issues of social justice, drawing on the work of Foucault and other post-structuralist writers. Fraser (2000) has recently acknowledged the importance of this dimension of equality also.

Much research on education does not focus on power relations *per se*; frequently power relations between students and teachers are not problematised, they are taken as a hierarchical given. The focus is on 'discipline', on order and control, on how to use power 'over' others effectively. The language of adults is used to name the issues of power. Wilson and Cowell describe school discipline as 'a kind of sophisticated common sense' (1990: xiv). Others suggest discipline strategies and techniques for teachers in their classrooms (Blandford 1998; Charles 1996; Heffernan 1998; McHugh *et al.* 1997; Moles 1990; Robertson 1996; Rogers 1997; Wolfenden 1994). Within Ireland there are regular proposals to introduce new disciplinary policies, systems and procedures to ensure the more effective functioning of schools (ASTI 1995, 1996b; Martin 1997).

Control and discipline are regarded as the necessary precursor of learning (Elton Report 1989; Haroun and O'Hanlon 1997; Clark 1998). Teachers are expected to exercise some authority over learners (Lortie 1984; Tirri and Puolinatha 2000). While discipline, in the sense of fair rules and regulations, is undoubtedly a pre-requisite for the running of a complex organisation such as a school, it is a very narrow and restrictive perspective to take on student–teacher relations. The neglect of the power dimension of relations is not surprising, however, when seen in the light of the relations of research production and dissemination. Education research is produced by adults who are 'experts' for other adult educators and policy makers. Students have not been party to the research dialogue. Moreover, positivism dominates methodologies and theoretical practice in educational research. The world of schooling is named and known by academics who lay claim to objectivity and impartiality in the analysis of the research subject. Dialogue and partnership with the research subject (students in this case) are not part of the stock in trade, certainly not in relation to research on children and young persons.

Without intent, traditional positivist research can and does operate as a form of colonisation. It creates public images about young people (in both the academic and the policy world) over which they have little or no control. This phenomenon is similar to the researched experience of other subordinate groups in society. Poor people, Travellers, asylum seekers, disabled people, and increasingly, women, become the subjects of books and papers in which their lives are recorded by professional middle-class experts who are frequently removed from their culture and lifestyle (Lynch and O'Neill 1994; Bourdieu 1993). By owning data about subordinate groups, the 'experts' (and the policy institutions and state departments that pay them) own part of them. The very owning and controlling of the stories of subordinates adds further to the subordination as it means that there are now people who can claim to know and understand you better than you understand yourself, and to speak on your behalf (Lynch 1999a). However unwittingly, education researchers have all too often played this role in relation to their analysis of the power relations between teachers and students in compulsory education.

The net effect of interpreting the world from the perspective of the 'expert' is that the viewpoint of the outsider is privileged over that of the insider, the adult expert over the child in the case of much of educational research. The privileging of the expert produces perspectives on power and inequality therefore that are politically and emotionally detached from the experiences that generated their articulation in the first place. In education we rarely name the domination of young people as an injustice, it is accepted as a political and institutional inevitable.

Arising from the work of Foucault (1977a, b, 1980) in particular, however, there is a growing awareness among educationalists of the importance of power as a research problematic (Francis 1998). The conceptualisation of power as a static entity, divided between those who have it and those over whom it is exercised, has been deconstructed and problematised. There is a realisation that power is not simply localised in a person or a position, that it is not a possession. Power is increasingly regarded as a series of relations that may be neither readily visible nor observable, but which are of profound educational importance none the less (Baker 1998; Devine 2000; Holligan 1999; Oyler 1996; Walkerdine 1990; Welland 2001).

The problematising of authority by post-structuralists has been paralleled by the rise of new 'rights' and 'voice' discourses among educationalists (Archard 1993; Epp and Watkinson 1996). Researchers have increasingly begun to realise that the adult perspective on schooling is just one standpoint and that it need not have any more authority than that of the student. There is a growing realisation that only those affected by something can speak about it in a practical way on their own behalf (Foucault 1977b: 209). What the new research work *with* young people (as opposed to research on them) has led to is a realisation that schools may be harming children and young people by the way in which they exercise control and authority. There is a growing body of evidence suggesting that schooling practices that fail to respect the autonomy and individuality of the student, that fail to manage power relations between students and teachers in a respectful manner, may have quite negative educational consequences (Best 1983; Collins 2000; Fagan 1995; John 1996; Herr and Anderson 1997; Pomeroy 1999; Rudduck *et al.* 1996; Yoneyama 2000). Within this literature, there is also a recognition of the importance of teachers in the lives of young people in school. Schools are experienced through the medium of individual teachers, both positively and negatively. Relationships with teachers are crucial in terms of how students define school.

Recognising the importance of relationships or the circulatory nature of power does not take away from the fact that schooling is not a matter of choice for children or young people in most societies. It is compulsory in practice if not in law. Its compulsory nature means that conflict is endemic to relationships between students and teachers (Bourne 2001; Candela 1999; Cothran and Ennis 1997). As Waller (1932) noted many years ago, schooling is there for the 'good' of children and young people, as defined by adults, consequently:

> The teacher-pupil relationship is a form of institutionalised dominance and subordination. Teacher and pupil confront each other in the school with an original conflict of desires, and however much that conflict may be reduced in amount, or however much it may be hidden it still remains. The teacher represents the adult group, ever the enemy of the spontaneous life of groups of children.
>
> (Waller 1932: 195)

Power relations pose equality problems, not only in terms of student–teacher relations, but also in terms of relations between teachers, relations between students, and relations between teachers and school managers. Neither students nor teachers are homogeneous in terms of the power resources they exercise. Consequently, in the following two chapters we explore how power relations operate in schools, first between students and teachers (Chapter 9) and then between teachers themselves (Chapter 10). We explore student and teacher views on the way power and authority are exercised in schools, and the challenges for equality that arise.

It is worth noting that the relationship of power and authority that teachers are expected to assume over young people is not one with which many of them necessarily feel easy. Teachers can experience ambiguous feelings about the authoritarian aspect of their role. The power differentials that exist between adults and young people in a school context can distort relationships between them (Hargreaves 2000). Tirri (1999) reports that teachers' most common moral dilemmas relate to their exercise of power over students. They do not feel that their training has adequately prepared them to deal with this aspect of their job (Tirri and Puolinatha 2000). They are also aware that their professional competence is judged by the level of control they have over the young people they teach (Denscombe 1985).

Chapter 9

Regimes of power and resistance

Introduction

One of the objectives of this research was to examine the equality agenda in schools as defined by young persons themselves. Both our own pilot study, and the findings of similar studies focused on student voice (Blatchford 1996; Nieto 1994; Rudduck *et al.* 1996; Woods 1990), indicated that if we were to hear what young people understood by equality in education, we needed to employ a diverse and age-sensitive range of research procedures.

A number of different research techniques were employed therefore to listen to young people, including focus groups, informal meetings and discussions, and essays. In addition, a more structured questionnaire was devised for measuring attitudes to schooling, and to a variety of equality issues.

In this chapter we report the findings from student essays about equality in school. A total of 1,202 students (77 per cent of the total sample population) completed essays in response to the following questions:

> We would like you to write here about any time or place when you think you've been unfairly or unequally treated since you came to this school, either by other students or teachers.

> To make school a fairer and more equal place, what kinds of changes would you like to see in it?

The essays were analysed in terms of the major equality issues arising and the sub-themes within these. As the issues raised by students in their essays were also the subject of discussion in the focus groups and other informal meetings, the analysis below will draw on these sources also when examining the voiced concerns of students about equality.

When we set out to do this research, our assumptions as to what constituted the 'equality' problem in schools were framed by the relevant literature. As the literature had indicated the issues of social class, race, gender, ethnicity, disability and sexual orientation were the major equality problematics in education, we set out to examine the microphysics of these inequalities in schools. To that end we set out to listen to students and to hear what their equality priorities were. We listened to the 'voices' of young people, expressed through their essays, their informal 'chats' with us, and focus group discussions. Rather than treating views about teachers, school and peers as a set of predictable 'complaints' about schooling, we analysed these concerns in the light of current debates about equality, difference and power. In taking their perspectives seriously, we identified a more varied and complex set of equality concerns among young people than what is defined by sociologists and other researchers. Most especially it became clear that the distributive view of social justice, that which viewed education as an unproblematic good to be distributed equally across all students, was only one dimension of the equality problem as seen by students.

The study also devoted time to listening to teachers' spontaneously articulated concerns about equality issues in their schools. Their comments and concerns resonated strongly with those of their students, especially in relation to the exercise of authority. Power was an equality problematic therefore for both students and teachers.

Student essays on school

When those who are managed and controlled, as young people are in schools, begin to speak for themselves, Foucault (1977b: 209) reminds us that theirs is a discourse against power, a counter-discourse. This chapter is therefore, in several respects, a counter-discourse against power as told essentially by young people. It presents a challenge to the way in which power and control are exercised in schools.

Relations with teachers, rather than relations with peers, were the principal focus of student essays and discussions about equality. Within this context, issues of respect, differential power, and the exercise of authority were the over-riding themes (Figure 9.1). Other equality issues (such as differentiation by social class, gender identity, sexual orientation, ethnicity) featured in student essays, but were not given the prominence accorded to issues of power, authority and respect (see Figure A3).

Lukes (1977: 77–78) argues that, beyond the satisfaction of certain basic needs, respect involves the entitlement to realise a number of basic capacities; namely, the capacity to act with autonomy, the capacity to act, think and experience within private spaces, and the capacity to realise individual potential. Much of the essay material focused around the schools' failure to grant students sufficient autonomy and privacy in particular. A smaller number of students expressed an awareness of how existing power relations within schools impair their capacity to develop as persons.

Almost half of all those who wrote essays (47 per cent) expressed concerns regarding the level of respect afforded to them as young people. They noted in particular the respect differential between themselves and teachers. A similar proportion of the essays (48 per cent) were concerned about specific instances

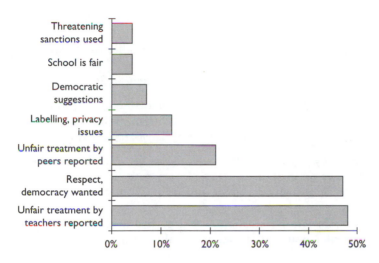

Figure 9.1 Essays on school: comments on the exercise of power and authority (*n* = 1,202)

involving either teachers or school administration in which they felt that they as students had been unfairly treated. Power differentials between members of the peer group were also a cause for complaint, with approximately one-fifth of all student essays (21 per cent) being concerned with some aspect of unfair or unequal treatment within the peer group.

Student concern with issues of power and authority did not focus only on negative experiences or problems. Many also expressed aspirations for improved respect or democratic participation between young people and adults. A small number of students (6.8 per cent) made concrete suggestions regarding the establishment of procedures or structures to facilitate the democratisation of relations between students and teachers.

A question of respect

> I'd like to see teachers treating students equally, they don't. They should have respect for students and listen to their opinions – after all we're people too. . . . I think that a lot of the time teachers abuse their positions of power.
>
> (A second year student in Ollan [co-ed Com Col])

The arbitrary or unfair use of authority by adults was the issue that received most comment in student essays. While students clearly accepted the exercise of regulation and control when they perceived it to be fair and reasonable, they firmly rejected authority that was seen as arbitrary or unnecessary.

Students were keenly aware not only of the power differential between teachers and students in schools, but also of the respect differential.

> [I would like] for teachers to act as they [do] with other adults. For them to show respect.
>
> (A third year student in St Peter's [ssg fr])

> [They should show] more respect to the students because in order for teachers to gain respect from students, the teachers must first give respect.
>
> (A fifth year male student in Ballydara [co-ed Com Col])

> I would like if they were nicer. This school is not that nice. I would like if people were nicer, some of the teachers are very hard.
>
> (A first year female student in Ollan [co-ed Com Col])

The use of sarcasm and humiliating sanctions was deeply resented and regarded as disrespectful of students. It was an issue that received much comment in essays:

> A teacher in our school if you do the smallest thing wrong in [subject], she makes you feel about 2 inches tall. She humiliates you in front of the whole class and sometimes makes people cry.
>
> (A third year student in St Cecilia's [ssg fp])

> They [teachers] bully many students with unnecessary punishments for innocent enough things and some extremely hurtful comments.
>
> (A fifth year male student in St Ita's [co-ed fp])

> She [the subject teacher] made us stand for the whole class and embarrassed us in front of the whole class. She told us we were pathetic little children and that we made her feel sick. She made me feel like shit.
>
> (A fifth year student in St Peter's [ssg fr])

> The punishments which [Ms L] had given us e.g. standing with our faces against the door are unjust.
>
> (A third year student in St Cecilia's [ssg fp])

Shouting at students and not giving them a right of reply evoked some strong comments in the focus groups:

> The teachers are all really moany. I get so fucking pissed off with it and you can't shout back at them no matter how much they shout at you. I think we should be treated like normal fucking human beings.
>
> (A second year female student in Ballydara [co-ed Com Col])

While critical comments in all schools only referred to a few teachers, when students had problems or negative interaction with even one individual teacher, this tended to colour their attitude to the school as a whole. Dislike of school was often due to the negative experiences students had with a very small number of teachers.

The prison image

A number of students resorted to the metaphor of the prison to express their sense of being overly regulated and controlled:

> This school is like a jail because they even lock the classrooms at lunch.
>
> (A first year student in Our Lady's [ssg fr])

> [The school] should change its prison image.
>
> (A fifth year student in St Patrick's [ssg fr])

> This school is like a prison. Teachers don't listen to anything you have to say. They're right and you're wrong.
>
> (A fifth year male student in St Ita's [co-ed fp])

Although the view that schooling is a form of imprisonment was not widely cited, it was a deeply held view among the minority with that opinion.

The desire for change: having your say

To understand the challenge and resistance of students to the way authority is managed in schools, one needs to locate it in a wider cultural context. One of the most significant, but unexamined, developments among second-level students in Ireland in recent years has been the growth in the numbers of students engaged in part-time work, either at weekends or during the week. While a considerable amount of this work among girls is babysitting work, it is paid work. In addition, new forms of work have emerged especially in the unskilled services area, including casual work in supermarkets, shops, pubs, fast food restaurants, hotels, garages, etc. While the availability of work varies between towns, cities and rural areas, and even within cities, depending on one's location, there may even be a choice of work, and ample opportunities to avail of it after school. The importance of this work in financial terms for families cannot be underestimated; however, it is also of significance in social and cultural terms. Students who have the ability to earn money to fund their leisure and/or their living costs, are likely to have a sense of autonomy and control over their lives that simply cannot be left at the school gate or classroom door as soon as they enter. They work in an adult world on adult terms; they have experience of exercising control over their lives, of being relatively autonomous, an experience that cannot be ignored when they come to school.

A large number of students across all schools reported having part-time work: 41 per cent were working part-time throughout the school year (Table 9.1). While most (55 per cent) of these were working less than ten hours per week, almost 30 per cent had from ten to thirty hours' work each week; the remainder had a series of different working arrangements. The pattern of working did not vary significantly by social class although the children of farmers were more likely to be working part-time than any other social group. While girls were more likely to be working than boys (49 per cent had work compared with 38 per cent of boys), the girls' work comprised babysitting in 57 per cent of cases; only 19 per cent of boys reported babysitting as their job. While all age groups were involved in paid work, the Leaving Certificate age cohort was the least likely to be working.

The fact that many students worked, and exercised a good deal of control over their personal lives outside of school, seemed to have contributed to a sense of frustration with the way authority was exercised within schools. The stated wish of almost 50 per cent of students for greater democratic engagement in the running of schools represents the clearest expression of their desire for greater autonomy. Seniors in particular were interested in having greater democratic involvement in issues directly affecting them at school. Students wanted to have their opinions taken seriously; they wanted to be involved in decisions that affected them.

> What we need in this school is a Student Council where students' rights will be held up for. At the moment it is what the teacher says goes. But I think we need student representatives.
>
> (A fifth year student in St Patrick's [ssg fr])

Many were interested either in having a Student Council established or in the existing Council being given real authority, rather than just being allowed to carry

Table 9.1 Proportion of students undertaking part-time work[a] (*n* = 1,556)

	n	% of total
Students with part-time work through the year	631	40.5
Students with part-time summer work only	30	1.9
Students without part-time work	863	55.4
Students not responding	32	2.2
Total student respondents	1,556	100

Note

[a] Levels of participation by school ranged from 17.6 per cent in one fee-paying boys' school (St David's [ssb fp]) to 68.6 per cent in one free scheme girls' rural secondary school (Our Lady's [ssg fr]). Junior as well as senior students were involved in part-time employment. A total of 41.2 per cent of all those in the 12–14 age group reported having part-time jobs, as did 40 per cent of all those in the 15–16 age group; 18.8 per cent of those in the 17–19 age group said that they were working part-time. A larger proportion of female students reported part-time employment (49.4 per cent) than did their male peers (37.5 per cent). Students from across the different bands and streams all reported participation in part-time employment.

out activities (such as running discos) which they regarded as unimportant. They wanted to have some genuine input into the way in which school rules were drawn up.

> I would like a student board to be set up especially for our 5th, 6th and RLCs [Repeat Leaving Certificate Students] so that we can have our say.
>
> (A sixth year student, St Dominic's [ssb fr])

> I think that students are not asked for their opinions on most things – everything is decided for them.
>
> (A fourth year student in St Peter's [ssg fr])

When student views about democratising schools were presented to teachers (at the research dialogues), some staff members expressed the view that such a development would 'lead to anarchy'. Although there were schools where Student Councils existed and were viewed positively by the teachers, overall there was a feeling among students that such bodies had little influence. In one of the boys' schools (Dunely [ssb fr]) students effectively boycotted an attempt by staff to set up a Students Council (by voting for the most unsuitable candidates) as they had not been consulted about either the setting up of the Council or its functions. They believed it would have had no real impact on the way the school was run so they did not see much point in supporting it.

In general, there appeared to be a communication gap between students and teachers about the nature and purpose of democratic structures. Students who had no involvement in exercising authority in the schools seemed to be genuinely interested in being a part of the institution, and in having the opportunity to dialogue with the teachers on a partnership basis about these issues. They did not wish to take complete control or 'wreak havoc', yet some of the teachers expressed fears of such occurrences. Teachers' fears seemed to stem from their lack of understanding and experience of participatory democracy in schools. The sense of exasperation that many senior cycle students expressed was summed up well by a fifth year student in Ballycorish (co-ed Com Col):

> In my opinion, if you're not treated like a child, you won't act like a child. Take for example, teachers who make us stand up when they come into the class. I mean, who do they think they are! We're seniors and we don't need to be treated as if we are in baby infants. The teacher says it is to get our attention, but to us it is more about intimidation than anything else. It feels as if that teacher thinks that they are in such high authority that we have to stand before her. I just feel that if we are treated with respect we, in return, will treat them with respect. I think a school should be a more democratic place where we have a say in what is done. Treat us like adults!

Differences between schools

While there were no differences between school types in the reporting of unfair incidents with teachers, there were differences between schools in terms of complaints about general democracy. Girls in all-girls' schools were much more likely to complain about the lack of equality of respect and the lack of democratic procedures than boys or girls in other schools. Almost two-thirds of all essays (65 per cent) written by students in single-sex girls' schools were concerned with this issue, in comparison with approximately one-third (32 per cent) of those from single-sex boys' schools (Table 9.2). Interestingly, a similar gender difference was not evident among students in co-educational environments. Girls in co-educational schools made approximately the same proportion of complaints about lack of democracy and respect as did boys in the co-educational schools.

The level of concern that girls expressed about the lack of democracy in all-girls' schools is not unduly surprising as these schools exercised much more control over students than other schools (see Chapter 5). The girls in these schools regarded the strong exercise of regulations and rules as a form of surveillance. They resisted this surveillance however, especially when it involved the policing of their bodies and their personal behaviour outside of school.

Reports of unfair treatment did not vary greatly, however, by school type. Although girls in both all-girls' schools and co-educational schools were more likely to report unequal treatment than boys in either school type, the differences across and within schools were not significant: 51 per cent of girls and 46 per cent of boys in single-sex schools complained of unfair treatment. The aggregate figure for the co-educational schools was lower at 44.6 per cent, with a slightly higher proportion of girls (46 per cent) expressing concern than their male peers (42 per cent).

Unfair treatment from peers

Conflicts over power and control were not confined to relations between students and teachers. Students also exercised control and regulation over each other and one in five of the students surveyed reported some incidence of unfair treatment from their peers. As the question asked of students did not expressly seek information about bullying, we cannot comment definitively on this matter.

Table 9.2 Student essays with the theme of lack of democracy and equality of respect (n = 1,202)

	Single-sex girls' school	Single-sex boys' school	Co-ed school
% within school type	64.5%	32.1%	40.4%
Total no. of essays by school type	453	390	359

Note
Chi-square significance: p<0.001

What is clear, however, from some of the examples cited, and from incidents that we observed, is that the unequal treatment students were subjected to on occasions was of a bullying type.

Most of the comments students made in their essays about unequal treatment by peers related to friendship and relationship problems. However, there were some complaints (and indeed, observed instances) of peer bullying. Overall, there was a higher incidence of 'unequal or unfair treatment' reported by female students in both single-sex and co-educational schools. Although they comprised half the sample, they reported 61 per cent of all incidences. The reported levels of threatening and excluding behaviour by peers were also highest among younger students (44 per cent of these were reported by 12–14-year-olds with the remainder being reported by the other two cohorts combined, 15–16-year-olds and 17–18/19-year-olds). Incidents of bullying and general unfair treatment were reported across all bands and tracks.

Boys' schools were least likely to document incidents of unfair treatment by peers in their essays, while co-educational schools reported a somewhat higher incidence than single-sex girls' schools (Table 9.3). Within co-educational schools girls were slightly more likely to report unfair treatment by peers than boys. It should be noted, however, that the unfair treatment and teasing reported in essays and observed in schools tended to occur within same-sex groups. Most girls' complaints centred on exclusion from friendships and unfair treatment by other girls in co-educational schools, and the same was true of boys.

While much of the unfair treatment reported among students related to the inevitable conflicts arising between young people around friends and associations, some of what was reported was much more negative and could be construed as bullying. The negative exercise of power by peers took a number of forms, although verbal abuse was the most common form reported. Teasing and 'slagging' were often related to a student's physical appearance:

> Because of my thin build, I have been bullied in the past which led to low self-confidence and often being looked down on by other physically bigger students.
>
> (A sixth year student in Ballinroe [ssb fr])

Table 9.3 Reports of unfair treatment by peers: differences between schools (*n* = 1,202)

	Single-sex girls' school	Single-sex boys' school	Co-ed school
% within school type	22.7 %	16.4 %	24.0 %
Total no. of essays by school type	453	390	359

Note
Chi-square significance value: $p < 0.022$

I am larger than most of the girls in the school. I am always being slagged about my size and especially my breast size. I am in third year and I have bigger breasts than some of the girls in sixth year. Sometimes even the teachers tease me about my weight.

(A third year girl in St Ita's [co-ed fp])

In a number of cases, students reported on bullying by older students of younger members of the same school:

I got bullied by some of the older boys on the corridor.

(A first year male student in Ollan [co-ed Com Col])

Verbal abuse by peers was also linked to other aspects of identity such as ascribed academic ability, religion, sexual orientation, race and social class, or a combination of these:

Some of the students are prejudiced against others. Say one person from our class who lives in . . . [local area] thinks she is brilliant and that people from . . . [outlying suburb] are poor, which is not true. She is a snobby cow. She is always telling people they are poor because they don't have a new school jumper, etc.

(A third year student in St Peter's [ssg fr])

Some people who are rich look down on me because I am from the poorest and the roughest area in [the locality].

(A third year student in Ollan [co-ed Com Col])

When I came to the school people began to slag me on account of my accent and background. They began to slag me, putting me down as being gay and homosexual. The school acted once at my request but their 'prevention' had no effect. I am too scared of these people to rat on them but I want it to stop. It is awful that people shout derogatory remarks at you for fun.

(A third year male student in St Ita's [co-ed fp])

The experience of regulation and control therefore was not confined to teacher–student relations. Students exercised controls and sanctions over each other, in diverse ways. As we will see in the following chapter, students also exercised control over teachers at times through their use of negative comment; some had indirect control via the influence of their parents on the school.

Privacy and surveillance

One of the most striking features of schooling is the extent to which students' lives within schools are tightly controlled in terms of time and space. This is such an accepted practice that we rarely stop to reflect on it. Yet, it is something that impinges heavily on students and results in a sense of being monitored at all times. There is little privacy in the sense of having personally managed time for oneself; there is also very little personal physical space.

Time is measured out in lots, it is a commodity that the schools control and over which students exercise little control, unless they can win time for themselves by deviating from expectations or by being rewarded with time for high levels of conformity. Students did not comment much on the lack of time but they did comment on the general phenomenon of privacy, particularly in relation to physical space. Classrooms and recreation areas, toilets and changing areas are shared. The only private space students possess in many schools is a locker, and in three of the twelve schools participating in the study, lockers were either unavailable or inadequate. In Ballydara (co-ed Com Col) there were no lockers at all, which meant that students had to carry all of their belongings around the school with them throughout the day. In St Peter's (ssg fr) there were insufficient lockers for all of the students, while in St Dominic's (ssb fr), lockers were broken into and students' belongings (including school books) taken. The lack of privacy for changing and dressing after Physical Education was another cause of concern for students; very often the toilets were used for changing clothes.

Some essays were concerned with privacy of space or of property. Female students in both co-educational and single-sex schools objected to male teachers and other school employees having access to their private spaces such as their lockers, diaries or journals, and the toilets, and to the use of toilets as the only place to have private space for changing clothes.

It was clear that schools managed space and resources in a stratified manner. Staff had access to comfortable and relatively private places (staffrooms with carpets, comfortable chairs, etc.) where they could sit and have lunch or a chat; this was a privilege that was not available to students in most schools.[1] While this was seen as 'natural' by both staff and students, it none the less symbolises the lowly status of students within the school organisation. In the three fee-paying schools, senior students had access to a space (a common room) which was off-limits to more junior students. The right to this privilege on the basis of age or seniority was challenged by the younger students in these schools as they did not accept status differentiation between students.

Confidentiality and labelling

The privacy issues that were of greatest concern to students related to the use of personal information about themselves. A small number of students in all schools expressed concern about being labelled by teachers, or by the peer group, as a 'troublemaker'. Students felt these labels arose for many different reasons (due to difficult behaviour as a junior student, being perceived as a part of an undesirable friendship group, or by having older siblings or relations whose behaviour had been poorly regarded). In all cases, labelling was felt to be an injustice. The students believed it could become a self-fulfilling prophecy.

I was unfairly treated in first year when [MrY] called me names just because he disliked my brother in 6th year. He discriminated against me even though he knew nothing about me.

(A second year student, Dunely [ssb fr])

If you get into trouble once, [then] it is always you.

(A third year student, St Peter's [ssg fr])

When you get a bad name for yourself in first year, it sticks with you for the rest of your school life no matter how hard you try to work or how well you try to behave. Teachers never praise you for the good work you do, they only see anything bad you do. In the end there's no point in trying to do well. The only praise you get is from yourself and often that is not enough.

(A fifth year student, St Peter's [ssg fr])

I am unfairly treated by one teacher. She compares us to other students which she taught. My name was also mentioned to older students. She told them that I didn't have enough confidence as I had dropped out of an extra-curricular activity.

(A third year female student, Ollan [co-ed Com Col])

Concern was also expressed by students about the lack of respect for confidential information. A number of students noted that any interactions they had with teachers, particularly of a negative nature, or any confidential information about their health or family background which became known to one teacher, would be discussed with the rest of the staff. This issue emerged in all of the single-sex girls' schools in particular (where 54 per cent of all such incidents were reported). Thirty per cent of the remainder were reported in co-educational schools and 16 per cent in boys' schools.

Teachers should keep out of students' personal lives.

(A second year student in Our Lady's [ssg fr])

Records of students shouldn't be made available to new teachers because this could give them a prejudiced opinion of students with a bad reputation.

(A third year student in St Peter's [ssg fr])

I know that one of the teachers who did not teach me was going around talking about me. [The teacher] lives in the same neighbourhood and therefore I heard about it.

(A sixth year female student in Ballycorish [co-ed Com Sch])

The teachers [should] not be talking about what happens in class, and sub/new teachers [should] not be told to watch out for certain people, etc.

(A fifth year student in Ballinroe [ssb fr])

The policing of girls' behaviour, which students complained of in single-sex schools especially, is reflected in the concerns which girls expressed about privacy, confidentiality and labelling. Girls were keenly aware of being monitored and controlled and resented the invasion of privacy which that entailed. It is interesting that almost three times as many girls in girls' schools complained about confidentiality and privacy violations as boys in boys' schools, while twice as many girls in co-educational schools complained about it compared with boys in these schools (see Chapters 5, 6 and 7 for further discussion of gender differences).

Teachers are not always right

It is clear, therefore, that while students realised and recognised their subordination, a large number of them did not accept it, in particular they did not accept the way power was exercised over them. In some respects, students and schools were working out of a different set of cultural premises about the exercise of authority and power. The school organisation relied heavily on the operation and exercise of traditional authority, the assumption that certain positions demanded respect irrespective of the position holder.

> The [senior teacher] doesn't listen to anything you have to say. She/he is right, you're wrong.
>
> (A male fifth year student, St Ita's [co-ed fp])

> Teachers should listen to pupils' points of view more often and not think they are always right because they are not.
>
> (A fourth year student, St Peter's [ssg fr])

The schools were generally hierarchical organisations with power being vested centrally in the principal and, sometimes, other senior staff. At the classroom level the teacher was assumed to have authority by virtue of her/his position. It was generally assumed that the students would accept that authority without challenge. However, students were visibly resistant to this form of traditional authority; many (not all) saw power as something to be negotiated. They operated out of a concept of both rational and charismatic authority.[2]

> Encouraging the students to do their work and not forcing them to do it [would make school more fair and equal].
>
> (A sixth year student, St Dominic's [ssb fr])

School rules were to be obeyed if they were reasonable. Teachers were to be respected if they commanded respect.

> I wish all the teachers were like [Ms M]. All she cares about is how the students do and not for her reputation. Just for us. She may seem tough but it's only because she cares.
>
> (A fourth year student, Our Lady's [ssg fr])

Neither school nor teachers were regarded as being deserving of respect by virtue of the authority vested in them by the institution. There were therefore real conflicts of perception as to what were the boundaries that were to be respected in the operation of power. As most schools did not have democratic forums in which such issues should be raised, there were no contexts where teachers and students could discuss issues of power and authority on even terms.

Undoubtedly one reason why schools and young people share different cultural assumptions about the exercise of authority is the fact that young people attending second-level schools are increasingly financially independent. Greater material autonomy can provide a challenge to traditional relationships of domination and subordination. Harris (1984) documented the impact on traditional patriarchal structures in rural Ireland of increased female paid employment outside the home. Greater financial independence for women meant that they no longer had to define their class position in terms of their relationship to men. Given that so many school-going children have a reasonable level of financial independence, it is not surprising that they no longer accept traditional relations of authority including those between students and teachers. Their financial means enable them to make choices and act autonomously, outside of school. The evolving cultural mores of the home and the high street are challenging the traditional authority relations of the school and the classroom.

Conclusion

While educationalists have addressed the issue of power and authority, it has frequently been from a managerialist perspective, how to manage schools more effectively, how to 'keep discipline'. Undoubtedly one of the reasons why we have failed to problematise power as an equality problematic is because of the research culture within the academy itself. Positivist analysis has been the dominant tradition in educational research, and within this there has been little emphasis on reflexive analysis. The power relations between students and teachers especially have been taken as a given, and the analyses have been undertaken from a 'top-down' perspective (Ball 1989). Young people's concerns regarding the exercise of power have been named as the predictable complaints of disgruntled teenagers.

In addition, the equality debate within the wider social sciences has not encouraged an analysis of age (and youth especially) as a signifier of difference, particular differences in capacity to exercise power. Where differences have been examined as a source of unequal treatment in education, the focus has been on social class, gender, ethnicity, race, sexual orientation and disability. In addition, achieving equality in education has been defined in distributive terms, as a matter of increasing access, participation and success for particular socially excluded groups. Democratising the internal relations of education has been a minority interest in relation to compulsory education although it has a long history, especially in the USA (Dewey 1916, 1938; Gutmann 1987; Apple and Beane 1999). Moreover promoting equality in pedagogical relations has become a core equality objective in adult education (Mezirow 1990) due to the influence of Freire (1972) in particular.

What the essay and focus group data suggest is that the exercise of power and authority is a major concern among young people in second-level schools. While other equality issues were raised in the essays, most notably issues relating to injustices arising from ability grouping, gender, social class, race, sexual orientation and disability, these did not warrant at all as much commentary as the issue of power.

What the data also show is that schools as institutions operate out of a strong developmentalist and protectionist model in the way in which they manage relations of authority (see Archard 1993, for a discussion of the importance of the protectionist position). A universalistic assumption seems to exist about the subordinate status of young persons which is not subjected to serious critical scrutiny. What appears to be happening in schools therefore is that while there is a recognition of difference between students and teachers, differences are defined in terms of subordination–superordination. Being young, one is assumed to be subordinate.

For their part, young people seem to be operating out of a different conception of authority to educationalists and teachers; in particular, they rejected the exercise of traditional authority, the assumption that a teacher was to be obeyed because of the authority vested in her or his role. They sought a greater democratisation of schooling, both at the organisational and at the classroom levels. This expectation is not surprising given that many young people are now working part-time while in school, and given the major cultural changes which are occurring in contemporary Irish society in terms of familial and other social institutions (Fahey 2000; O'Connor 1998). They often exercise a high level of autonomy in relation to both work and leisure outside of school, an autonomy that is greatly facilitated by their relative financial independence.

Chapter 10

Vertical and horizontal power
Teachers' experiences

Introduction

Young people in school perceive power principally as something that is exercised over them by adults (teachers and others in positions of authority). Students are positioned at the bottom of the school organisation's hierarchy, and as a result, have relatively little access to power positions, particularly in terms of their relationships with adults. Teachers' perceptions of power in the school are more complex. They experience power both vertically and laterally, both as something that is exercised by others in positions of authority *vis-à-vis* themselves, and in terms of relations with colleagues. Power is not something to which all teachers have equal access therefore. Some are given formal power as a consequence of their role or position within the school organisation; others have greater access to power as a consequence of belonging to a higher status group within the school.

Teachers: powerful and powerless

Schools and the teaching profession are subject to a high degree of external control and influence (Meyer and Rowan 1988; Giroux and MacLaren 1996). Curriculum content, modes of assessment and quality assurance are regulated externally. Educational policies and innovations are established by state bodies and are subject to the influence of other powerful stakeholders. Both schools and the teaching profession are the focus of public scrutiny, particularly in terms of measured attainment and because of ongoing concerns regarding quality and effectiveness (Harold 1998; Mahony 2001; Smyth 1999). Teachers and schools are the focus of interest and pressure by increasing numbers of educational stakeholders. While the teacher unions are recognised as powerful educational players in the Irish context (Drudy and Lynch 1993) this is not necessarily the case elsewhere (van Veen *et al.* 2001).

Teachers are relatively autonomous in their own classrooms in terms of the pedagogical approaches they employ. However, they are subject to a range of internal as well as external controls. School principals and senior management regulate their access to resources and structure their time and location through timetabling (Meyer and Rowan 1988). In general, they work in isolation from their colleagues (van Veen *et al.* 2001) with an expectation that they will maintain a high level of constant vigilance over their students (Travers and Cooper 1996). The emphasis on quality assurance, as well as the pressures caused by terminal state examinations, not only creates a stressful climate but also operates to curtail teachers' willingness to use exploratory or innovative teaching methods (Broadfoot 1979; Murphy and Torrance 1988; Hargreaves *et al.* 1996).

Furthermore, the multiple roles that teachers and schools are now expected to fulfil have become increasingly complex (van Veen *et al.* 2001). While it is true that teachers are in a position to exercise power over young people in schools, they themselves are subject to control by external bodies and the authority of those in superordinate positions within their own institution. Thus, teachers experience their own role as both powerful and powerless (Davies 1996).

Much of what is written about the operation of power in schools is primarily concerned with ensuring or increasing educational quality and outcomes, or developing effective leadership (Gray *et al.* 1999; Preedy *et al.* 1997; Law and Glover 2000). Schools are understood within a management science framework as hierarchical bureaucracies (Bennett deMarrais and LeCompte 1999; Packwood 1988) in which power is invested in certain roles and accompanies specific responsibilities (Handy and Aitken 1986). Within such a framework, power is exercised vertically downwards. Ball (1989) is critical of this interpretation, arguing that it operates out of, and legitimates, a managerial perspective.

Davies (2001) regards schools as highly complex organisations in which power is dispersed, albeit unequally, throughout the organisation. Ball (1987, 1989) argues that power is not only exercised vertically, but also laterally between colleagues and is the result of the actions in which individuals and groups engage. Schools are limited democracies in which those in leadership positions attempt to dominate definitions of the institution's purpose, while those in subordinate positions may well resist this (Ball 1989). At the same time, groups of colleagues engage in power struggles regarding access to resources, information, level of influence and position within the school. Sikes *et al.* (1985) argue that the hierarchical nature of schools can lead to the establishment of cliques or interest groups with different levels of power or value within that institution. Power struggles can occur between interest groups united by a particular aspect of identity (e.g. gender, subject taught, career status, age). Teacher identities can result in some being hierarchically ordered in the school according to whether these are afforded higher or lower status, resulting in unequal recognition and representation in relationships with superordinates and peers. Maguire (2001) has observed that there are few key texts considering the ways that adult–adult power relationships are played out in a school context, and notes the silence that has surrounded negative staffroom power relations (whether between colleagues or with superordinates) until very recently.

Teacher equality concerns regarding power relations

Teachers were provided with the opportunity to outline their own equality concerns at a research dialogue that was facilitated with the staff of each school. They were given a short open-ended questionnaire asking if they had ever experienced unfair or unequal treatment in their current school, and what the primary equality concerns in their school were. The issues they identified as significant reflected the contested nature of power and the limited nature of democracy within their school communities.

The issues most frequently raised by teachers concerned the operation of power and authority in their school. Their concerns also reflected the hierarchical nature of status positions within the teaching cohort, including the differential status accorded to teachers teaching different subjects, and different levels within a given subject. Gender was mentioned more frequently than any other aspect of identity as a source of unfair treatment.

One-quarter of all the teachers who filled out this questionnaire said that they had experienced unequal treatment at some time in their current school (Table 10.1). Among those who responded, the four most frequently cited issues were: personal experience of unfair treatment by school management (36.7 per cent); problematic or negative relations with colleagues (15.5 per cent); lack of democratic participation by teachers in the running of the school (12.2 per cent); and problems experienced by part-time and temporary staff (11.1 per cent). It is interesting to note that teachers identified similar equality concerns regarding the way in which power was exercised over students in the school. Over a quarter (26.8 per cent) identified unfair or harsh treatment of students as a source of injustice; 8.7 per cent regarded the lack of student voice and democratic input for students as an inequality; a small proportion (4 per cent) cited peer bullying among students as an issue of concern.

The equality issues raised by teachers regarding the ways in which power was exercised by other adults in school were concerned with both vertical and lateral power relationships. They expressed concerns about the ways in which resources, information and privileges were distributed by those in managerial positions. They were also aware of bias in attitudes and treatment by colleagues based on labelling of themselves as inferior due to particular aspects of their identity. Some respondents noted that the failure of their peers, or superiors, to afford them equal respect arose from an unwillingness to recognise and accommodate difference.

The exercise of authority: control of timetabling and resources

Many teachers were conscious of their relative lack of power *vis-à-vis* senior personnel, such as the school principal and others in management positions. Their own lack of control over time, work activity and location was one of the reasons commonly cited for unfair treatment. Time, resources and certain work

Table 10.1 Incidences of unequal treatment experienced in their own school listed by teachers (open question) (*n* = 93)

	% of those naming incidences[a]
Unfair exercise of authority	36.7
Unfair treatment by colleagues	15.5
General lack of democracy	12.2
Unfair treatment of part-time staff	11.1
Gender discrimination issues	6.7
Age discrimination issues	6.7
Status differentiation between subjects	5.6
Lack of promotional prospects	3.3
Advantage taken of teachers	3.3
Work pressure/stress	2.2
Racial discrimination	1.1
Sexual orientation discrimination	1.1
Bullying by students	1.1
Total no of teachers listing incidences	93

Note
[a] Percentages add to over 100 per cent as more than one answer was given by some teachers.

activities were potential privileges. When it was believed that power exercised by those in authority was giving rise to unequal access to these benefits, teachers felt they were treated unjustly:

> [There is] unequal timetabling. A colleague was given time off (class period) when work was done by someone else.
>
> > (Female permanent teacher, St Patrick's [ssg fr])
>
> Yes [I was unfairly treated when] a class I loved was taken off me at 6th year level to suit an older teacher [a religious order member].
>
> > (Female permanent teacher, St Dominic's [ssb fr]
>
> Equality of treatment for all teachers is important, including half days and time off.
>
> > (Female permanent teacher, Our Lady's [ssg fr])

Being outside the 'in-group'

Some of those who documented unfair or unequal treatment by their school principal, focused on a sense of being excluded from a powerful or influential group because they were not personally close to management, or because they held alternative opinions on educational or school matters. Individual teachers perceived that opportunities for promotion were tied to membership of groups that were either friendly with management, or were believed to hold the same political or philosophical views.

A power elite group holding personal friendship with the principal dictates policy and their own personal views are filtered through to the majority of the staff.

(Female temporary teacher, Ballydara [co-ed Com Col])

Yes [I am unfairly treated] if my opinion does not coincide with that of the powers that be I am reprimanded in a subtle way. I feel that teachers must behave in a politically acceptable way.

(Female permanent teacher, Ballydara [co-ed Com Col])

[There is] an inner circle who seem to know more about what's happening than anyone else.

(Female permanent teacher, Ballycorish [co-ed Com Sch])

Some teachers' opinions are listened to and others ignored or treated as being insignificant – the 'golden circle'.

(Female permanent teacher, Our Lady's [ssg fr])

Teachers also raised concerns regarding the perceived inequality of access to information and resources in the school. Again, there appeared to be a belief in some schools that certain members of staff who belonged to a privileged group were more likely to benefit.

[An important equality issue in this school is] access to information about school finance.

(Female permanent teacher, St Patrick's [ssg fr])

[An important equality issue in this school is] equal facilities, budgets, etc.

(Male temporary teacher, Ballinroe [ssb fr])

Lack of exam notification is an issue. Information is given to one teacher and not to others.

(Female permanent teacher, Ollan [co-ed Com Col])

The impact of assertive colleagues

A small number of very assertive or demanding individuals were perceived to be dominating the staff and school environment in some instances, with negative and unfair consequences for others.

I feel that I have suffered over the years from a good deal of moral bullying from a *minority* of vociferous, radical and dissatisfied colleagues.

(Male permanent teacher, Dunely [ssb fr])

[An important equality issue in the school is] allocation of classes, timetabling, etc. The power is handed by management to a 'bullying' group/individuals on staff.

(Female permanent teacher, St Patrick's [ssg fr])

Unequal access to resources and information was not only an issue in the exercise of authority by senior school personnel. It could also become a source of contention between colleagues, particularly where individuals denied peers access to shared resources.

Some [teachers] withhold information/sharing, e.g. videos, TV, rooms, tape recorders, and this can become a power struggle in a few cases.

(Female temporary teacher, St Ita's [co-ed fp])

Who gets the top stream?

It was clear from comments made by teachers during visits to schools, and in the questionnaires they filled out, that many of them regarded being allocated certain classes (honours sets, high stream or band groups) as a privilege that was unequally distributed in schools. Lortie (1984) argues that teaching has never been characterised by extrinsic rewards and therefore psychic rewards are of particular significance to teachers. Higher track classes, characterised by positive teacher–student relationships and significant levels of time on-task (Boaler 1997b), are regarded by many teachers as intrinsically more rewarding to teach. Comments from teachers across different schools made it clear that there was no stated school policy in most regarding the distribution of these popular classes between teachers.

[An important equality issue in this school is] for teachers to get a fair crack of the whip when it comes to getting honours and pass classes.

(Male permanent teacher, Dunely [ssb fr])

There should be much more obvious policy in existence within departments regarding rotation of ordinary and higher level classes and syllabus 'C' where applicable.

(Female permanent teacher, St Peter's [ssg fr])

The status of the subject and the status of the teacher

Particular subjects or subject areas have higher status in schools than others (Goodson 1988; Bennett deMarrais and LeCompte 1999). This can result in those who teach these subjects having greater influence over school policy and the allocation of resources than others (Ball and Lacey 1984; Ball 1987). It can also result in messages being given to students, and other members of the school community, indicating where different subjects stand in a hierarchy of importance and seriousness.

Teachers in this study were keenly aware of the fact that there was a hierarchy in terms of how subjects were perceived in their school. From informal conversations, questionnaire comments, and staffroom visits, it was evident that the subjects most often regarded as having low status included the more applied subjects, in particular Home Economics and Art. Although this was not true across all of the participating schools, it was very evident in two of the single-sex girls' schools (Our Lady's and St Peter's) that Home Economics was of low status. Junior students were encouraged by senior staff to opt away from Home Economics, and into Science, if they were regarded as high attainers academically. Similarly, in one of the single-sex boys' schools, the Art teacher clearly felt that his subject was of low status in the school and drew the researchers' attention to the fact that it was the only subject allocated to a prefabricated classroom.

> [One example of demeaning treatment was] not including Art in the exam timetable because it is not one of the more academic subject areas. I think that the various subject areas within schools should be treated equally and that areas such as Art, Music, Religion, etc. should be placed on an equal footing with other areas. I think that the real educational benefits of Art are generally unrecognised.
>
> (Female temporary teacher, St Peter's [ssg fr])

> Feedback [from other teachers], and overheard conversations in my classes, have indicated to me that my subject (Art and Design) has been denigrated by a few other teachers in their classes as being only suitable for 'weak underachievers'.
>
> (Female permanent teacher, St Patrick's [ssg fr])

Subjects such as Mathematics or Science were regarded as being more highly valued subjects, thus more likely to be given privileges.

> Some subjects are being facilitated by having fewer students in a class, e.g. small classes in Science, when this would not be allowed as viable in other subjects.
>
> (Female permanent teacher, St Peter's [ssg fr])

Teachers associated with the less valued subjects expressed a sense of alienation or perceived lack of regard by colleagues. Not only did teachers of poorly regarded subjects experience a sense of relative exclusion by school management personnel, but they also felt that some of their peers viewed them as inferior.

> Teachers of less academic subjects are seldom asked opinions on important issues.
>
> (Female permanent teacher, St Patrick's [ssg fr])

All subjects are not given equal importance by all teachers. There is one particular teacher who thinks his subject has precedence over others – particularly non-exam subjects.

(Female permanent teacher, Ollan [co-ed Com Col])

Status within the staff hierarchy – issues for the young and the temporary

Many of the teachers in this study expressed concerns about the way in which the teaching staff was ordered hierarchically according to age and seniority. There was a sense that the more senior teachers dominated, and that younger or more junior teachers were not afforded the same level of respect or recognition. Older or more senior teachers could treat their junior colleagues in ways that were regarded as disrespectful or condescending. Maguire (2001) noted that those teachers most likely to report bullying and a negative exercise of power over them by colleagues are young and inexperienced teachers, particularly those who are student teachers.

Older members of staff dominate at staff meetings.

(Male permanent teacher, St Dominic's [ssb fr])

At times in this school, I feel seniority is given too much importance. The opinions of younger members of staff should be taken into account. At times the attitude towards younger teachers is condescending.

(Female temporary teacher, St Peter's [ssg fr])

Some teachers feel that they do not have the right to raise issues because they are not post-holders.

(Female permanent teacher, Ballydara [co-ed Com Col])

In particular, there were concerns regarding the low status of non-permanent members of staff resulting in their exclusion from full participation in the life of the school.

At times part-time/substitute teachers may be excluded from the decision-making process.

(Female permanent teacher, St Peter's [ssg fr])

Some younger, less experienced teachers claimed that they were patronised by older colleagues (Richie *et al.* 2000).

[I was unfairly treated when I was] labelled or grouped as a young, new teacher lacking in experience.

(Female temporary teacher, St Peter's [ssg fr])

As a 'new' teacher in this school (but very experienced in other schools – I was redeployed) I was treated very badly by long-time teachers. At subject meetings I was given (a) the academically weakest students, (b) the most unattractive classrooms. Established teachers in subject areas tend to be undemocratic towards newer/temporary staff.

(Female permanent teacher, St Patrick's [ssg fr])

[I experienced unfair treatment] on the basis that youth implies inexperience rather than new knowledge and ideas.

(Male permanent teacher, Dunely [ssb fr])

Many teachers reported unfair treatment, either of themselves or others, due to junior and/or temporary status, involving school management or more senior colleagues. One practice involved giving less established teachers low status classes, such as lower track groups (Sikes *et al.* 1985; Taylor, 1993).

As a junior teacher at the beginning of my career I was unfairly treated by a senior member of staff – [I was] forced to take certain classes or difficult students, etc. This only happened in the early years of my career.

(Female permanent teacher, St Cecilia's [ssg fp])

[I experienced unfair treatment because of my] relative youth compared to other teachers, e.g. being asked to do things older teachers would not be asked to do.

(Male permanent teacher, St Ita's [co-ed fp])

[I experienced unfair treatment by] not having a proper spread of classes within the school. Being asked to take large classes that permanent teachers won't be asked to do.

(Female temporary teacher, Ballycorish [co-ed Com Sch])

The issue of unequal pay and unreasonable working hours for those in temporary or substitute positions was a concern.

[I was unfairly treated] as a part-time teacher [I was given an] exam rota of 22 hours even though I was teaching 18 [hours] and being told that I would not be paid if I did not supervise.

(Female temporary teacher, St David's [ssb fp])

[I experienced unfair treatment] doing the same work as a full-time teacher and getting much less pay.

(Male permanent teacher, Ollan [co-ed Com Col])

Asking temporary teachers to take on unpaid duties, such as extra-curricular activities, was also named by a number of such staff as an injustice:

Temporary teachers are sometimes taken advantage of and asked to do extra-curricular activities.

(Male permanent teacher, Dunely [ssb fr])

The attitudes of students towards temporary staff reflected their low organisational status.

> As a part-time teacher, the students do not have the same (if any) respect for you as they would have for full-time teachers. But this changes the longer you are here.
>
> (Female temporary teacher, Ballydara [co-ed Com Col])

Those teachers who held non-permanent positions in schools (whether in full-time or part-time temporary posts, or as substitute teachers) were keenly aware of their precarious employment situation. They felt a sense of pressure to conform to organisational expectations and demands even where these might be unfair or unreasonable. They lacked the status, power and training to be in a position to resist (Buendia 2000; Phelan 2001).

> As a temporary, part-time teacher I am very aware that I cannot voice any opinion management does not like, as otherwise I will not have a job next year as has happened to others.
>
> (Female temporary teacher, St Cecilia's [ssg fp])

> I'm always aware I'm not permanent and cannot always say what I want in case of prejudice against permanency. Non-permanent staff or part-time staff have very little status.
>
> (Female temporary teacher, St Patrick's [ssg fr])

> Because I'm only part-time I feel that when I may be asked to help (in relation to serving tea, etc., graduations, etc. in school) that I'm obliged to say 'yes, no problem' when even the permanent teachers may not be asked – it feels that it could be a black mark for me if I don't.
>
> (Female temporary teacher, Ballydara [co-ed Com Col])

New teachers in some of the schools had a sense of being isolated from the established groups of permanent teachers.

> [I experienced unfair treatment by] being isolated at first (as if one had to pass a test before being accepted); felt I was under observation.
>
> (Female permanent teacher, St Patrick's [ssg fr])

Gender and minority issues

Most comments and claims of unfair treatment with respect to gender were made by female teachers, although there were a small number of complaints made by men regarding perceived bias against themselves in one school.

Female teachers reported difficulties in being treated as equals by male colleagues.

Being taken seriously by male teachers is sometimes a problem.
                        (Female permanent teacher, Ballydara [co-ed Com Col])

Yes [I was unfairly treated] by fellow male teachers – two in particular –
who passed sexist comments, e.g. 'this school is gone to hell since women
teachers came' and remarks of this ilk.
                        (Female temporary teacher, Dunely [ssb fr])

Female teachers do not seem to be taken seriously in the staffroom.
                        (Female temporary teacher, Dunely [ssb fr])

Female teachers can be, and are, subjected to sexist behaviour by adolescent
male students (Tirri and Puolinatha 2000). The negative views of female teachers
expressed by some male colleagues in Dunely (ssb fr) were perceived as reinforcing the sexist behaviour and attitudes of students.

As a female teacher I feel that the students have different expectations of me
than of their male teachers and behave accordingly. The male dominated staff
includes certain members who are openly sexist to female members of staff.
                        (Female permanent teacher, Dunely [ssb fr])

The treatment of female teachers by the pupil body, particularly new teachers
to the school, is a problem. There is discriminatory behaviour towards female
teachers.
                        (Male permanent teacher, Dunely [ssb fr])

The belief that female teachers had lower status than their male colleagues in
mixed staff situations was not confined to Dunely:

There is a perception among students that male teachers are 'better' and that
male teachers have superior roles to female teachers.
                        (Female permanent teacher, St Patrick's [ssg fr])

Warren and O'Connor (1999) reported that some female teachers in their
study had decided against applying for promotions because of the sexist and
negative banter to which male colleagues subjected them. In one school, there
was a perception that some of the male teachers lacked respect for the principal
on gender grounds.

[There is] criticism of the principal because she is female and non co-
operation by older men on staff.
                        (Female permanent teacher, Ballycorish [co-ed Com Sch])

The lack of gender balance in the management of a number of schools was
regarded as problematic.

[An important equality issue in this school is that it is an] all–girls' school and has a male principal.

> (Female permanent teacher, St Patrick's [ssg fr])

[An important equality issue in this school is] female/male balance in management. Most teachers are female in this school and most senior posts are held by men!!

> (Female permanent teacher, Ballydara [co-ed Com Col])

Research findings demonstrate clearly that female teachers are less likely to occupy senior positions in schools, especially the principalship, than are their male colleagues (Lynch 1999a; Mahony 2000). Not surprisingly, one of the gender-related issues raised by teachers in co-educational schools concerned access to promotion. While the majority of such concerns were raised by women, in Ballydara (co-ed Com Col) a small number of male staff believed that there was a bias against them in terms of accessing promotion on gender grounds. The largest number of complaints about gender bias in promotions was in Ollan:

Men will get priority regarding posts of responsibility.

> (Female permanent teacher, Ollan [co-ed Com Col])

The general perception in this school is that there is no notice taken of female opinion. There is a small core of male teachers in the inner circle.

> (Female permanent teacher, Ollan [co-ed Com Col])

I applied for an 'A' post because I was doing the duties I felt. I was not considered because I am female.

> (Female permanent teacher, Ollan [co-ed Com Col])

Female teachers are first to get promotion in relation to 'B' posts and 'A' posts. Male staff feel they are in a minority situation. [There is a] perception that female staff receive more favourable timetables.

> (Male permanent teacher, Ballydara [co-ed Com Col])

Among the other equality concerns raised by a small number of the participating teachers were issues relating to family status. Two teachers in different schools asserted that they had been discriminated against while on maternity leave.

I felt that I was passed over (although holding a temporary position for three years) for promotion because I was on maternity leave that spanned six months, i.e. experience counted for nothing.

> (Female permanent teacher, Ollan [co-ed Com Col])

My conditions of work were changed while on maternity leave.

> (Female permanent teacher, Ollan [co-ed Com Col])

Another female teacher was concerned that additional (after-school) duties such as extra-curricular involvement were incompatible with family life and that there was a lack of recognition by school management of this. Some teachers felt under pressure to assist in extra-curricular duties although it was not feasible given their family status.

> I feel it is difficult to be involved in extra-curricular activities after school when you have young children and this is not always recognised.
>
> (Female permanent teacher, Ballycorish [co-ed Com Sch])

Lack of respect for minorities

Membership of identifiable minority groups (particularly those with low status) can result in individuals experiencing, or being fearful of, lack of recognition or even harassment. This is particularly true of those who are gay, lesbian or bisexual (Epstein and Johnson 1994; Gowran 2000). A very small proportion of teachers who participated in this study described experiencing unfair treatment based on their membership of minority groups. One respondent claimed that she had experienced discrimination by senior school personnel because of suspicion that she was lesbian.

> [I was] passed over for a job because of influence of senior staff on decisions. There were allegations about my lifestyle, etc. that I'm gay.
>
> (Female temporary teacher, Ballydara [co-ed Com Col])

Another teacher, who had been working in Ireland for many years but was not Irish, noted that he occasionally experienced workplace bias on the basis of his nationality:

> Despite teaching and living in Ireland for over 20 years I am still judged by some solely on my nationality and, on occasion, this has resulted in unequal treatment.
>
> (Male permanent teacher, St Ita's [co-ed fr])

Conclusion

Power is a dimension of the interactive relations between individuals and groups (Ball 1989). However, it is not equally accessible to all participants in these relationships and engagements; it is asymmetrically distributed (Davies 2001). Schools are not genuinely democratic institutions, but are organised on hierarchical terms where the ability to exercise degrees of power is associated both with formal roles (principal, teacher, student) and with particular identities afforded higher or lower status (adult, young person).

While students' concerns about the exercise of power focused on the vertical power relations between themselves and teachers, more so than on the lateral relations with their peers, teachers' experiences of power were more complex. On the one hand they were expected to exercise authority in their roles as teachers and adults; yet they were also subject to the vertical power of those in formal roles of authority over them both within and without the school institution. Furthermore, power was exercised laterally between colleagues. Those who had higher status identities (because of age, experience, job status, subjects taught, gender) were more likely to be in a position to exercise power over lower status colleagues.

What the teachers' questionnaires and discussions with individual teachers indicate is that a sizeable minority of teachers had experienced unfair treatment in the way that power was exercised by those in senior managerial positions in the school, as well as by their colleagues. Their experiences demonstrate that power is exercised both vertically and laterally in an organisation such as a school. Younger, temporary and part-time teachers were especially vulnerable to both vertical control by management, and the horizontal regulation of colleagues. Gender was also an important factor in determining the pattern of power relations between staff, not least because women tended to occupy more junior positions, especially in co-educational schools.

Power is not a binary system therefore where students have no power and teachers have absolute authority and control. Teachers feel constrained by the way in which authority is exercised in relation to themselves, both by school management and by colleagues. Students also exercise some control over staff.

While school managers exercise control over resources such as 'easy classes', good timetables and promotion, colleagues exercise power by their ability to determine the school's agenda, to influence the distribution of resources, and by their capacity to include or exclude. Teachers are keenly aware that the exercise of power is a process, and that teachers can and do engage in conflict with their peers over resources, information, privileges and status.

Power relations therefore comprise an important site for the investigation of equality in schools, not only the power relations between students and teachers, but also the power relations between teachers themselves. No more than the student body, the teaching body is not homogeneous. Status divisions arising from subject divisions, seniority, permanence, gender, subject, sexuality and ethnicity, can and do impact on how power is exercised within the school organisation. Those who are either temporary or part-time seem to be especially vulnerable to the abuse of power.

Chapter 11

Inequality and the 3Rs – redistribution, recognition and representation

The purpose of this final chapter is to present an overview of the study and its major findings in the light of the equality framework presented in Chapter 1. Drawing on our data, we demonstrate the need for a more inclusive and eclectic approach to the understanding of inequality in education. The chapter also engages with some of the major social scientific debates about the nature and implications of inequality in education, especially in terms of the role schools play in this matter. We highlight not only the separateness of different forms of inequality, but also their inter-relationship, and their relative significance for different social groups.

As schools are highly complex institutions, the research design for this study was complex and multifaceted (Ball 1997). We used a triangular approach, and a range of research tools to explore the life inside schools and classrooms. We listened, observed and dialogued with the major actors in the school setting, principals, teachers and most especially students. We used different media, including informal discussion, tape recordings, essay writing, focus groups, questionnaires and observations in classrooms, playgrounds and school events, to go deep inside schools. When our analysis was in draft form we went back on a visit to each school and presented a summary of our findings to the staff for comment and response. Draft papers were also circulated to schools for comments as they developed, and discussion with students took place in focus groups with students as the research progressed.

From this lengthy process of research and dialogue a number of issues about the way in which we had come to understand equality in education became evident. This first realisation was that while social scientific frameworks are essential for explaining the why and how of inequality in education, they often lack the conceptual tools that enable us to differentiate between different forms of inequality in the deeper philosophical sense. Drawing on the work of egalitarian theory, we suggest that schools reproduce unequal social outcomes in three primary domains, the socio-economic, the socio-political and the socio-cultural. The way in which interpersonal relations are organised in school also has implications for equality in affective terms, although we do not examine this matter in any depth in this book.

The second insight derived from the dialogue with political theory relates to the importance of normative discourses for the realisation of change, particularly in relation to a subject such as inequality. Not to explore the ethical implications of injustice and inequality is to ignore the value or normative dimension of the research subject. Yet, mainstream social scientific work eschews questions of ethics (Sayer 2000a). While critical theoretical and feminist work does engage with normative issues, the ethical justifications for change are not posted in any systematic way. The reluctance to engage with the normative issues arising from inequality has meant that the discourse of change has been impoverished. Social scientists have been effective in identifying the scope of the equality problem but not in presenting solutions. There needs to be a dialogue therefore between the social scientific explanatory perspective, and the normative, ethical perspective on any given inequality. If we utilise both discourses for naming the inequality problem in education we open the way for transformative action. We open up a new language for naming the processes of change.

In this study we have made a tentative attempt to marry the insights from normative egalitarian theory with social science frameworks in the analysis of equality issues in schools. Allying analytical frameworks with normative perspectives suggests that the solution to the economically generated inequality in schools is primarily, albeit not exclusively, a distributive issue; it is about ensuring equality of access, participation, outcome and condition for all students to all forms of knowledge and understanding (Lynch 1999a: 287–309). It is about challenging practices at all stages of education that result in privileged outcomes for some at the expense of others, be that through selective schooling, tracking, subject choice or differential treatment within the classroom. The data also indicate that, in the public context of school life, while the distributive concept of justice has considerable salience, it is only applicable in the contexts of those social goods that are distributable. Not all social goods within and through which inequality can be created can be distributed. Not all social contexts in which inequality arises are contexts involving distribution or redistribution (Baker 1998; Young 1990). Our findings suggest that while the distributive view of social justice is especially important for challenging inequalities arising in the material sphere of goods and resources, and opportunities relating to the same, it is not salient when the issues of inequality pertain to power or status. The latter are ontologically of a different order to money, resources and opportunities.

Inequalities of recognition arise from status differentiations; they are primarily socio-cultural and symbolic injustices. These are rooted in patterns of representation, interpretation and communication. They take the form of cultural domination, symbolic misrepresentation or non-recognition, all leading to a lack of respect (Baker 1998; Fraser 1995, 1997; Young 1990). The changes that are required to address such injustices are changes that focus on symbolic and communication systems, and institutionalised status-related structures and practices. They are about managing difference in schools in a respectful way, organisationally, pedagogically and intellectually in terms of curricula, syllabi and assessment systems. They are about the textbooks and the materials that are used to teach, the images of differences we portray, and the silences that need to be broken about demonised and marginalised differences.

Political or representational injustice occurs when and wherever power is enacted, in the realms of decision-making, including policy-making, and in political life generally. It may take the form of political exclusion, political marginalisation, political trivialisation or political misrepresentation (Young 1990). In schools, power is a core equality problematic as it is imbricated in all social relations, between teachers and students, between teachers themselves and students themselves, and between parents, teachers and students. Promoting equality in the exercise of power requires changes in the way power is exercised 'over' students and 'over' particular teachers and parents. It requires changes in the procedures for the representation of interests by all parties to the education process, so that subordinate voices can be heard and heeded. It requires the introduction of new structures for dialogue, and changes in attitudes that trivialise and disregard the political interests of the 'other'.

Although distributive, recognition and power-related injustices are identified as discrete entities for heuristic purposes, in reality they are deeply interactive (Phillips 1999). The reason that student voices are not heard is not simply because they lack institutional power, it is also because they are defined as subordinate in status terms. Although working-class students experience direct distributive injustices in terms of curricula, resources, etc., they also experience injustices in terms of power and status. Their parents do not exercise the same influence on schools as middle-class parents; there are numerous ways in which they are not given equal status, not least in the way that textbooks and materials often do not engage with the histories, stories or issues of working-class life.

Finally, as noted already in our analysis, schooling is an enterprise that involves emotional work on behalf of both students and teachers. While this was recognised many years ago by writers such as Dan Lortie (1975), from a teacher's perspective, it has not received much attention until recent times (see Hargreaves 2000). And even to date, the focus has been on the feelings of teachers and the effect of these on their performance. Yet schooling relations are relations of dependency and interdependency that are deeply affective in character. Although we do not analyse affective relations in any systematic way, in this study, we recognise that inequality may arise in the affective sphere of educational relations, especially when caring is neglected, be that in relations between students, or between teachers themselves, or in relations between students and teachers.

Issues of distributive justice – the primacy of social class

Economic equality is fundamentally a problem of distributive justice, including ownership and control, and redistribution of primary goods and opportunities. Within education, economic inequality manifests itself fundamentally as a social class problem, an issue of unequal access, participation, outcome and condition. It is about students from low income and welfare-dependent backgrounds being unable to access, participate and achieve in education on equal terms with other students. The inability to avail of educational opportunities on the same terms as other, more economically advantaged, students is itself an outcome of the unequal economic conditions between classes in the wider society (Tawney 1964; Nielsen 1985).

This is not to suggest that the redistribution issue in education is purely a class issue, it is not. The failure to provide the resources for all types of social groups to avail fully of education, be it women availing of technological or scientific education, or disabled people or migrant workers being able to participate equally with others in education, is essentially a distributive problem. However, the generative cause of the inequality that the latter groups experience in education is not in the first instance a distributive one. The generative cause of their marginalisation is their lack of status in terms of citizenship and/or ethnic recognition. It is the latter that is the primary determinant of their economic subordinacy and consequentially of their experience of educational inequality. For those who come from low income working-class backgrounds, however, the reason why they cannot avail of education is most often because they cannot compete on the same terms as other classes for educational advantages, and derivatively, for the advantages and privileges that accrue from education (Bourdieu 1996; Gambetta 1987; Lynch and O'Riordan 1998; Shavit and Blossfeld 1993). Their educational marginalisation is economically generated even though it may subsequently take cultural and political manifestations.

Our data on school selection, streaming and banding, and classroom interaction (Chapters 3 and 4) demonstrate clearly how particular class differences in schooling outcomes are achieved, and how these, in turn, are related to but not dependent on the way different abilities are managed in schools. Although students from different classes are all theoretically receiving the same education, the reality of educational practice is different. First, public policies in the form of taxation, social expenditures and legislative provisions are biased to create serious economic inequalities between classes. These economic inequalities generate differences in resources for schooling that are, in turn, translated into differences in both school choices and schooling experience (Cantillon and O'Shea 2001; Healy and Reynolds 1998; Nolan et al. 2000). The first stage of what we term the Class Act takes place therefore away from the school site. It takes place when wages and salaries are being negotiated, when tax rates and social expenditures are being established, when laws are being enacted to the benefit of particular interests, enabling some to live with resources that are several multiples of those of others (Fischer et al. 1996). Stage 2 of the Class Act is set when parents 'choose' a school for their children. Low income working-class households are seriously disadvantaged at this stage as they frequently lack the money, transport, time, and sometimes even knowledge, to discriminate between schools. It is middle-class families who exercise the freest choice. The data show, however, that class exclusions are not only operating in the demand side of the choice equation, they are also operating in the supply side as schools position themselves to attract the most educationally attractive students through a host of mechanisms that are clearly class biased: requirements regarding voluntary contributions and uniforms, and selection mechanisms that favour past pupils' children and those from targeted primary schools, are all examples of procedures that advantage students from middle-class families.

The third stage of the Class Act opens with the grouping of students on the basis of prior attainment. This is an invisible stage of the play as it is screened away from the public eye. It is also a profoundly problematic stage in terms of how students are screened and selected for different classes. In Ireland as in many other countries tests used for such selection are linguistic and mathematical in focus, so students with good skills in these two areas are generally strongly advantaged in their set, band or stream allocation.[1] The data suggest that both the type of grouping one is likely to experience and the group into which one is allocated are influenced by social class. Middle-class students are least likely to be in low streams or bands within banded/streamed schools, and they dominate the fee-paying schools where 'mixed ability' is the normal form of grouping in the junior cycle.

Stage 4 moves inside the classroom door. Given that the classroom environment in top sets or tracks and in mixed classes is frequently more work-oriented and more positive than that in low bands/streams, this means that middle-class students are once again advantaged educationally, even if they have not attended one of the more socially elite schools. The data do indicate, however, that not only is there between-class stratification in schools, there is also within-class stratification that is not necessarily social-class related.

Social class was always present on the school stage, but it was a relatively silent actor in the course of the research. When trying to discuss the issues associated with class inequality, we sensed a great unease, especially about being named as 'working-class'. The students who were most willing to claim their class were upper middle-class students. Those in fee-paying schools in particular named and claimed their own class. They were aware that the schools they attended were a mechanism for maintaining their class advantage, something that they accepted and even welcomed in some cases. Among the majority of students, however, there was ambivalence and denial about social class differences with most students simply claiming they were middle-class, including a clear majority of students from manual working-class backgrounds.

Students from low income working-class backgrounds generally named social class differences in terms of perceived social demeanour, including accent, and sometimes wealth: the 'others' were those who 'were posh', or 'snobs', or who had 'rich' parents. They also equated being middle-class with being 'swots' or 'brainy'. The term 'social background' was used most often to denote social class, and even this term was used very rarely. Middle-class students (especially) defined students in terms of the housing they lived in; they referred to the fact that they lived in a 'good area' and that others were from 'rough' areas. In many cases the name of the housing estate or the address was a surrogate term for class.

The segregation of students from different social classes both across schools, and across streams and bands within schools, meant however that the most and least advantaged in social class terms were institutionally segregated from each other on a day-to-day basis. The segregation was most visible in the fee-paying and designated disadvantaged schools, but it also operated within schools, between top and bottom sets, streams or bands. Social class segregation and the denial of difference made challenges to unequal social class outcomes difficult. By naming a number of the generative contexts of inequality in this study, however, we hope that we will stimulate a debate about change. The data suggest that taxation systems, school entrance procedures, grouping practices, definitions of intelligence and ability, and personal attitudes, all need to be challenged and changed if class inequalities in education are to be systematically addressed. Inequality is endemic in a class-driven capitalist society and education has become a major tool in the realisation of this project. The breaking down of class inequality in education requires levels of intervention that are as multi-faceted as class inequality itself.

The non-recognition of differences: equal status issues

Inequalities of recognition are fundamentally status injustices. They are not about some esoteric process of identity construction, but rather about institutional practices of denial, denigration and subordination (Fraser 2000). Cultural non-recognition or misrepresentation is not only operating in the symbolic realms; it is also grounded in the practices and processes of social life, including the life of schools.

While it is evident that all subordinate groups in society experience some forms of non-recognition (including working-class groups) recognition is much more likely to be the generative source of inequality or injustice for groups that are culturally marginalised in the first instance. Fraser (1997) suggests that for people who are gay, lesbian or bisexual, the principal cause of the injustice they experience is the failure to recognise their sexuality, the unwillingness to name it and facilitate it on equal terms with heterosexuality. Other groups also experience misrecognition including people with disabilities or different abilities and religious minorities. The level of non-recognition that occurs in all of these areas varies with the unique cultural and historical contexts of schools.

The data indicate that the groups that experienced the strongest form of misrecognition and non-recognition in schools were those who were gay or lesbian, and Travellers. The analysis of attitude statements in particular, but also essays and focus groups, indicated that those who were gay or lesbian and those who were Travellers were often not seen as suitable friends or even school companions. Their differences were judged as inferiorities or as abnormalities.

Overall, more than half of the students said they would terminate a friendship if they found out that their friend was lesbian or gay, while almost the same number believed that if they were friendly with students who were Travellers, their other friends might abandon them. In all cases male attitudes were more negative than those of females, significantly so in many cases.

While students were open in their expression of views about Travellers, this was in sharp contrast to their views on sexuality. Silence and reticence characterised the limited discussions that took place on sexual orientation. Those who were gay, lesbian or bisexual were generally invisible in public discourse in schools. Ten of the twelve schools in the study did not deal with differences in sexual orientation in any systematic way in their school programmes. This was equally true of schools which were Catholic, Protestant and non-denominational. The issue of sexual orientation was a taboo subject in several respects. Neither school prospectuses nor year books made any explicit reference to sexual difference. Moreover, only in one of the twelve schools was the subject raised by teachers in our research dialogues with them, although we presented attitudinal data in all schools indicating the high levels of homophobia among students.

This institutional invisibility was reinforced by the lack of vocabulary to name and discuss sexual differences. Students were generally not accustomed to addressing the subject of sexual orientation, so they literally did not know what to say or how to say what they did feel or know. While the new *Relationships and Sexuality Programme* does allow space for the examination of the subject of sexual orientation in schools, it was not fully implemented at the time of our data collection. Research by O'Carroll and Szalacha (2000) suggests, however, that few schools actually address issues of sexual orientation, even since the programme was initiated. The fact that the issue of sexual orientation was only raised spontaneously in eight of the twelve hundred essays as a cause of unequal treatment in schools is itself indicative of the silence that prevails.

The limited research in Ireland on the educational experiences of those who are lesbian, gay or bisexual strongly supports our findings about the silence that exists about sexual difference (Rose 1994; Glen/NEXUS 1995; Barron 1999; Foyle Friend 1999; Gowran 2000; O'Carroll and Szalacha 2000). While this has been often attributed to the influence of Roman Catholic teaching on matters of sexuality, in particular their interpretation of same-sex relationships as deviant and disordered (Dillon 1999), all the religious bodies involved in managing the schools we studied did not give parity of esteem to same-sex relationships.

It was notable, however, that where an individual teacher or a specific school programme had addressed the issue, as had occurred in two of the schools, pupils in focus groups were better able to examine their own feelings and fears about their sexuality. A proactive approach by their school or teacher was judged by them to have helped to create a space in which this aspect of sexuality could be explored.

Although non-recognition was most acute in relation to sexual orientation, it also operated in relation to ethnicity (Traveller status especially), racial identity (especially colour), disability and religious differences. The nomadic lifestyle of most Travellers was minimally understood, leading to deep fear and hostility at times. Discussions in focus groups on religious differences indicated a profound lack of knowledge on the subject, with some students observing that they had never met anyone from a different religious background to themselves. They felt they would not know how to relate to them if they met. Yet, there was no context or forum where differences between students were discussed or dealt with systematically. Although differences were discussed in religion classes in some cases, whether or not this happened depended on the teacher and their interpretation of their subject.[2]

The management of cultural, religious, ability, sexual, ethnic and other differences was not a matter that received much attention in most schools. Assumptions of homogeneity tended to prevail among both teachers and students. Student response to differences in particular tended to vary between denial and silence (in relation to different sexualities), expressions of overt hostility (most common in relation to Travellers), caution (with respect to religious differences), pity (for disabled students) and acceptance (of all groups by some students). While ethnic differences have emerged as important sources of social tension in Ireland over the last two years due to rising immigration, at the time we were in schools there were relatively few ethnic minority students. In the one school in the study with a small number of ethnic minority students there were tensions however between the minority and majority students; minority students claimed their lifestyles were denigrated by other students.

The fact that students lacked the vocabulary to discuss differences, and seemed unable to express views on differences in a non-judgemental way, says much about the urgent need to explore issues of difference in schools. We need to move away from a narrow liberal discourse of tolerance, with its hierarchical connotations of the dominant tolerating the subordinate, to a perspective that respects and celebrates differences (Young 1990).

Powerlessness – presence and effective representation

The work of distribution and recognition in education takes place in the institutional context of a particular school. Schools operate structures of decision-making, methods of engagement and control, and systems for the construction and dissemination of meaning that assume particular relations of power between the parties involved in the education process. Relations between students and teachers, between teachers and school managers, and between students, parents and teachers are defined in terms of relations of power, control and regulation. Power relations are deeply imbricated therefore in the fabric of school life.

When we listened to the voices of young people about their experience of schooling, through essays, informal discussions and focus groups, their equality issues were framed in a different way from that which dominated the intellectual discourse of educationalists and academics. The most deeply felt and articulated sense of injustice arose around issues of power and control by adults, both in school, but also out of school, by parents. Power relations constituted a constituency of concern in its own right independent of, albeit related to, redistributive and recognition issues.

The data bring into fresh relief Waller's (1932: 19) claim many years ago, that the teacher–pupil relationship is a form of institutionalised dominance and subordination, in which the spontaneous life of groups of children is pitted against the interests and concerns of adults. While issues of gender, social class, racial and ethnic inequalities did emerge from the spontaneous voices of the young people in the schools, these did not hold the significance in their consciousness that might be attributed to them by social scientists. Interestingly also, students' concerns about unequal treatments by peers did not receive as much attention in essays or focus groups as unfair treatments by teachers; only one-fifth named peers as persons responsible for their unequal treatment in school while almost half of all essays cited teachers as the persons responsible for unequal treatment. The issues cited included concerns regarding perceived arbitrary or unfair use of authority by teachers or other adults in school and the lack of democratic procedures for managing staff–student conflict.

The way in which power is exercised was not only a concern for students however, it was also a focus of teachers' comment. Teachers' experience of power was both vertical and horizontal. While teachers exercised control over students (and almost 50 per cent observed that authority was not always exercised fairly in the school), teachers themselves were also subject to numerous controls and regulations by an increasingly diverse range of stakeholders, including State agencies, parents, students and school managers. They were simultaneously powerful but powerless *vis-à-vis* different stakeholders (Davies 1996). Power was not only experienced vertically, it was also exercised laterally (Ball 1987, 1989). Teachers who were temporary, younger, part-time and/or female were the most likely to claim they were relatively powerless in the school organisation.

Power is everywhere in schools, although the ability to control and influence events is by no means evenly dispersed (Davies 2001). Creating equality in education demands that we treat power as an equality problematic. We need to set up structures to democratise power relations in all their manifestations. We need to move to more participatory forms of democratic engagement if those who are currently marginalised in power terms are to be enabled to exercise real control over decision-making. Moreover, the more vulnerable parties to partici-patory democratic engagements need to be informed, resourced and supported if they are to exercise power effectively (Phillips 1995).

Gender – a paradigm case of a multivalent status

Although the paradigm cases of economically-driven, status-dependent, and power-related inequalities in these schools may be those arising from social class, sexuality and age (youth) respectively, for any given person in a given social group, the generative causes of inequality are not singular. Women or men who experience inequality do not experience it in singular terms, they also experience it in terms of their age, abilities, social class, sexuality, ethnicity, etc. Notwithstanding the layered nature of social experience and the interpenetration of different forms of inequality with each other, the importance of certain statuses in the determination of inequality is greater than that of others, in terms of the forms of inequality that it generates. Fraser (1995) claims that gender and race are examples of status positions that generate inequality in terms of both recognition and redistribution in relatively equal measure. Not only do gender and race structure one's experience culturally and symbolically, they also exercise a profound influence on one materially, in the economic sphere.

While our data lend support to Fraser's hypothesis, they also indicate that we need to go beyond it. They suggest that gender-related inequalities are not bivalent but multivalent in character. They arise in the realms of power-relations as well as in the realms of economic and cultural relations. Within schools, it is the power and status differentiations between women and men that are most visible.

Power

As noted in Chapter 9, the teachers who exercised least control either vertically or laterally in schools were women. Overall women were disproportionately over-represented in the posts where power was least concentrated, that is in non-promotional posts, and in temporary and part-time positions. Although the subordinate position of women was most visible in one of the co-educational schools in particular (Ollan), it was an issue in all types of schools. Female (and sometimes male) teachers commented on the inequalities arising either because the most senior posts were held by men although women comprised the majority of the staff (Ballydara, co-educational), or because the principal was male and almost all the staff were female (St Patrick's, girls' school), or because male teachers and students made sexist remarks that were allowed to go unchallenged (Dunely, boys' school). There was one co-educational school in the study (Ballydara) however in which male teachers claimed the male principal was biased against them in promotional terms. Female teachers within the same school countered this with evidence of the over-representation of men in promotional posts despite the fact that women comprised the majority of the teaching staff.

The gendered nature of the hierarchical relations between teachers themselves was but one aspect of the power equation. Student–teacher relations were also hierarchical, and especially so in girls' schools. The data suggest that young female students are more stringently monitored and controlled in schools than young men, particularly in girls' schools. Almost three times as many girls in girls' schools complained about confidentiality and privacy violations by teachers as boys in boys' schools, while twice as many girls in co-educational schools complained about it compared with boys in these schools. Control of dress, demeanour and general behaviour was also much more stringently exercised in girls' schools than in either boys' or co-educational schools. (Given that both the boys' and the girls' schools in the study were all under Catholic management, one cannot simply attribute the differences between them to the type of religious management in the school.) Classroom surveillance[3] procedures were also more visible in girls' than in boys' schools or co-educational schools. Although we only recorded incidences of surveillance in a small minority of classes (18 per cent), a disproportionately high number of single-sex girls' classes involved such incidences. Girls across the schools, and especially in the girls' schools, did not accept the regulation and control of their body, demeanour and behaviour in a passive way. Their essays on school and their comments during focus groups and informal discussions indicated that many regarded the regulations imposed on them as arbitrary and anachronistic. They resisted them in their discourse about schooling, and in occasional refusals to conform to codes of dress, hairstyles and demeanour.

The control of masculinity in boys' schools was most visibly exercised within the peer groups. Hegemonic conceptions of masculinity, based on notions of dominance (Connell 1995), seemed to prevail strongly in three of the four boys' schools. Boys who were successful in valued male sports and/or who were physically strong and able to defend themselves in fights, were respected above those who were not. While dominance-driven notions of masculinity were also very visible in one of the co-educational schools in particular, this was less true in the others. School authorities did not promote dominance-driven views of masculinity, and one boys' school clearly challenged them. However, there was a sense in which teachers in boys' schools especially, and in one of the co-educational schools, ignored, and in some cases condoned, dominance-style behaviours among boys.

Status differentiations – gender differences in levels of recognition

As in most countries, there are no Women's Studies, Equality Studies or related subjects on the second-level school curriculum in Irish schools. In addition, there are few female images and authors in school texts: the poets, the novelists, the scientists, historians, geographers, mathematicians, economists, etc., that students study are overwhelmingly male. The world they read about is a world overwhelmingly recorded by men. While this is not problematised in any serious or systematic way, it is none the less something that needs to be recorded as it signifies to all those who are educated that women do not name the world, that the voice that is recorded is a male voice (Harding 1991). At a deep structural level, it assigns things female a lower status in the world of education without declaring it. It forms the backdrop against which other status distinctions are framed and placed.

There were a number of subtle ways in which the subordinate status of women found expression in the life of the schools, including life within the classroom. Within co-educational classes, teachers were more likely to use the first names of male students in class than those of female students: in the forty-seven co-educational classes observed, girls were twice as likely as boys not to be spoken to by name for the duration of the lesson (see Chapter 7). The subordinate status of girls' work was also visible in the area of extra-curricular activities, where boys' sports were given greater prominence both symbolically in the public spaces of the school (in terms of being recorded in pictures, plaques, school magazines, etc.) and in terms of resources (money invested in coaching). The practices in girls' schools of monitoring and regulating students' dress, sexuality and demeanour, while interpreted in power terms by students, could be interpreted from a structural perspective as being indicative of the lowly and more subservient status of women generally. While the girls were being prepared for jobs, and careers (the latter if they were middle-class or with middle-class ambitions), their servicing, compliant role in society was always part of their predicted future. They were learning to regulate their person and their behaviour is a way that made them 'feminine' as opposed to 'feminist', where the feminine required obedience to codes of dress and behaviour that were not only outdated but were also inappropriate. One student commented wryly on the inconvenience of wearing a skirt and knee socks; it made cycling to school in winter a hazardous occupation, something to be avoided. Not surprisingly, far fewer girls (3 per cent) cycled to school compared with boys (10 per cent). Yet girls were expected to endure this inconvenience; the outdated and restricted character of their uniform was only a subject for discussion in one of the four girls' schools.

While most girls did not remark in essays or focus groups on gender differentiation in the co-educational schools, a small number did claim that girls had lower status in the school than the boys. Direct references to incidences of gender inequality in the school emerged most prominently from St Ita's (co-ed fp), a school with a predominantly urban, middle- and upper middle-class intake. Over one-fifth of the essays from this school had some comments about gender inequality. The students in this school, and particularly the girls, displayed an awareness of their rights relating to gender issues, and an ability to name gender inequality that was not evident to the same degree in the other co-educational schools.

Redistribution – the interface of social class and gender

While girls experienced schooling within their social class, their experience within their class was also a gendered and subordinated one. One example of this was the notable differences in resources between the fee-paying girls' and boys' schools in our study. St David's and St Cecilia's were located in neigbourhoods that were very similar in social class terms. However, St Cecilia's fees were much lower than those in St David's (less than IR£900 compared with IR£1,400) and its resources and facilities, on *pro rata* terms, were also poorer. It lacked the extensive grounds and the sports facilities of St David's.

Neither did it have the paid coaches for the sports teams that St David's had. While it was true that St David's attracted more than twice as many students from Social Class 1 as St Cecilia's, none the less St Cecilia's was a largely upper middle-class school with 82 per cent being from Classes 1 and 2 compared with 93 per cent of those in St David's (see Chapter 3). It would seem therefore that within the upper middle classes, somewhat more money was being invested in the education of boys than girls. Given the fact that considerably more boys than girls attend single-sex fee-paying schools in Ireland generally (58 per cent of those in single-sex fee-paying schools are boys), this is also proof of the extent to which elite education is a greater priority for boys than girls. While both girls and boys from upper middle-class backgrounds are expected to enter elite positions, the placing of boys in schools where the culture and social life of the school anticipates such positions is a higher priority for them than it is for girls.

The differing expectations of girls and boys from all classes were evident in relation to the study of Home Economics. It was promoted as a Junior Certificate subject for girls within both girls' and co-educational schools. While it was available to boys in co-educational schools, albeit not strongly promoted, it was not available in any of the all-boys' schools in the main curriculum. Home Economics (Social and Scientific) was made available, however, as an optional extra subject for fifth-year boys in St David's where students could attend lectures two evenings a week after school. The more practical subject of Home Economics (General) was not offered. Home Economics (Social and Scientific) was regarded by the principal as an easy additional subject for boosting one's overall grades in the Leaving Certificate examination. There was a clear assumption, institutionalised in the curriculum provisions of the schools, that domestic work, for which Home Economics (General) was seen as a preparation, was not an upper middle-class boy's responsibility.

While one's experience of class was gendered, one's experience of gender was also classed. The way in which gender and social class interface was visible in the co-educational schools, most especially in the way that class influenced even the experience of sexism and gendered practices. St Ita's was an upper middle-class school, where 91 per cent of the students were from Social Classes 1 and 2, most being from Class 1. No more than 5 per cent of the students in each of the other three co-educational schools were from Class 1; Ballydara had the highest of the three from Classes 1 and 2, at 34 per cent, while Ballycorish had only 15 per cent (see Table A5). Although St Ita's was one of the less gender biased of the four co-educational schools in terms of its policies and procedures, especially less so than Ollan, it was the school in which there were most complaints about gender discrimination from girls. In two of the other co-educational schools, which were more working class and lower middle class in composition than St Ita's, sexist practices and procedures that were more pronounced than those in St Ita's either went unnoticed or were discounted by students. Boys in one of the schools frequently formed a line in the corridor and touched girls and some female teachers (and sometimes younger boys) as they passed at break times; this was described by the boys as 'just a bit of fun'. Yet, while a teacher in the school described the experience as 'running the gauntlet', girls in the school did not comment on this practice in either essays or focus groups. There was a sense in which the practice was normalised in the school. Students seemed to lack both the language and the general awareness to articulate concerns about gender issues. The girls (and to some degree younger boys who were also targeted) also seemed to lack a sense of power to control the situation, something that was less true in St Ita's. It appeared that the more upper middle class the girls, the greater their ability to name and challenge the stereotyping or inequalities that occurred.

The types of extra-curricular activities students engaged in were also structured along both social class and gender lines. In most schools, girls and boys were socialised into sports that were highly gendered – rugby, boxing, Gaelic football and hurling for boys, hockey, camogie and basketball for girls. While roughly equal proportions of girls and boys (50 per cent of each) were involved in extra-curricular activities in their schools, 80 per cent of the boys involved were involved in sport only, compared with 49 per cent of girls. Girls were much more likely than boys to be involved in non-sporting activities, especially music, but also drama. The type of extra-curricular activity that one could engage in within a school was strongly class and gender driven.

Our Lady's girls' school was a mixed school in terms of social class intake, in a rural area. It did not devote much time to sport; however, a lot of time was devoted by staff and students to drama and musical productions. Insofar as it had a public extra-curricular profile, it was cultural rather than sporting. St Peter's girls' school had a large working-class and lower middle-class intake; here again cultural (music and choir) rather than sporting extra-curricular activities predominated. Although St Peter's did promote basketball, volleyball, athletics and swimming, these tended to involve relatively small numbers of students and not to receive high priority in the school organisation. The more upper middle-class schools in the study tended to play either hockey as their main sport if they were girls' schools (St Cecilia's and St Patrick's), rugby if they were boys' schools (St David's), and rugby for boys and hockey for girls if co-educational (St Ita's). Hurling dominated the more rural boys' school, Dunely; it had a sizeable minority from farming backgrounds but few upper middle-class students. The co-educational community schools and colleges did not prioritise particular sports, some offered Gaelic football, others athletics, basketball, hurling or soccer. None offered rugby or hockey. We were informed in two schools that they had deliberately prioritised certain sports over others and precluded the introduction of competitor sports. This was true in St David's (boys' school) where one teacher pointed out (after our research presentation to the staff) that the school had refused to promote hurling or Gaelic football, as it was claimed these games might take players from rugby. This, he believed, was not simply a matter of maintaining the status of rugby, it was also about the social class profile of the school. Both hurling and Gaelic football were seen as lower middle-class and working-class sports for boys, and the school did not want to promote that kind of image. A not dissimilar issue arose in St Cecilia's, a girls' school, with a large middle-class intake and a strong interest in hockey. While there had been a proposal to introduce soccer by a small number of senior staff, this proposal was rejected as some teachers pointed out to us that it might 'give a wrong image' about the school, namely a male working-class image.

It is clear therefore that the type of subjects one studied, the extra-curricular activities in which one was engaged, the social climate within which one lived, and the discourse about gender (or lack of it) to which one was exposed, were all class based, and they were also clearly gendered. Social class and gender were important, interfacing signifiers of difference and differentiation. There was no class without gender and no gender without social class.

Gender inequalities in education also had multiple origins. In terms of the knowledge taught, the pedagogy employed, the symbols portrayed on school walls, gender divisions are status driven with the female being generally subordinate to the male; in terms of the career or jobs expected, the extra-curricular activities promoted, gender differentiations are materially or economically driven, with much socialisation encouraging girls into areas of work or recreation that are economically subordinated in later life; in terms of the way authority is exercised, gender subordination has a power dimension with men dominating positions of authority in schools, and girls being subordinated by an array of procedures around dress, demeanour and behaviour that are absent for boys generally, and in boys' schools in particular.

Conclusion

Although sociological research has relied heavily on concepts of distributive justice to understand inequality in education, a distributive model does not enable us to understand inequalities of power and status. It tends to underestimate the importance of the 'institutional contexts within which distributions take place, and which is often at least partly the cause of patterns of distribution of jobs and wealth' (Young 1990: 21–22). It underestimates the importance of structures of decision-making, engagement and control, the systems for the construction of meaning, interpretation and dissemination, the importance of language, and the codes, norms and values which govern what is defined as common sense in everyday educational life.

Our data suggest that inequality in education has at least three major generative roots: it is rooted in socio-culturally-based systems of recognition, non-recognition and misrecognition; it is rooted in all contexts where power is enacted, in the realms of decision-making and in systems of inclusion or exclusion in the exercise of power; and it is rooted in the socio-economic systems in terms of patterns of ownership, control, distribution and consumption. The relative significance of any one of these contexts for the generation of inequality for a given group can be empirically investigated. Detailed analysis of the microphysics of inequality helps guide us in developing counterfactual positions to unequal educational relations.

Drawing on our research data a schematic outline of a range of different groups that experience inequality in our education system is presented in Figure 11.1. We realise that this is an ideal-type model and is open to empirical refinement and theoretical advancement. It is presented as a heuristic device to enable us to summarise the range and types of inequality arising across social groups.

What is clear from Figure 11.1 is that the contexts that generate inequality vary with different groups. The differences between groups are most visible where economic, political or cultural inequalities are highly polarised (for children, gays and lesbians and working-class groups respectively). It is less clear, however, for those groups that are internally diverse and where inequalities are cumulative across all three areas with no one context predominating.

While social-class-related inequality in education is clearly an economically generated injustice, and as such cannot be resolved in the educational site alone, other groups may experience economic inequality or poverty as a derivative of either cultural and/or political inequalities. Equally while powerlessness is a key equality issue for young people, adults in schools may also experience relative powerlessness in vertical and/or horizontal terms depending on their age, status and gender. Other groups can experience powerlessness in a derived way, due to their lack of cultural recognition (religious minorities) or lack of resources to make their voices heard (working-class parents). Finally, those who experience cultural and symbolic inequalities in the form of non-recognition or misrecognition (such as gays, lesbians) may experience powerlessness and exclusions from decision-making arising from their low cultural status. Their low cultural status may also contribute to their economic marginalisation and subordination (Phillips 1999).

Attempts to respond to inequality in education by focusing on one manifestation of inequality alone are not likely to produce much by way of social change. Different forms of inequality are deeply implicated with one another, and their resolution requires a multi-faceted response. This is especially the case for large internally diverse groups such as women. Women experience inequalities in education that are economically, politically and culturally generated in relatively equal measure. Resolving these means working on a range of political, economic and cultural sites both within and without schools simultaneously.

Although class inequalities require resolution in terms of distributive justice, the class problem is not solely a distributive one; it also involves redressing power relations between working-class families and schools, and status considerations relating to class cultures and values. Equally while children and young people in school experience their primary inequality problem as power-related, the factors that exacerbate their powerlessness such as low legal status, and economic

Figure 11.1 Key contexts for the generation of inequality and means of redress for selected social groups[a]

Key contexts of inequality	Typical forms of inequality	Primary form of redress	Ethnic minorities	Religious minorities	Age groups	Social class	Gender		Sexual orientation	Dis/Ability
			Travellers		Children	Low income welfare/ working class	Girls generally	Working-class girls/boys	Lesbian/ gay/bisexual	
Political	Powerlessness	Effective representation – democratisation	*	*	**	*	*	*	*	*
Economic	Lack of adequate resources	Redistribution of goods and wealth	*	*	*	**	*	**	*	*
Socio-cultural	Lack of respect	Recognition of culture, values, lifestyles	**	**	*	*	*	**	**	**

Note
[a] This figure is based on ongoing work at the Equality Studies Centre with our colleagues John Baker and Sara Cantillon in the preparation of an Equality Framework for the National Economic and Social Forum (see Lynch et al. 2001)

The focus in this schema is on the primacy of particular contexts in generating inequality in the first instance. Each context is defined as being of some (*) or of major (**) significance for a particular group in generating inequality.

dependency, also need to be reconsidered. What this points to also is that while inequalities may be reproduced in the education site they are also reproduced and generated in the fields of economic, socio-cultural and political relations outside of school. School is a major player in the inequality game but by no means the only one.

Appendix A: Tables

Table A1 The gender profile of second-level schools in the Republic of Ireland

School type	School gender intake	No. of schools	No. of students
Secondary schools Free-scheme	Single-sex girls	142	83,617
	Single-sex boys	109	54,548
	Co-educational	137	61,646
Fee-paying	Single-sex girls	17	6,195
	Single-sex boys	17	8,284
	Co-educational	23	9,315
Vocational schools/ community colleges	Single-sex girls	3	342
	Single-sex boys	2	459
	Co-educational	241	94,008
Community schools	Single-sex girls	0	0
	Single-sex boys	2	1,196
	Co-educational	59	41,128
Comprehensive schools	Single-sex girls	1	286
	Single-sex boys	1	298
	Co-educational	14	8,543
Total *n*		768	369,865

Source: Figures compiled from full database of pupil and school numbers for the academic year 1995/96 provided by the Statistical Section, Department of Education and Science, Department of Education (1997) *Statistical Report 1995/96*, Dublin: Stationery Office

Table A2 Breakdown of teaching staffs by school showing number of whole-time, part-time, and student teachers, and giving student–teacher ratio

School	Description	Student n	Total tchr n	Whole-time tchrs	Part-time tchrs	hDip.s	Student /tchr ratio[b]
St Peter's	ssg, city, fr (disadv)	950	72[a]	63	2	7	14.6 : 1
Ballydara	co-ed, city, Com Col	950	71	46	24	1	16.6 : 1
St Patrick's	ssg, town, fr	800	57	45	10	2	15.8 : 1
St Ita's	co-ed, city, fp	800	80[a]	80	0	0	10.3 : 1
Ballinroe	ssb, town, fr	700	36	36	0	0	18.0 : 1
Ollan	co-ed, town, Com Col	650	45	43	2	0	14.3 : 1
Ballycorish	co-ed, rural, Com Sch (disadv)	650	40	40	0	0	16.0 : 1
St David's	ssb, city, fp	550	47[a]	45	0	2	12.2 : 1
Dunely	ssb, town, fr	500	31	31	0	0	16.5 : 1
St Dominic's	ssb, city, fr (disadv)	500	32	32	0	0	15.5 : 1
St Cecilia's	ssg, city, fp	400	36[a]	22	10	4	15.6 : 1
Our Lady's	ssg, rural, fr	250	20	14	6	0	14.8 : 1

Notes

[a] The teacher numbers in these instances include ex-quota members of staff. In the case of St Peter's, one part-time teacher is paid by school funds to teach an additional six hours per week over her Department of Education allocation; in the case of St David's, thirteen of the forty-seven staff members are ex-quota; in the case of St Ita's, thirty-five of the eighty staff members are ex-quota.

[b] These calculations are based on the total number of whole-time teachers and the number of part-time posts combined to make equivalent whole-time posts. Student teachers are excluded from this calculation. However, in St Peter's, student teachers were regarded as necessary to be able to complete the timetable. In Ballydara, the principal stated that as far as he was concerned, everyone teaching in the school, permanent, temporary or student, was a teacher.

Table A3 Provision of academic facilities and supports by school

School	Type	Student no.	Science labs	Art rooms	Tech. rooms	Home ec. rooms	Music facils	PE facils	Comp. room	No. of comps	Video + audio	Remed tchr	Library
St Peter's	ssg, city, fr (disd)	950	✓4	✓2	✓1	✓3	✓	✓ in/out-door		25	✓	✓	✓
Ballydara	Co-ed, city, Com Col	950	✓6	✓2	✓6	✓3	✓	✓ in/outdoor*		18	✓	✓	✓
St Patrick's	ssg, town, fr	800	✓3	✓1	0	✓2	✓	✓ in/outdoor		26	✓	✓	✓
St Ita's	Co-ed, city, fp	800	✓6	✓3	✓1	✓1	✓	✓ in/outdoor		24	✓	✓(p/time)	✓
Ballinroe	ssb, town, fr	700	✓3	0	✓1	0	0	✓ outdoor		15	✓		✓
Ollan	Co-ed, town, Com Col	650	✓3	✓1	✓6	✓2	✓	✓ indoor		35	✓	✓	✓
Ballycorish	Co-ed, rural, Com Sch (disd)	650	✓3	✓1	✓5	✓2	✓	✓ in/outdoor		15	✓	✓	✓
St David's	ssb, city, fp	550	✓3	✓1	✓1	0	0	✓ in/outdoor		17	✓	✓	✓
St Dominic's	ssb, city, fr (disd)	500	✓3	✓1	✓2	0	0			60	✓	✓	✓
Dunely	ssb, town, fr	500	✓3	✓1	✓2	0	✓	✓ outdoor*		30	✓	Vol. only	0
St Cecilia's	ssg, city, fp	400	✓2	✓1	0	✓2	✓	✓ in/outdoor		12	✓	Vol. only	✓
Our Lady's	ssg, rural, fr	250	✓1	✓1	0	✓1	✓	✓ in/outdoor	0	0	✓	Vol. only	✓

Table A4 Provision of extra-curricular facilities and resources by school

School	Type	Studnt no.	F'ball pitches	Hurl/ camogie	Hockey pitches	Court games	Swim pool	Full gym	Games hall	Change rooms + shower	Hall with stage	Spec coach	Green-space
St Peter's	ssg, city, fr (disad)	950	0	0	✓1	✓4	0	0	✓+ stage	✓✓	✓	Vol staff time	✓
Ballydara	co-ed, city, Com Col	950	✓1	✓1	0	✓2	0	0	✓+ stage	✓✓	✓	Vol staff time	✓
St Patrick's	ssg, town, fr	800	0	0	✓1	✓3	0	0	0	0	✓	Coach p/time staff	✓
St Ita's	co-ed, city, fp	800	✓2 (+ prac. fields)	0	✓2	✓2	0	✓	0	✓✓	✓	Coaches p/time staff	✓
Ballinroe	ssb, town, fr	700	✓1 (also hurling)	✓1 (also f'ball)	0	✓1	0	0	0	0	0	Vol staff time	
Ollan	co-ed, town, Com Col	650	0	0	0	0	0	0	✓+ stage	0	✓	Vol staff time	0
Ballycorish	co-ed, rural, Com Sch (disad)	650	✓1 (also hurling)	✓1 (also f'ball)	0	✓1	0	✓	0	✓✓	✓	Vol staff time	✓
St David's	ssb, city, fp	550	✓4	0	0	✓2	✓	✓	0	✓✓	✓	Coaches p/time staff	✓
St Dominic's	ssb, city, fr (disad)	500	0	0	0	0	0	0	0	0	0	Vol staff time	0
Dunely	ssb, town, fr	500	✓2 (used for hurling)	✓2	0	✓2	0	0	0	0	✓	Vol staff time	✓
St Cecilia's	ssg, city, fp	400	0	0	✓1	✓2	0	0	✓+ stage	0	✓	Coaches p/time staff	✓
Our Lady's	ssg, rural. fr	250	0	0	0	✓1	0	0	✓(social area)	0	0	Vol staff time	✓

Table A5 Breakdown of student sample in each participating school by father's social class [Total n (questionnaires) = 1,411]

School	Description	Soc cls 1 (%)	Soc cls 2 (%)	Soc cls 3 (%)	Soc cls 4 (%)	Soc cls 5 (%)	Soc cls 6 (%)	Soc cls 7 (%)	Farmers[b] (%)	Total (%)
St Peter's	ssg, fr (disad), city	8.7 (3.5)[a]	20.5 (5.9)	18.9 (16.2)	29.1 (17.2)	9.4 (9.7)	7.9 (15.6)	5.5 (14.6)	0 (0)	9.0
Ballydara	co-ed, Com Col, city	5.4 (2.3)	28.7 (8.3)	15.5 (13.5)	29.5 (17.7)	10.9 (11.3)	4.7 (9.4)	5.4 (14.6)	0 (0)	9.1
St Patrick's	ssg, fr, town	22.0 (8.7)	42.3 (11.7)	12.2 (10.1)	13.8 (7.9)	4.9 (4.8)	2.4 (4.7)	1.6 (4.2)	0.8 (1.8)	8.7
St Ita's	Co-ed, fp, city	45.5 (18.0)	45.5 (12.6)	4.1 (3.4)	3.3 (1.9)	0 (0)	0 (0)	1.6 (4.2)	0 (0)	8.7
Ballinroe	ssb, fr, town	23.6 (10.6)	39.3 (12.4)	9.3 (8.8)	14.3 (9.3)	5.0 (5.6)	1.4 (3.1)	5.0 (14.6)	2.1 (5.3)	9.9
Ollan	co-ed, Com Col, town	3.9 (1.3)	24.5 (5.6)	8.8 (6.1)	22.5 (10.7)	23.5 (19.4)	5.9 (9.4)	3.9 (8.3)	6.9 (12.3)	7.2
Ballycorish	co-ed, Com Sch, (disad) rural	2.2 (0.6)	13.2 (2.7)	12.1 (7.4)	30.8 (13.0)	25.3 (18.5)	4.4 (6.3)	3.3 (6.3)	8.8 (14.0)	6.4
St David's	ssb, fp, city	78.8 (37.0)	14.4 (4.7)	2.7 (2.7)	2.1 (1.4)	0.7 (0.8)	0 (0)	1.4 (4.2)	0 (0)	10.3
Dunely	ssb, fr, town	5.6 (2.6)	36.6 (11.7)	14.8 (14.2)	8.5 (5.6)	9.9 (11.3)	7.0 (15.6)	3.5 (10.4)	14.1 (35.1)	10.1
St Dominic's	ssb, fr (disad)	3.6 (0.6)	21.4 (2.7)	7.1 (2.7)	26.8 (7.0)	17.9 (8.1)	19.6 (17.2)	3.6 (4.2)	0 (0)	4.0
St Cecilia's	ssg, fp, city	31.9 (13.8)	49.6 (15.1)	8.9 (8.1)	4.4 (2.8)	2.2 (2.4)	1.5 (3.1)	1.5 (4.2)	0 (0)	9.6
Our Lady's	ssg, fr, rural	3.1 (1.0)	29.9 (6.5)	10.3 (6.8)	12.4 (5.6)	10.3 (8.1)	10.3 (15.6)	5.2 (10.4)	18.6 (31.6)	6.9
n Total (%)		311 22.0	444 31.5	148 10.5	215 15.2	124 8.8	64 4.5	48 3.4	57 4.0	1411 100

Notes
[a] Column percentages in parentheses.
[b] Farmers were categorised separately in this study because it was not possible for students to give sufficiently accurate data on family farms in order to be able to group them correctly into the occupational categories used by the Central Statistics Office.

Key (as by Clancy 1995)
Soc Cls 1 = Higher Professional, Higher Managerial, Proprietors
Soc Cls 2 = Lower Professional, Lower Managerial, Proprietors
Soc Cls 3 = Other Non-Manual
Soc Cls 4 = Skilled Manual
Soc Cls 5 = Semi-Skilled Manual
Soc Cls 6 = Unskilled Manual
Soc Cls 7 = Social Class Unknown
Farmers = all students indicating their father's main work was farming

Table A6 Most frequent modes of transport to and from school reported by student sample by school (*n* = 1,524)

School	Description	Walk/ cycle (%)	Public bus/ train (%)	Car (%)	Other (%)	Total n
St Peter's	ssg, city, fr (disadv)	48.9	32.6	10.1	8.4	129
Ballydara	co-ed, city, Com Col	87.7	5.4	6.8	0.1	147
St Patrick's	ssg, town, fr	52	22	16.5	9.5	127
St Ita's	co-ed, city, fp	16.7	50	31	2.3	126
Ballinroe	ssb, town, fr	53.1	22.8	23.4	0.7	145
Ollan	co-ed, town, Com Col	32.6	45.5	21.2	0.7	132
Ballycorish	co-ed, rural, Com Sch (disadv)	34	48	15	3	100
St David's	ssb, city, fp	13.1	40.8	46.1	0	152
Dunely	ssb, town, fr	31.3	34	28.7	6	150
St Dominic's	ssb, city, fr (disadv)	49.3	24.6	15.9	10.2	69
St Cecilia's	ssg, city, fp	32.9	0.7	57.9	8.5	140
Our Lady's	ssg, rural, fr	12.1	48.6	34.6	4.7	107
Total n		593	465	402	64	1524
Total %		38.9	30.5	26.4	4.2	100

Table A7 The relationship between social class and streaming/banding in junior cycle of streamed/banded schools

Ability grouping	Prof./ man. (%)	Salaried white-collar/ skilled (%)	Semi/ unskilled other (%)	Farmers (%)	Total (%)
Lower band/ stream	30.4 (36.6)	34.2 (53.5)	32.3 (67.1)	3.2 (35.7)	49.1
Upper band/ stream	50.6 (63.4)	28.7 (46.5)	15.2 (32.9)	5.5 (64.3)	50.9
Total (%)	40.7 %	31.4 %	23.6 %	4.3 %	100 %
Total n	131	101	76	14	322

Note
Column percentages in parentheses.

Table A8 Comments in student essays about unequal treatment on the basis of social class by school (*n* = 50)

School	Type	Essays from each school containing claims about differential treatment on the basis of social class (%)	n
St Peter's	ssg, city, fr (disadv)	7.9	9
Ballydara	co-ed, city, Com Col	5.8	6
St Patrick's	ssg, town, fr	2.5	3
St Ita's	co-ed, city, fp	4.0	4
Ballinroe	ssb, town, fr	0.9	1
Ollan	co-ed, town, Com Col	3.4	3
Ballycorish	co-ed, rural, Com Sch (disadv)	11.9	8
St David's	ssb, city, fp	2.6	3
St Dominic's	ssb, city, fr (disadv)	0	0
Dunely	ssb, town, fr	2.9	3
St Cecilia's	ssg, city, fp	2.4	3
Our Lady's	ssg, rural, fr	7.4	7
Total *n*			50
Total essays (%)		4.2	

Table A9 Gender composition of primary and post-primary schools in Ireland

School type	All schools (%)	All pupils (%)
Primary schools		
Single-sex girls	11.4	17.2
Single-sex boys	9.7	17.2
Co-educational	78.9	65.3
Second-level schools		
Single-sex girls	21.2	24.5
Single-sex boys	17.1	17.5
Co-educational	61.7	58.0

Source: Department of Education and Science Statistics Section, figures for 1999/2000.

Table A10 Differences in the responses to the statement: 'Boys and girls are treated equally well in this school' in the four co-educational schools (n = 522)

School	Gender of students	Agree range (%)	Disagree range (%)
Ballydara	female	4	96
(n = 127)	male	18	82
Ollan	female	58	42
(n = 125)	male	49	51
St Ita's	female	22	78
(n = 110)	male	20	80
Ballycorish	female	41	59
(n = 72)	male	55	45

Table A11 Proportion of student essays in which explicit complaints about gender inequality or sexism in sport were reported (n = 359)

	Ballydara Com Col		Ollan Com Col		St Ita's fp		Ballycorish Com Sch		Total co-ed essays
	female	male	female	male	female	male	female	male	
Complaint about gender inequality	8 16.7%	1 1.8%	11 17.5%	3 12.0%	18 38.3%	4 7.4%	4 10.0%	0	13.6%
Sexism in sport	2 4.2%	0	0	2 8.0%	16 34.0%	3 5.5%	1 2.5%	0	6.7%
Gender-related complaints about lack of opportunities for self-expression, individuality	1 2.0%	7 12.7%	9 14.3%	0	4 8.5%	20 37.0%	3 7.5%	1 3.7%	12.5%
Total n of essays in co-ed schools	48	55	63	25	47	54	40	27	359

Note
Student concerns may be expressed in more than one category.

Appendix B: Figures

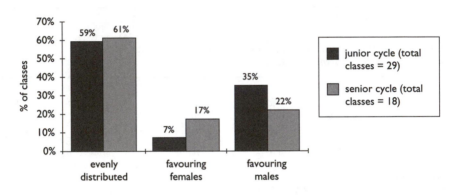

Figure A I Recorded public work interactions in observed co-educational classes by gender and seniority of class (*n* = 47)

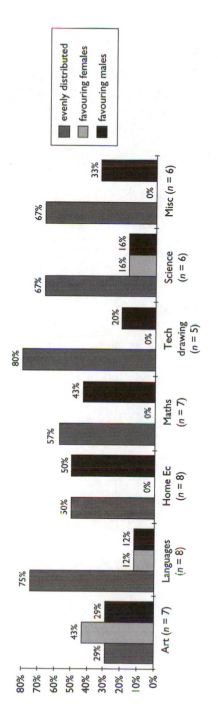

Legend:
- evenly distributed
- favouring females
- favouring males

Chart values by subject:

Art (n = 7): 29%, 43%, 29%

Languages (n = 8): 75%, 12%, 12%

Home Ec (n = 8): 0%, 50%, 50%

Maths (n = 7): 57%, 0%, 43%

Tech drawing (n = 5): 80%, 0%, 20%

Science (n = 6): 67%, 16%, 16%

Misc (n = 6): 67%, 0%, 33%

Y-axis: 0%, 10%, 20%, 30%, 40%, 50%, 60%, 70%, 80%

Figure A2 Recorded public work interactions in observed co-educational classes by gender and subject area (*n* = 47)

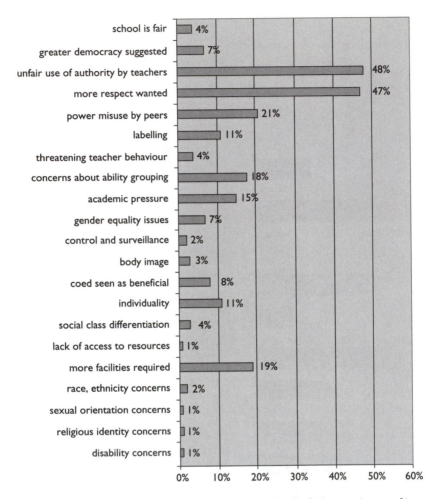

Figure A3 Breakdown of topics arising in student essays on their experiences of inequality and suggestions for improvement (*n* = 1,202)

Notes

Setting the scene

1   From the work with colleagues at the Equality Studies Centre at University College Dublin, we recognise that inequalities in the affective domain are also of major importance although we do not examine them in this study.

I The equality debates

1   The challenge to universalising which is part of the post-modernist project, is of course a form of universalising in itself. Furthermore, to deconstruct to the point of complete relativism is a form of universalising which is deeply apolitical.

2 The design of the study and a profile of the schools

1   Designated disadvantaged status is granted to schools on the basis of a number of indicators of deprivation. The schools are entitled to some additional resources owing to the high numbers of students attending from socio-economically and educationally deprived backgrounds. Despite the extra resources accruing to such schools, it was clear from visiting the schools, and spending one year living among them, that the resource differential between these schools and fee-paying schools in particular, remained considerable.

2   Since our study was completed, the Education Act, 1998 has been passed. This requires all second-level schools to support the setting up of student councils.

3   Transition Year refers to a very flexible and non-exam oriented education programme for those who have completed three years of junior cycle education (and have done the Junior Certificate Examination). Students enter Transition Year at age 15/16 approximately. It is widely regarded as an educationally beneficial year when students can experiment with new activities and interests although it varies widely across schools in terms of how it is organised. When students complete Transition Year they enter the two-year Leaving Certificate Programme up to age 18 approximately. While most schools offer Transition Year programmes, many have opted out of it for a variety of reasons, including opposition from parents and students who fear that it imposes extra costs and/or increases the risk that their children will not wish to return to study for their Leaving Certificate.

Issues of redistribution

1   By focusing on so-called 'ability grouping' and social class, we do not wish to deny the importance of other distributive problems arising in relation to ethnicity, disability, age, etc. The focus on the former arose because of the nature of the data we collected rather than from any preconceived view about the primacy of one form of distributive injustice over others.

3 The Class Act: a one-act play in four stages

1   These are the Irish version of the UK public schools although these are not as exclusive. First, they are a predominantly urban (mostly Dublin) phenomenon. As most of the teachers in these schools have their salaries paid by the State, the fees are not at all as high as in comparable UK schools. In 1996/7 the average day pupil fee was IR£1,000–IR£1,500 per annum; the 2001 rate was between IR£2,000 and IR£2,500 per annum.

2   During the late 1960s with the advent of the free secondary education scheme, a financial arrangement was made between the Department of Education and the Secondary Education Committee representing the four Protestant churches in the Republic whose schools have remained outside the 'free scheme'. A 'block grant' was made available to enable parents of minority Christian denominations (regardless of their personal means) to send their children to appropriate secondary schools, many of which took boarders. The grant awarded is paid directly to the school in question in order to cover fees or part of fees. Families are means tested to ensure allocation of this money according to need. Young people from the Jewish community who attended Protestant secondary schools were also assisted by this grant. Glendenning (1999) outlines how the 'block grant' supports the constitutional right of parents to have their children educated in denominationally appropriate schools. Recent research by Woulfe (2001) shows that, in large urban centres, the majority of students attending Protestant secondary fee-paying schools are not, in fact, members of the four main Protestant churches. This research also demonstrates that these schools are in receipt of a disproportionately high level of state subvention compared with free scheme secondary schools. This is not the case with all the Protestant schools, however. Protestant boarding schools in rural areas, particularly those situated in areas with a mixed religious population, can have almost exclusively Protestant attendance. In some of these schools up to 90 per cent of students are in receipt of some level of grant assistance.

3   One must remember that we only observed classes where teachers agreed to our visit, hence the likelihood of having a relatively low number of very disruptive classes.

4   (our note) The GAA is the Gaelic Athletic Association, the umbrella body for the national sports of Ireland, hurling, Gaelic football and handball. It is a largely male organisation.

4 The grouping process: selecting out, selecting in

1   The concept of ability grouping is highly problematic in and of itself. It implies that there is some generative educational ability on the basis of which students can be grouped fairly. In reality, no such 'generic' ability exists (Gardner 1985; Sternberg 1998). Students are generally grouped in schools on the basis of their academic achievement in particular subjects (in Ireland that is in terms of Irish, English and Mathematics) or related fields. We will avoid the use of the term 'ability grouping' wherever practicable therefore; we will refer to a student's academic achievement instead. Where 'ability grouping' is used it will be presented in inverted commas to highlight its problematic status.

2 The Junior Certificate syllabus, which included three-tier programmes for compulsory subjects, was introduced to schools in 1989; the first Junior Certificate examination took place in 1992.

3 So-called *Mixed-ability Grouping* refers to the practice of allocating students to classes across all subjects so that there is a range of different attainment levels in all classes. *Banding* refers to the practice of dividing students into broad 'ability' bands, with two or three mixed classes in each. It is a form of streaming in larger schools where numbers allow schools to stratify students into top, middle and lower bands. Students are mixed within each band, but not between bands. Although banding is formally a less stratified system than streaming, in our study we found that some teachers used the terms interchangeably, often referring to the bottom or top band as the bottom or top stream respectively. *Streaming* is a method of assigning students heirarchically to classes on some overall assessment of general attainment. The streamed classes are used as the teaching units for all subjects. *Setting* is a practice whereby students are grouped into streams or tracks according to their attainment in a given subject; at Junior level it is quite common for schools to set students for Mathematics and Irish, and sometimes English.

4 The Grade Point Average that one achieves in one's Leaving Certificate Examination (the equivalent of 'A' levels or the baccalaureate) is known as the 'Points' system. One's Points or Leaving Certificate Grade Point Average is used to determine access to all higher education courses.

5 Girls' schools: diligence, surveillance and resistance

1 We have defined *surveillance* in this context as teacher criticism or correction of the student's person (appearance, demeanour, posture, expression) rather than of any specific misbehaviour, such as lack of attention or active disruption.

2 It is arguable, however, that the pressure to achieve reported in girls' schools is indicative of the greater value placed on such achievement by parents (and students) who send their children to single-sex girls' schools in the first instance. There is some evidence from New Zealand that parents do sometimes choose single-sex schools for girls so that they will not be 'distracted' from their studies (Harker 2000).

3 RTCs (Regional Technical Colleges) have been renamed as ITs (Institutes of Technology) since the fieldwork was completed.

4 Public evaluation denotes any public assessment of individual students' progress, understanding or ability. It includes any situation during a lesson when a teacher asked students to publicly declare the level of correct answers they had achieved in an individual exercise; when individuals in the class were publicly ranked in terms of marks or achievement at a specific task; when individuals were asked to admit failure to understand work in front of their peers; and when the teacher made public judgement upon the value and quality of individuals' written or oral work in the classroom setting.

7 The complex cultures of co-educational schools: diversity, silence and hegemony

1 On-task, or work-related, interactions included all interactions observed in each classroom that were directly related to the academic task in hand. Unlike the Flanders schedule for example (Flanders 1970), the focus in this study was not on the behaviour of teachers, or on subject pedagogy or learning styles; rather, it was broader examination of the social and equality climate of classrooms. For that reason, a categorical system was devised, based on a similar one used in research of primary classrooms (Lodge 1998), which gave equal weight to the interactions of students and teachers, and which took account of on- as well as off-task behaviours. The

broad on-task categories included teacher-initiated questions, student responses, teacher reactions; student on-task initiated interactions, teacher response. A range of sub-categories were contained within these broad headings.

2 There were four different teachers across the co-educational schools observed teaching classes that had highly visible disruption. In the case of two of these teachers, they had deliberately chosen to invite the researcher to observe classes they termed as 'difficult' in order to facilitate the research process.

3 Across all observed classrooms ($n = 162$), social interactions accounted for a small proportion of all interactions. There were no social interactions at all recorded in 41 per cent of all observed classes. In those classes ($n = 96$) where social interactions were observed, they accounted for between 1 per cent and 8 per cent of all recorded interactions in almost all cases (94 per cent).

4 The strong sense of gender inequality that was reported in Ballydara by both girls and boys was linked to a critical incident that occurred in the school the week before the questionnaire was distributed. Some of the teachers' cars had been damaged (scraped) in the car park and students of both genders had been severely reprimanded over this. As most students had nothing to do with the incident, they resented the public rebuke; this was especially true in the case of girls.

5 In girls' schools, 7 per cent of the essays cited ways in which girls felt they experienced gender-related inequality within their single-sex schools. Only one essay from the boys' schools listed their gender as a cause of the inequality they experienced in school.

6 The four co-educational schools chosen for this study differed considerably: they comprised a community school in a rural area, a community college in a large town, a community college in a large urban area and a fee-paying secondary school. As was outlined in Chapter 3, co-educational schools vary greatly in character: vocational schools and community colleges have traditionally catered for a relatively large proportion of lower middle-class, small farming and working-class students, while fee-paying co-educational schools are predominantly upper middle-class in intake. Community/comprehensive schools, and co-educational free scheme secondary schools, tend to have the most heterogeneous social class intake.

8 The diversity deficit: minorities and the recognition of difference

1 Travellers are a small indigenous ethnic minority whose economic and social structures are fundamentally based on nomadism. They have a range of social and cultural practices which make them distinctive from the settled community.

2 In the 1991 Census, 95.7 per cent of the population indicated that they were affiliated, at least nominally, to a religious group; 91.6 per cent described themselves as Roman Catholic. Only 1.9 per cent of the population described themselves as being of *No Religion, Atheist or Agnostic* and a further 2.4 per cent of respondents gave no religious affiliation.

3 All 1,557 students in the study were invited to write a short essay on their experiences of inequality in their school, and outline their ideas as to how to make their school more equal and just; 1,202 wrote essays. The essay question was in two parts and worded as follows:

> We would like you to write here about any time or place when you think you've been unfairly or unequally treated since you came to this school, either by other students or teachers.

To make school a fairer and more equal place, what kinds of changes would you like to see in it?

4   Since we have completed the fieldwork, there has been a very significant increase in the number of migrant workers, refugees and asylum seekers entering Ireland. Such groups are now experiencing the same type of recognition problems as the more marginalised indigenous groups (see Lentin 1999).

9 Regimes of power and resistance

1   In some schools, privacy and access to space was a problematic issue for teachers as well as students. In two of the participating schools, the existing staffrooms were too small, and there was insufficient space for all of the teachers to have even a space to store work-related material, coats and bags. This was a reported cause of tension and stress for staff in these schools.
2   Weber (Gerth and Mills 1975) defined traditional authority as the acceptance of the unchanging, unchallengeable and almost sacrosanct nature of institutional norms and routines; charismatic authority as that invested in the person of the leader by others due to her/his extraordinary qualities; rational authority as that established by known, established and accepted rules and regulations.

11 Inequality and the 3Rs – redistribution, recognition and representation

1   See Gardner's work (1983, 1999) for a discussion on the multiple abilities and intelligences that people possess, and the way in which schooling neglects many of these.
2   At the time of the study the new Civil Social and Political Education course for second-level students was just beginning to be introduced in schools. This is a subject in which differences can be explored.
3   We have defined *surveillance* in this context as teacher criticism or correction of the student's person (appearance, demeanour, posture, expression) rather than of any specific misbehaviour, such as lack of attention or active disruption.

Bibliography

Abbott-Chapman, J., Hughes, P. and Wyld, C. (1986) *Participation and Retention Rates and Social and Educational Factors which are Related to Them in Tasmania* (2 vols, Hobart Centre for Gender Equity in Schools), Manchester: Equal Opportunities Commission.

Akenson, D.H. (1975) *A Mirror to Kathleen's Face: Education in Independent Ireland, 1922–1960*, Montreal: McGill–Queen's University Press.

Allen, K. (2000) *The Celtic Tiger: the Myth of Social Partnership in Ireland*, Manchester: Manchester University Press.

Ambler, J.S. and Neathery, J. (1999) 'Education policy and equality: some evidence from Europe', *Social Science Quarterly* 80, 3: 437–456.

Anthias, F. (2001) 'The material and the symbolic in theorizing social stratification: issues of gender, ethnicity and class', *British Journal of Sociology* 52, 3: 367–390.

Apple, M.W. (1982) *Education and Power*, New York: Routledge & Kegan Paul.

—— (1986) *Teachers and Texts: a Political Economy of Class and Gender Relations in Education*, New York: Routledge & Kegan Paul.

—— (1996) 'Power, meaning and identity: critical sociology of education in the United States', *British Journal of Sociology of Education* 17: 125–144.

—— (2000) 'Away with all Teachers: the cultural politics of home schooling', *International Studies in Sociology of Education* 10, 1: 61–80.

Apple, M.W. and Beane, J.A. (eds) (1999) *Democratic Schools: Lessons from the Chalk Face*, Buckingham: Open University Press.

Apple, M.W. and Weis, L. (eds) (1983) *Ideology and Practice in Schooling*, Philadelphia: Temple University Press.

Archard, D. (1993) *Children: Rights and Childhood*, London: Routledge.

Archer, P. (2001) 'Public spending on education, inequality and poverty', in S. Cantillon, C. Corrigan, P. Kirby and J. O'Flynn (eds) *Rich and Poor: Perspectives on Tackling Inequality in Ireland*, Dublin: Oak Tree Press.

Argys, L. M., Rees, D.I. and Brewer, D.J. (1996) 'Detracking America's schools: equality at zero cost?' *Journal of Policy Analysis and Management* 15, 4: 623–645.

Arnot, M. (1991) 'Equality and democracy: a decade of struggle over education', *British Journal of Sociology of Education* 12, 4: 447–466.

Arnot, M. and Barton, L. (eds) (1992) *Voicing Concerns: Sociological Perspectives on Contemporary Education Reforms*, Wallingford, Oxfordshire: Triangle Books Ltd.

Arnot, M. and Dillabough, J. (1999) 'Feminist politics and democratic values in education', *Curriculum Inquiry* 29, 2: 159–190.

Arnot, M. and Weiler, K. (eds) (1993) *Feminism and Social Justice in Education*, London: Falmer Press.

Arnot, M. and Weiner, G. (eds) (1987) *Gender and the Politics of Schooling*, London: Hutchinson.

Arnot, M., David, M. and Weiner, G. (1999) *Closing the Gender Gap*, Cambridge: Polity Press.

Aronwitz, S. and Giroux, H. (1991) *Post-Modern Education: Politics, Culture and Social Criticism*, Minneapolis: University of Minnesota Press.

Askew, S. and Ross, C. (1988) *Boys Don't Cry: Boys and Sexism in Education*, Milton Keynes: Open University Press.

ASTI (Association of Secondary Teachers, Ireland) (1995) *School Discipline: Advice for Teachers and School Authorities*, Dublin: ASTI.

—— (1996a) *Staffing, Funding and Facilities in Irish Second Level Schools*, Dublin: ASTI.

—— (1996b) *Submission on Discipline in Second Level Schools*, Dublin: ASTI.

Baker, J. (1987) *Arguing for Equality*, New York: Verso.

—— (1997) 'Studying equality', *Imprints* 2, 1: 57–71.

—— (1998) 'Equality', in S. Healy and B. Reynolds (eds) *Social Policy in Ireland*, Dublin: Oak Tree Press.

Ball, S.J. (1981) *Beachside Comprehensive*, Cambridge: Cambridge University Press.

—— (1987) *The Micro-politics of the School: Towards a Theory of School Organization*, London: Methuen.

—— (1989) 'Micro-politics versus management', in S. Walker and L. Barton (eds) *Politics and the Processes of Schooling*, Milton Keynes: Open University Press.

—— (1993) 'Education markets, choice and social-class – the market as a class strategy in the UK and the USA', *British Journal of Sociology of Education* 14, 1: 3–19.

—— (1997) 'Good school/bad school: paradox and fabrication', *British Journal of Sociology of Education* 18, 3: 317–335.

Ball, S.J. and Gewirtz, S. (1997) 'Girls in the educational market: choice, competition and complexity', *Gender and Education* 19, 2: 207–222.

Ball, S.J. and Lacey, C. (1984) 'Subject disciplines as the opportunity for group action: a measured critique', in A. Hargreaves and P. Woods (eds) *Classrooms and Staffrooms: the Sociology of Teachers and Teaching*, Milton Keynes: Open University Press.

Ball, S.J., Bowe, R. and Gewirtz, S. (1995) 'Circuits of schooling – a sociological exploration of parental choice of school in social-class contexts', *Sociological Review* 43, 1: 52–78.

Barker Lunn, J. (1970) *Streaming in the Primary School*, Slough: National Foundation for Educational Research (NFER).

Barron, M. (1999) 'Lesbian, gay and bisexual experiences of school', Unpublished thesis in Youth Studies, National University of Ireland Maynooth.

Barton, L. (1995) *Making Difficulties: Research in the Construction of Special Educational Needs*, London: Paul Chapman.

—— (ed.) (1996) *Disability and Society: Emerging Issues and Insights*, Harlow, Essex: Addison Wesley Longman.

Beechey, V. (1987) *Unequal Work*, London: Verso.

Bell, L.A. (1997) 'Theoretical foundations for social justice education', in M. Adams, L.A. Bell and P. Griffin (eds) *Teaching for Diversity and Social Justice: A Sourcebook*, London: Routledge.

Bennett deMarrais, K. and LeCompte, M.D. (1999) *The Way Schools Work: a Sociological Analysis of Education*, third edition, New York: Longman.

Berends, M. (1991) *High School Tracking and Students' School Orientations*, Madison, Wis.: National Center on Effective Secondary Schools.

—— (1995) 'Educational stratification and students' social bonding to school', *British Journal of Sociology of Education* 16, 3: 327–351.

Bernstein, B. (1983) *Beyond Objectivism and Relativism: Science, Hermeneutics and Praxis*, Pittsburgh: University of Pennsylvania Press.

Best, R. (1983) *We've All Got Scars: What Boys and Girls Learn in Elementary Schools*, Bloomington: Indiana University Press.

Betts, J.R. and Shkolnik, J.L. (2000) 'Key difficulties in identifying the effects of ability grouping on student achievement', *Economics of Education Review* 19, 1: 21–26.

Beynon, J. (1989) '"A school for men": an ethnographic case study of routine violence in schooling', in S. Walker and L. Barton (eds) *Politics and the Processes of Schooling*, Milton Keynes: Open University Press.

Biddulph, S. (1994) *Manhood: A Book about Setting Men Free*, Sydney: Finch Publishing.

Blandford, S. (1998) *Managing Discipline in Schools*, London: Routledge.

Blatchford, P. (1996) *Social Life in School: Pupils' Experience of Breaktime and Recess from 7 to 16 Years*, London: Falmer.

Blatchford, P. and Sharpe, S. (eds) (1994) *Breaktime and the School*, London: Routledge.

Bly, R. (1991) *Iron John: A Book about Men*, London: Element.

Boaler, J. (1997a) 'Setting, social class and survival of the quickest', *British Educational Research Journal* 23, 5: 575–595.

—— (1997b) 'When even the winners are losers: evaluating the experiences of "top set" students', *Journal of Curriculum Studies* 29, 2: 165–182.

—— (2000) 'Mathematics from another world: traditional communities and the alienation of learners', *Journal of Mathematical Behaviour* 18, 4: 379–397.

Bourdieu, P. (1993) *Sociology in Question*, London: Sage.

—— (1996) *The State Nobility: Elite Schools in the Field of Power*, Oxford: Polity Press.

—— (1998) *Acts of Resistance: Against the Tyranny of the Market*, New York: The New Press and Polity Press.

Bourne, J. (2001) 'Discourses and identities in a multi-lingual primary classroom', *Oxford Review of Education* 27, 1: 103–114.

Bowles, S. and Gintis, H. (1976) *Schooling in Capitalist America*, New York: Basic Books.

Brantlinger, E., Majd-Jabbari, M. and Guskin, S.L. (1996) 'Self-interest and liberal educational discourse: how ideology works for middle-class mothers', *American Educational Research Journal* 33, 3: 571–597.

Breen, R. (1998) 'The persistence of class origin inequalities among school leavers in the Republic of Ireland, 1984–1993', *British Journal of Sociology of Education* 49, 2: 275–298.

Breen, R. and Goldthorpe, J.H. (1997) 'Explaining educational differential: towards a formal rational choice theory', *Rationality and Society* 9, 3: 275–305.

Breen, R. and Whelan, C.T. (1995) 'Gender and class mobility: evidence from the Republic of Ireland', *Sociology* 29, 1: 1–22.

Breen, R. and Whelan, C.T. (1996) *Social Mobility and Social Class in Ireland*, Dublin: Gill and Macmillan.

Breen, R., Hannan, D.F., Rottmann, D.B. and Whelan, C.T. (1990) *Understanding Contemporary Ireland: State, Class and Development in the Republic of Ireland*, Dublin: Gill and Macmillan.

Brighouse, H. (1996) 'Egalitarianism and equal availability of political influence', *Journal of Political Philosophy* 4, 2: 118–141.

Broadfoot, P. (1979) *Assessment, Schools and Society*, London: Methuen.

Brown, D. (1999) 'Complicity and reproduction in teaching physical education', *Sport Education and Society* 4, 2: 143–159.

Bryck, A.S., Lee, V.E. and Holland, P.B. (1993) *Catholic Schools and the Common Good*, Cambridge, Mass.: Harvard University Press.

Buendia, E. (2000) 'Power and possibility: the construction of a pedagogical practice', *Teaching and Teacher Education* 16: 147–163.

Burgess, R. (1988) 'Conversations with a purpose: the ethnographic interview in educational research', *Studies in Qualitative Methodology* 1: 137–155.

Burstyn, V. (1999) *The Rites of Men: Manhood, Politics, and the Culture of Sport*, Toronto: University of Toronto Press.

Butler, I. and Shaw, I. (1996) *A Case of Neglect: Children's Experiences and the Sociology of Childhood*, Aldershot: Avebury.

Byrne, A. and Lentin, R. (eds.) (2000) *(Re)searching Women: Feminist Research Methodologies in the Social Sciences in Ireland*, Dublin: Institute of Public Administration.

Byrne, E.M. (1993) *Women and Science: The Snack Syndrome*, London: Falmer Press.

Callewaert, S. (1999) 'Philosophy of education, Frankfurt critical theory and the sociology of Pierre Bourdieu', in T. Popkewitz and L. Fendler *Critical Theories in Education*, New York: Routledge.

Candela, A. (1999) 'Students' power in classroom discourse', *Linguistics and Education* 10, 2: 139–163.

Cantillon, S. and O'Shea, E. (2001) 'Social expenditure, redistribution and participation', in S. Cantillon, C. Corrigan, P. Kirby and J. O'Flynn (eds) *Rich and Poor: Perspectives on Tackling Inequality in Ireland*, Dublin: Oak Tree Press.

Carroll, S. and Walford, G. (1996) 'A panic about school choice', *Educational Studies* 22, 3: 393–407.

Central Statistics Office (1991) *Census of Ireland*, Dublin: Government Publications Office.

Charles, C.M. (1996) *Building Classroom Discipline*, fifth edition, London: Longman.

Clancy, P. (1995) *Access to College: Patterns of Continuity and Change*, Dublin: Higher Education Authority.

Clancy, P. and Wall, J. (2000) *Social Backgrounds of Higher Education Entrants*, Dublin: Higher Education Authority.

Clark, C. (1998) 'Discipline in schools', *British Journal of Educational Studies* 46, 3: 289–301.

Clarke, D. (1998) 'Education, the state and sectarian schools', in T. Murphy and P. Twomey (eds) *Ireland's Evolving Constitution, 1937–1997: Collected Essays*, Oxford: Hart Publishing.

Clarricoates, K. (1983) '"The importance of being Ernest . . . Emma . . . Tom . . . Jane" the perception and categorisation of gender conformity and gender deviation in primary schools', in J. Purvis and M. Hales (eds) *Achievement and Inequality in Education*, London: Routledge & Kegan Paul.

Clear, C. (1990) 'The limits of female autonomy: nuns in nineteenth century Ireland', in M. Luddy and C. Murphy (eds) *Women Surviving*, Dublin: Poolbeg.

Cohen, G.A. (1995) *Self-Ownership, Freedom and Equality*, Cambridge: Cambridge University Press.

—— (1997) 'Back to socialist basics', in J. Franklin (ed.) *Equality*, London: IPPR, pp. 29–47.

—— (2000) *If You're an Egalitarian, How Come You're so Rich?* Cambridge, Mass.: Harvard University Press.

Cohen, M. (1998) '"A habit of healthy idleness": boys' underachievement in historical perspective', in D. Epstein, J. Elwood, V. Hey and J. Maw (eds) *Failing Boys? Issues in Gender and Achievement*, Buckingham: Open University Press.

Cole, M. (ed.) (2000) *Education, Equality and Human Rights*, London: RoutledgeFalmer.

Cole, M. and Hill, D. (1995) 'Games of despair and rhetorics of resistance – postmodernism, education and reaction', *British Journal of Sociology of Education* 16, 2: 165–182.

Coleman, J.S. (1961) *The Adolescent Society*, New York: Free Press.

Collins, J. (2000) 'Are you talking to me? The need to respect and develop a pupil's self image', *Educational Research* 42, 2: 157–166.

Combat Poverty Agency (1998) *Educational Disadvantage and Early School Leaving*, Dublin: Combat Poverty Agency.

Connell, R.W. (1989) 'Cool guys, swots and wimps: the interplay of masculinity and education', *Oxford Review of Education* 15, 3: 291–303.

—— (1993) *Schools and Social Justice*, Philadelphia: Temple University Press.

—— (1995) *Masculinities*, Cambridge: Polity Press.

Connell, R. W., Ashenden, D., Kessler, S. and Dowsett, G.W. (1982) *Making the Difference*, Sydney: Allen and Unwin.

Connolly, P. (1998) *Racism, Gender Identities and Young Children*, London: Routledge.

Cooke, J. (1997) *Marley Grange Multi-denominational School Challenge 1973–1978*, Dublin: Author.

Coolahan, J. (1981) *Irish Education*, Dublin: IPA.

Corrigan, P. (1979) *Schooling the Smash Street Kids*, London: Macmillan.

Corsaro, W.A. (1997) *The Sociology of Childhood*, London: Pine Forge Press.

Cothran, D.J. and Ennis, C.D. (1997) 'Students' and teachers' perceptions of conflict and power', *Teaching and Teacher Education* 13, 5: 541–553.

Creemers, B.P.M. and Scheerens, J. (1994) 'Developments in the educational effectiveness research programme', in R. J. Bosker, B.P.M. Creemers and J. Scheerens (eds) *Conceptual and Methodological Advances in Educational Effectiveness Research*, Oxford: Elsevier.

Crocker, T. and Cheeseman, R. (1991) 'The ability of young children to rank themselves for academic ability', in M. Woodhead, P. Light and R. Carr (eds) *Growing up in a Changing Society*, London: Routledge/Open University.

Crompton, R. (1998) *Class and Stratification*, second edition, Cambridge: Polity Press.

Crozier, G. (1997) 'Empowering the powerful: a discussion of the interrelation of government policies and consumerism with social class factors and the impact of this upon parent interventions in their children's schooling', *British Journal of Sociology of Education* 18, 2: 187–200.

Cusick, P. (1973) *Inside High School: the Student's World*, New York: Holt, Rinehart and Winston.

Dale, R.R. (1974) *Mixed or Single-sex Schooling: Vol. 3 Attainment, Attitudes and Overview*, London: Routledge & Kegan Paul.

Daly, P. (1996) 'The effects of single sex and co-educational schooling on girls', *Research Papers in Education* 11, 3: 289–306.

Daly, T.G. (1999) 'An action research study of the application of information and communication technologies in meeting the special educational needs of pupils with physical and sensory impairments in mainstream second-level education', Unpublished MA thesis, University of Limerick.

Darmarin, M. (1995) 'Classroom practices and class pedagogies', in J. Salisbury and S. Delamont (eds) *Qualitative Studies in Education*, London: Avebury.

Davidson, A.L. (1996) *Making and Molding Identity in Schools: Student Narratives on Race, Gender and Academic Achievement*, New York: State University of New York Press.

Davies, B. (1982) *Life in the Classroom and Playground: The Accounts of Primary School Children*, London: Routledge & Kegan Paul.

—— (1996) *Power/Knowledge/Desire: Changing School Organisation and Management Practices*, Canberra: Department of Employment, Education, Training and Youth Affairs.

Davies, L. (1984) *Pupil Power: Deviance and Gender in School Leavers*, London: Falmer Press.

—— (2001) 'Development, democracy and deviance in contemporary sociology of education', in J. Demaine (ed.) *Sociology of Education Today*, Basingstoke: Palgrave.

Davies, S. (1995) 'Leaps of faith: shifting currents in critical sociology of education', *American Journal of Sociology* 100, 6: 1448–1478.

Deem, R. (1978) *Women and Schooling*, London: Routledge & Kegan Paul.

de Koning, K. and Martin, M. (eds) (1996) *Participatory Research in Health*, London: Zed Books.

Delamont, S. (1980) *Sex Roles and the School*, London: Methuen.

Delphy, C. and Leonard, D. (1992) *Familiar Exploitation: a New Analysis of Marriage and Family Life*, London: Polity Press.

Denscombe, M. (1985) *Classroom Control: a Sociological Perspective*, London: Allen and Unwin.

Department of Education (1997) *Statistical Report 1995/96*, Dublin: Government Publications Office.

Department of Education and Science (1995) *Charting Our Education Future: White Paper on Education*, Dublin: Stationery Office.

—— (2000) *Learning for Life: White Paper on Adult Education*, Dublin: Stationery Office.

Devine, D. (1991) 'A study of reading ability groups, primary school children's experiences and views', Unpublished M.Ed thesis, Education Department, University College Dublin.

—— (1998) 'Structure, agency and the exercise of power in children's experience of school', Unpublished Ph.D. thesis, Education Department, University College Dublin.

—— (2000) 'Constructions of childhood in school: power, policy and practice in Irish education', *International Studies in Sociology of Education* 10, 1: 23–41.

Devlin, B., Fineberg, S., Resnick, D.P. and Roeder, K. (eds) (1997) *Intelligence, Genes and Success: Scientists Respond to 'The Bell Curve'*, New York: Springer-Verlag.

Dewey, J. (1916) *Democracy and Education*, New York: Macmillan.

Dewey, J. (1938) *Experience and Education*, Bloomington Ind.: Kappa Delta Pi.

Dillon, M. (1999) *Catholic Identity: Balancing Reason, Faith and Power*, Cambridge: Cambridge University Press.

Donnelly, C. (2000) 'In pursuit of school ethos', *British Journal of Educational Studies* 48, 2: 134–154.

Douglas, J.W.B. (1964) *The Home and the School: a Study of Ability and Attainment in the Primary School*, London: MacGibbon, Kee.

Drudy, S. and Lynch, K. (1993) *Schools and Society in Ireland*, Dublin: Gill & Macmillan.

Drudy, S. and Ui Cathain, M. (1999) *Gender Equality in Classroom Interaction*, Maynooth: Education Department, National University of Ireland, Maynooth.

Dunden, P. (1993) 'Teacher–pupil interaction in the Irish coeducational primary school', Unpublished MA in Education thesis, University of Limerick.

Dunning, E. (1999) *Sport Matters: Sociological Study of Sport, Violence and Civilisation*, London: Routledge.

Dworkin, R. (2000) *Sovereign Virtue: The Theory and Practice of Equality*, Cambridge, Mass.: Harvard University Press.

Edley, N. and Wetherell, M. (1997) 'Jockeying for position: the construction of masculine identities', *Discourse and Society* 8, 2: 203–217.

Eivers, E., Ryan, E. and Brickley, A. (2000) *Characteristics of Early School Leavers: Results of the Research Strand of the 8 to 16 year old Early Leaving Initiative.* Report to the Department of Education and Science, Dublin: Educational Research Centre.

Ellis, C. and Flaherty, M. (eds) (1992) 'An agenda for the interpretation of lived experience', *Investigating Subjectivity: Researching Lived Experience*, California: Sage.

Ellsworth, E. (1989) 'Why doesn't this feel empowering? Working through the repressive myths of critical pedagogy', *Harvard Educational Review* 59, 3: 297–324.

Elton Report (1989) *Discipline in Schools*, Department of Education and Science, Great Britain, Committee of Inquiry into Discipline in Schools, London: Department of Education and Science.

Epp, J.R. and Watkinson, A.M. (eds) (1996) *Systemic Violence: How Schools Hurt Children*, London: Falmer.

Epstein, D. (ed.) (1994) *Challenging Lesbian and Gay Inequalities in Education*, Buckingham: Open University Press.

Epstein, D. and Johnson, R. (1994) 'On the straight and the narrow: the heterosexual presumption, homophobias and schools', in D. Epstein (ed.) *Challenging Lesbian and Gay Inequalities in Education*, Buckingham: Open University Press.

Epstein, D., Elwood, J., Hey, V. and Maw, J. (1998) 'School frictions: feminisms and "failing" boys', in D. Epstein, J. Elwood, V. Hey and J. Maw (eds) *Failing Boys? Issues in Gender and Achievement*, Buckingham: Open University Press.

Erikson, R. and Jonsson, J.O. (1998) 'Social origin as an interest-bearing asset: family background and labour-market rewards among employees in Sweden', *Acta Sociologica* 41, 1: 19–36.

Erikson, R.E. and Jonsson, J.O. (1996) *Can Education be Equalized: The Swedish Case in Comparative Perspective*, New York: Westview Press.

Everhart, R.B. (1983) *Reading, Writing and Resistance: Adolescence and Labour in a Junior High School*, London: Routledge & Kegan Paul.

Fagan, H. (1995) *Culture, Politics, and Irish School Dropouts*, London: Bergin & Garvey.

Fahey, T. (1987) 'Nuns in the Catholic Church in Ireland in the nineteenth century', in M. Cullen (ed.) *Girls Don't Do Honours*, Dublin: WEB.

Fahey, T., Russell, H. and Smythe, E. (2000) 'Gender equality, fertility, decline and labour market patterns among women in Ireland', in B. Nolan *et al.* (eds) *Bust to Boom: The Irish Experience of Growth and Inequality*, Dublin: Institute of Public Administration.

Fejgin, N. (1994) 'Participation in high school competitive sports – a subversion of school mission or contribution to academic goals', *Sociology of Sport Journal* 11, 3: 211–230.

Finley, M.K. (1984) 'Teachers and tracking in a comprehensive high school', *Sociology of Education* 57, 4: 233–243.

Fischer, C., Hout, M., Janowski, M.S., Lucas, S.R., Swider, A. and Voss, K. (1996) (eds) *Inequality by Design: Cracking the Bell Curve Myth*, Princeton, NJ: Princeton University Press.

Flanders, N. (1970) *Analyzing Teaching Behaviour*, Reading, Mass.: Addison-Wesley Publishing.

Fontes, P.J. and Kelleghan, T. (1983) 'Opinions of the Irish public on intelligence', *Irish Journal of Education* XVII, 2: 55–67.

Foster, P., Gomm, R. and Hammersley, M. (2000) 'Case studies as spurious evaluations: the example of research on educational inequalities', *British Journal of Educational Studies* 48, 3: 215–230.

Foucault, M. (1977a) *Discipline and Punish*, Harmondsworth: Penguin.

—— (1977b) *Language, Counter Memory, Practice: Selected Essays and Interviews*, Oxford: Basil Blackwell.

—— (1980) *Power/Knowledge: Selected Interviews and Other Writings, 1972–1977*, Brighton: Harvester Press.

Foyle Friend (1999) *The Experiences of Lesbian, Gay and Bisexual Youth in the Northwest of Ireland*, Derry.

Francis, B. (1997) 'Discussing discrimination: children's construction of sexism between pupils in primary school', *British Journal of Sociology of Education* 18, 4: 519–532.

—— (1998) *Power Plays: Children's Construction of Gender, Power and Adult Work*, Stoke-on-Trent: Trentham Books.

—— (1999) 'An investigation into the discourses children draw on in their construction of gender', *Journal of Applied Social Psychology* 29: 300–316.

—— (2001) 'The creation and dissemination of feminist research in education: facts or fictions?', Paper presented to the 3rd International Gender and Education Conference: The Politics of Gender and Education, London: Institute of Education, 4–6 April.

Fraser, N. (1995) 'From redistribution to recognition? Dilemmas of justice in a "post-socialist" age', *New Left Review* 212: 68–93.

—— (1997) *Justice Interruptus: Critical Reflections on the 'Postsocialist' Condition*, New York: Routledge

—— (2000) 'Rethinking recognition', *New Left Review* 2, 3: 107–120.

Freeman, M.D.A. (ed.) (1996) *Children's Rights: A Comparative Perspective*, Aldershot: Dartmouth.

Freire, P. (1972) *Pedagogy of the Oppressed*, New York: Penguin.

—— (1973) *Education for Critical Consciousness*, New York: Continuum.

French, J. and French, P. (1984) 'Gender imbalances in the primary classroom: an interactional account', *Educational Research* 26, 2: 127–134.

French, S. and Swain, J. (1997) 'Young disabled people', in J. Roche and S. Tucker (eds) *Youth in Society*, Buckingham: Open University Press.

Fullan, M.J. with Stiegelbauer, S. (1991) *The New Meaning of Educational Change*, second edition, London: Cassell.

Gambetta, D. (1987) *Were They Pushed or Did They Jump?* Cambridge: Cambridge University Press.

Gamoran, A., Nystrand, M., Berends, M. and LePore, P.C. (1995) 'An organisational analysis of the effects of ability grouping', *American Educational Research Journal* 32, 4: 687–715.

Gardner, H. (1983) *Frames of Mind: the Theory of Multiple Intelligences*, New York: Basic Books.

—— (1985) *The Mind's New Science: a History of the Cognitive Revolution*, New York: Basic Books.

—— (1993) *Multiple Intelligences: the Theory in Practice*, New York: Basic Books.

—— (1997) *Leading Minds: an Anatomy of Leadership*, London: HarperCollins.

—— (1999) *Intelligence Reframed: Multiple Intelligences for the 21st Century*, New York: Basic Books.

Garner, J. and Bing, M. (1973) 'Inequalities of teacher-pupil contacts', *British Journal of Educational Psychology* 43, 5: 234–243.

Gay HIV Strategies/NEXUS (2000) *Education: Lesbian and Gay Students*, Dublin.

Gerth, H.H. and Mills, C.W. (1975 [1947]) *From Max Weber: Essays in Sociology*, London: Kegan Paul, Trench, Trubner & Co. Ltd.

Gewirtz, S., Ball, S.J. and Bowe, R. (1995) *Markets, Choice and Equity in Education*, Buckingham: Open University Press.

Gilbert, P. and Taylor, S. (1991) *Fashioning the Feminine: Girls, Popular Culture and Schooling*, London: Allen and Unwin.

Gilbert, R. and Gilbert, P. (1998) *Masculinity Goes to School*, London: Routledge.

Gill, D., Mayer, B. and Blair, M. (eds) (1992) *Racism and Education, Structures and Strategies*, London: Sage/OUP.

Giroux, H. (1983) *Theory and Resistance in Education*, London: Heinemann.

—— (1983) *Theory and Resistance in Education: A Pedagogy for the Opposition*, Amherst: Bergin & Garvey.

—— (1992) *Border Crossings*, New York: Routledge.

Giroux, H.A. and MacLaren, P. (1996) 'Teacher education and the politics of engagement: the case for democratic schooling', in P. Leistyna, A. Woodrum and S.A. Sherblom (eds) *Breaking Free: the Transformative Power of Critical Pedagogy*, Cambridge Mass.: Harvard Educational Review.

Glaser, B.G. and Strauss, A.I. (1967) *The Discovery of Grounded Theory: Strategies for Qualitative Research*, Chicago: Aldine.

Glen/NEXUS (1995) *Poverty: Lesbians and Gay Men*, Dublin: Combat Poverty.

Glendenning, D. (1999) *Education and the Law*, Dublin: Butterworths.

Glyn, A. and Miliband, D. (1994) *Paying for Inequality: The Economic Cost of Social Injustice*, London: IPPR/Rivers Oram Press.

Goffmann, E. (1968) *Stigma: Notes on the Management of a Spoiled Identity*, London: Penguin.

Goldstein, H., Rasbash, J., Yang, M., Woodhouse, G., Pan, H., Nuttall, D. and Thomas, S. (1993) 'A multilevel analysis of school examination results', *Oxford Review of Education* 19, 4: 425–433.

Goldthorpe, J. (1996) 'Class analysis and the re-orientation of class theory: the case of persisting differentials in educational attainment', *British Journal of Sociology* 47, 3: 481–505.

Goldthorpe, J.H., Llewellyn, C. and Payne, C. (1980) *Social Mobility and Class Structure in Modern Britain*, Oxford: Clarendon Press.

Goleman, D. (1995) *Emotional Intelligence*, London: Bantam Books.

Goodnow, J. and Burns, A. (1985) *Home and School: a Child's Eye View*, London: Allen & Unwin.

Goodson, I. (1988) 'Beyond the subject monolith: subject traditions and subcultures', in A. Westoby (ed.) *Culture and Power in Educational Organisations*, Milton Keynes: Open University Press.

Gouldner, A.V. (1970) *The Coming Crisis of Western Sociology*, London: Heinemann.

Government of Ireland (1997) *Sharing in Progress: The National Anti-Poverty Strategy*, Dublin: Government Publications Office.

Gowran, S. (2000) 'Minority sexualities in education: the experiences of teachers', Unpublished Masters in Equality Studies thesis, Equality Studies Centre, University College Dublin, Ireland.

Grant, C.A. and Sleeter, C.E. (1996) 'Race, class and gender in educational argument for interpretative analysis', *Review of Educational Research* 56, 195–211.

Gray, J. (1995) 'The quality of schooling: frameworks for judgement', in J. Gray and B. Wilcox, (eds) '*Good School, Bad School': Evaluating Performance and Encouraging Performance*, Milton Keynes: Open University Press.

Gray, J., Hopkins, D., Reynolds, D., Wilcox, B., Farrell, S. and Jesson, D. (1999) *Improving Schools: Performance and Potential*, Buckingham: Open University Press.

Griffiths, M. (1998) *Educational Research for Social Justice: Getting off the Fence*, Buckingham: Open University Press.

Gutmann, A. (1987) *Democratic Education*, Princeton, NJ: Princeton University Press.

Hacker, R.G., Rowe, M.J. and Evans, R.D. (1991) 'The influences of ability grouping for secondary science lessons upon classroom processes Part 1: homogeneous groupings', *School Science Review* 73, 262: 125–129.

Hallam, S. and Toutounji, I. (1996) 'What do we know about grouping pupils by ability?' *Education Review* 10, 2: 63–70.

Hallinan, M.T. (1994) 'School differences in tracking effects on achievement', *Social Forces* 72, 3: 799–820.

—— (1996) 'Bridging the gap between research and practice', *Sociology of Education*, Special Issue on Sociology and Educational Policy: 131–134.

Halsey, A.H., Lauder, H., Brown, P. and Wells, A.S. (1997) *Education Culture, Economy, Society*, Oxford: Oxford University Press.

Hammersley, M. (1992) 'On feminist methodology', *Sociology* 26, 2: 187–206.

—— (1995) *The Politics of Social Research*, London: Sage.

Hammersley, M. and Atkinson, P. (1995) *Ethnography: Principles in Practice*, second edition, London: Routledge.

Hammersley, M. and Woods, P. (eds) (1984) *Life in School: the Sociology of Pupil Culture*, Milton Keynes: Open University Press.

Hanafin, J. (1994) 'Moving beyond the figures: using quantitative methods in educational research', *Irish Educational Studies* 14: 184–201.

Handy, C. and Aitken, R. (1986) *Understanding Schools as Organisation*, Harmondsworth: Penguin Books.

Hanley, E. and McKeever, M. (1997) 'The persistence of educational inequalities in state-socialist Hungary: trajectory-maintenance versus counterselection', *Sociology of Education* 70: 1–18.

Hannan, D.F. and Boyle, M. (1987) *Schooling Decisions: The Origins and Consequences of Selection and Streaming in Irish Post-Primary Schools*, Dublin: ESRI.

Hannan, D., Breen, R., Murray, B., Hardiman, N., Watson, D. and O'Higgins, K. (1983) *Schooling and Sex Roles: Sex Differences in Subject Provision and Student Choice* (Paper No. 113), Dublin: ESRI.

Hannan, D., Smyth, E., McCullagh, J., O'Leary, R. and McMahon, D. (1996) *Coeducation and Gender Equality: Exam Performance, Stress and Personal Development*, Dublin: Oak Tree Press.

Harding, S. (1991) *Whose Science, Whose Knowledge? Thinking from Women's Lives*, Milton Keynes: Open University Press.

Hargreaves, A. (2000) 'Mixed emotions: teachers' perceptions of their interactions with students', *Teaching and Teacher Education* 16: 811–826.

Hargreaves, A., Earl, L. and Ryan, J. (1996) *Schooling for Change: Revisiting Education for Early Adolescents*, London: Falmer Press.

Hargreaves, D. (1967) *Social Relations in a Secondary School*, London: Routledge & Kegan Paul.

Harker, R. (2000) 'Achievement, gender and the single-sex/coeducation debate', *British Journal of Sociology of Education* 21, 2: 203–218.

Harlen, W. and Malcolm, H. (1997) *Setting and Streaming: A Research Review* (Using Research Series 18), Edinburgh: SCRE.

Harold, B. (1998) '"Head"ing into the future: the changing role of New Zealand principals', *International Journal of Educational Research* 29: 347–357.

Haroun, R. and O'Hanlon, C. (1997) 'Do teachers and students agree in their perception of what school discipline is?' *Educational Review* 49, 3: 237–250.

Harris, L. (1984) 'Class, community and sexual divisions in north Mayo', in C. Curtin, M. Kelly and L. O'Dowd (eds) *Culture and Ideology in Ireland*, Galway: Galway University Press.

Hart, C.H. (1993) *Children on Playgrounds – Research Perspectives and Applications*, New York: State University of New York Press.

Head, J. (1999) *Understanding the Boys: Issues in Behaviour and Achievement*, London: Falmer.

Healy, S. and Reynolds, B. (eds) (1998) *Social Policy in Ireland: Principles, Practice and Problems*, Dublin: Oak Tree Press.

Heffernan, J.P. (1998) 'Discipline in Irish schools: models of discipline and their influence on policy and practice', Unpublished M.Ed. thesis, Education Department, University College Dublin.

Held, D. (1995) *Democracy and the Global Order*, Cambridge: Polity Press.

Heron, J. (1981) 'Philosophical basis for a new paradigm', in P. Reason and J. Rowan (eds) *Human Inquiry: A Sourcebook of New Paradigm Research*, Chichester: John Wiley & Sons.

Herr, K. and Anderson, G. (1997) 'The cultural politics of identity: student narratives from two Mexican secondary schools', *Qualitative Studies in Education* 10, 1: 45–61.

Higher Education Authority (1996) *Report of the Steering Committee on the Future Development of Higher Education*, Dublin: Higher Education Authority.

Hill, P.W., Holmes-Smith, P. and Rowe, K.J. (1993) *School and Teacher Effectiveness in Victoria: Key Findings from Phase 1 of the Victoria Quality Schools Project*, Melbourne, Centre for Applied Educational Research, University of Melbourne.

Hochschild, A. (1983) *The Managed Heart*. Berkeley: University of California Press.

—— (1989) *The Second Shift: Working Parents and the Revolution at Home*, Harmondsworth: Penguin.

Holligan, C. (1999) 'Discipline and normalization in the nursery: the Foucaldian gaze', *Scottish Educational Review* 31, 2: 137–148.

Honneth, A. (1995) *The Struggle for Recognition: the Moral Grammar of Social Conflicts*, Cambridge: Polity Press.

hooks, bell (1994) *Teaching to Transgress: Education as the Practice of Freedom*, New York: Routledge.

Howe, C. (1997) *Gender and Classroom Interaction*, Edinburgh: The Scottish Council for Research in Education.

Humphries, B. and Truman, C. (eds) (1994) *Rethinking Social Research*. Aldershot: Avebury.

Inglis, T. (1998) *Moral Monopoly: the Rise and Fall of the Catholic Church in Ireland*, Dublin: UCD Press.

—— (1999) *Irish Lessons in Sexuality*, Dublin: UCD Press.

Ireson, J. and Hallam, S. (1999) 'Raising the standards: is ability grouping the answer?' *Oxford Review of Education* 25, 3: 343–358.

Jackson, B. (1964) *Streaming: an Education System in Miniature*, London: Routledge & Kegan Paul.

Jackson, D. (1998) 'Breaking out of the binary trap: boys' underachievement, schooling and gender relations', in D. Epstein, J. Elwood, V. Hey and J. Maw (eds) *Failing Boys? Issues in Gender and Achievement*, Buckingham: Open University Press.

James, A. and Prout, A. (eds) (1990) *Constructing and Reconstructing Childhood: Contemporary Issues in the Sociological Study of Childhood*, London: Falmer Press.

James, A., Jenks, C. and Prout, A. (1998) *Theorizing Childhood*, Cambridge: Polity Press.

Jenkins, P.H. (1997) 'School delinquency and the school social bond', *Journal of Research in Crime and Delinquency* 34, 3: 337–367.

Jenkins, R. (1981) *Lads, Citizens and Ordinary Kids: Working-Class Youth Lifestyles in Belfast*, London: Routledge & Kegan Paul.

—— (1982) *Hightown Rules: Growing Up in a Belfast Housing Estate*, Leicester: National Youth Bureau.

John, P. (1996) 'Damaged goods: an interpretation of excluded pupils' perception of schooling', in E. Blyth and J. Milner (eds) *Exclusion from School*, London: Routledge.

Jovanovic, J. and Steinback King, S. (1998) 'Boys and girls in the performance-based science classroom: who's doing the performing?' *American Educational Research Journal* 35, 3: 477–496.

Kariya, T. and Rosenbaum, J.E. (1999) 'Bright flight: unintended consequences of detracking policy in Japan', *American Journal of Education* 107: 210–230.

Kashti, Y. (1998) 'Nationhood, modernity and social class in Israeli education', *British Journal of Sociology of Education* 19, 3, 355–364.

Kaufmann, M. (1994) 'Men, feminism and men's contradictory experiences of power', in H. Brod and M. Kaufmann (eds) *Theorizing Masculinities*, London: Sage.

Kellaghan, T., Weir, S., O' hUallachain, S. and Morgan, M. (1995) *Educational Disadvantage in Ireland*, Dublin: Department of Education, Combat Poverty Agency, Educational Research Centre.

Kenny, M. (2000) 'Travellers, minorities and schools', in E. Sheehan (ed.) *Travellers: Citizens of Ireland*, Dublin: The Parish of the Travelling People.

Kenny, M., McNeela, E., Shevlin, M. and Daly, T. (2000) *Hidden Voices: Young People with Disabilities Speak about their Second-Level Schooling*, Cork: South West Regional Health Authority.

Kenway, J. (1996) 'Reasserting masculinity in Australian schools', *Women's Studies International Forum* 19, 4: 447–466.

Keogh, A. (2000) 'Talking about the other: a view of how secondary school pupils construct opinions about refugees and asylum-seekers', in M. McLachlan and M. O'Connell (eds) *Cultivating Pluralism*, Dublin: Oak Tree Press.

Kerchoff, A.C. (1984) 'The current state of mobility research', *Sociological Quarterly* 25: 139–153.

Kerchoff, A.C., Fogelman, K. and Manlove, J. (1997) 'Staying ahead: the middle class and school reform in England and Wales', *Sociology of Education* 70: 19–35.

Kimmel, M.S. (1996) *Men's Lives,* third edition, London: Allyn and Bacon.

Kittay, E. (1999) *Love's Labor: Essays on Women, Equality and Dependency*, New York: Routledge.

Kruse, A. (1996) 'Approaches to teaching girls and boys: current debates, practices, and perspectives in Denmark', *Women's Studies International Forum* 19, 4: 429–445.

Kubitschek, W.N. and Hallinan, M.T. (1998) 'Tracking and students' friendships', *Social Psychology Quarterly* 61, 1: 1–15.

Lacey, C. (1974) 'De-streaming in a pressured academic environment', in J. Eggleston (ed.) *Contemporary Research in the Sociology of Education*, London: Methuen.

Lareau, A. (1987) 'Social class differences in family–school relationships: the importance of cultural capital', *Sociology of Education* 60: 73–85.

Lather, P. (1991) *Getting Smart: Feminist Research and Pedagogy With/In the Postmodern*, New York: Routledge.

Lauder, H., Hughes, D. and Watson, S. (1999) 'The introduction of educational markets in New Zealand: questions and consequences', *New Zealand Journal of Educational Studies* 34, 1: 86–98.

Lave, J. and Wenger, E. (1991) *Situated Learning: Legitimate Peripheral Participation*, Cambridge: Cambridge University Press.

Law, S. and Glover, D. (2000) *Educational Leadership and Learning: Practice, Policy and Research*, Buckingham: Open University Press.

Layte, R. and Whelan, C.T. (2000) 'The rising tide and equality of opportunity: the changing class structure', in B. Nolan, P.J. O'Connell and C.T. Whelan (eds) *Bust to Boom? The Irish Experience of Growth and Inequality*, Dublin: IPA.

Lee, M. (1993) 'Gender, group composition, and peer interaction in computer-based co-operative learning', *Journal of Educational Computing Research* 9: 549–554.

Lee, V.E. and Bryck, A.S. (1986) 'Effects of single-sex secondary schooling on student achievement and attitudes', *Journal of Educational Psychology* 78: 381–395.

Lee, V.E., Marks, H. and Byrd, T. (1994) 'Sexism in single sex and coeducational independent secondary school classrooms', *Sociology of Education* 67: 92–120.

Lee, V.E., Croninger, R.G., Linn, E. and Chen, X. (1996) 'The culture of sexual harassment in secondary schools', *American Educational Research Journal* 33, 2: 383–417.

Lees, S. (1993) *Sugar and Spice: Sexuality and Adolescent Girls*, London: Penguin.

Lentin, R. (1999) *The Expanding Nation: Towards a Multi-Ethnic Ireland. Proceedings of a Conference 1*, Dublin: Department of Sociology, Trinity College Dublin.

LePore, P.C. and Warren, J.R. (1997) 'A comparison of single-sex and coeducational Catholic secondary schooling: evidence from the national educational longitudinal study of 1988', *American Educational Research Journal* 34, 3: 485–511.

Linehan, C. (1996) 'Irish experiments in sharing in education: educate together', in *Pluralism in Education: Conference Proceedings*, 227–238.

Lodge, A. (1998) 'Gender identity and schooling: a two-year ethnographic study of the expression, exploration and development of gender identity in 7–9 year-old children in their school environment', Unpublished Ph.D. thesis, National University of Ireland, Maynooth.

Lodge, A. and Flynn, M. (2001) 'Gender identity in the primary school playground', in A. Cleary, M. Nic Ghiolla Phadraig and S. Quin (eds) *Understanding Children 1, State, Education and the Economy*, Cork: Oak Tree Press.

Lodge, A. and Lynch, K. (2000) 'Power: a central educational relationship', *Irish Educational Studies* 19: 46–67.

Lortie, D. (1975) *The Schoolteacher*, Chicago: Chicago University Press.

—— (1984) 'Teacher career and work rewards', in A. Hargreaves and P. Woods (eds) *Classrooms and Staffrooms: the Sociology of Teachers and Teaching*, Milton Keynes: Open University Press.

Lukes, S. (1973) *Individualism*, Oxford: Basil Blackwell.

—— (1977) 'Socialism and equality', in L. Kolakowski and S. Hampshire (eds) *The Socialist Idea (Quartet)*, reproduced in S. Lukes, *Essays in Social Theory*, London: Macmillan (1977) *Reappraisal*, London: Falmer Press.

Lynch, K. (1985) 'An analysis of some presuppositions underlying the concepts of meritocracy and ability as presented in Greaney and Kelleghan's study', *Economic and Social Review* 16, 2: 83–102.

—— (1987a) 'Dominant ideologies in Irish educational thought', *Economic and Social Review* 16, 2: 101–122.

—— (1987b) 'Dominant ideologies in Irish educational thought: consensualism, essentialism and meritocratic individualism', *Economic and Social Review* 18, 2: 102–122.

—— (1989) *The Hidden Curriculum: Reproduction in Education: a Reappraisal*, Lewes: Falmer Press.

—— (1992) 'Intelligence, ability and education: challenging traditional views', *Oideas* Spring: 134–148.

—— (1995) 'Equality and resistance in higher education', *International Studies in Sociology of Education* 5: 93–111.

—— (1999a) *Equality in Education*, Dublin: Gill & Macmillan.

—— (1999b) 'Equality studies, the academy and the role of research in emancipatory social change', *Economic and Social Review* 30, 1: 41–69.

—— (1999c) 'Social class and social change: naming the silences and the differences', Paper presented at the Conference on *Understanding Class in Ireland*, University College Dublin, Sociology Department, 11–12 December.

—— (2000a) 'Research and theory on equality and education', in M.T. Hallinan (ed.) *Handbook of the Sociology of Education*, New York: KluwerAcademic/Plenum Publishers.

—— (2000b) 'Education for citizenship: the need for a major intervention in social and political education in Ireland', Invited paper presented to the CSPE Conference, Bunratty, Co. Clare, 29 September.

—— (2000c) 'Realising change: structural and ideological considerations', Paper presented to the 10th Anniversary conference of the Equality Studies Centre, University College Dublin, *Equality and Social Justice: Challenges for Theory and Practice*, University College Dublin, 15 December.

Lynch, K. and Lodge, A. (1999) 'Essays on school', in K. Lynch, *Equality in Education*, Dublin: Gill & Macmillan.

Lynch, K. and O'Neill, C. (1994) 'The colonisation of social class in education', *British Journal of Sociology of Education* 15: 307–324.

Lynch, K. and O'Riordan, C. (1998) 'Inequality in higher education: a study of class barriers', *British Journal of Sociology of Education* 19, 4: 445–478.

Lynch, K., Brannick, T., Clancy, P., Drudy, S. with Carpenter, A. and Murphy, M. (1999) *Points and Performance in Higher Education: The Predictive Validity of the Points System*, Research Paper No. 4, Commission on the Points System, Dublin: Brunswick Press.

Lynch, K., Baker, J. and Cantillon, S. (2001) 'Equality: frameworks for change', Paper presented to the *National Economic and Social Forum Plenary Meeting*, Dublin Castle, Dublin, 30 January 2001.

Lyons, M., Lynch, K., Sheerin, E., Close, S. and Boland, P. (2002) *Inside Classrooms: A Study of Teaching and Learning*, Dublin: Institute of Public Administration and Department of Education and Science.

Mac an Ghaill, M. (1994) *The Making of Men: Masculinities, Sexualities and Schooling*, Buckingham: Open University Press.

McDonagh, W. (2000) 'A Traveller woman's perspective on education', in E. Sheehan (ed.) *Travellers Citizens of Ireland*, Dublin: Parish of the Travelling People.

McDonnell, A. (1995) 'The ethos of Catholic voluntary secondary schools', Unpublished Ph.D. thesis, Education Department, University College Dublin.

McDonnell, P. (1995) 'Integration in education in Ireland: rhetoric and reality', Paper presented to the European Conference on Educational Research, University of Bath, 14–17 September.

McGrath, D.J. and Kuriloff, P.J. (1999) '"They're going to tear the doors off this place": upper-middle-class parent school involvement and the educational opportunities of other people's children', *Educational Policy* 13, 5: 603–629.

McHugh, B., McCutcheon, I. and Williams, J. (1997) *Classroom Management: Summer Course Summary*, Dublin: INTO.

McLaren, P. (1993) *Schooling as Ritual Performance: Towards a Political Economy of Education*, second revised edition, London: Routledge.

—— (1995) *Critical Pedagogy and Predatory Culture*, New York: Routledge.

McMinn, J. (2000) 'The changers and the changed: an analysis of women's community education groups in the North and South of Ireland', Unpublished Ph.D. thesis, Equality Studies Centre, UCD.

McRobbie, A. (1978) 'Working class girls and the culture of femininity', in Women's Studies Group, Centre for Contemporary Cultural Studies (eds), *Women Take Issue*, London: Hutchinson.

McVeigh, R. (1995) *The Racialization of Irishness*, Belfast: CRD.

Maguire, M. (2001) 'Bullying and the post-graduate secondary school trainee teacher: an English case study', *Journal of Education for Teaching* 27, 1: 95–109.

Mahony, P. (1985) *Schools for the Boys? Coeducation Reassessed*, London: Hutchinson.

—— (1996) 'Changing schools: some international feminist perspectives on teaching girls and boys', *Women's Studies International Forum* 19, 4: 1–2.

—— (1998) 'Girls will be boys and boys will be first', in D. Epstein, J. Elwood, V. Hey and W. Maw (eds) *Failing Boys? Issues in Gender and Achievement*, Buckingham: Open University Press.

—— (2000) 'Teacher education and feminism', *Women's Studies International Forum* 23, 6: 767–775.

Marsh, H.W. (1989a) 'Effects of attending single-sex and coeducational high schools on achievement, attitudes, behaviours and sex differences', *Journal of Educational Psychology* 81: 70–85.

—— (1989b) 'Effects of single-sex and coeducational schools: a response to Lee and Bryck', *Journal of Educational Psychology* 81: 651–653.

Martin, M. (1997) *Report to the Minister for Education Niamh Bhreathnach, T.D. on Discipline in Schools*, Dublin: Department of Education.

Mason, M. (1990) 'Disability equality in the classroom – a human rights issue', *Gender and Education 2*, 3: 363–366.

Meyer, J.W. and Rowan, B. (1988) 'The structure of educational organisations', in A. Westoby (ed.) *Culture and Power in Educational Organisations*, Milton Keynes: Open University Press.

Mezirow, J. (1990) *Fostering Critical Reflection in Adulthood: a Guide to Transformative and Emancipatory Learning*, San Francisco: Jossey-Bass Publishers.

Middleton, S. (1990) 'Women, equality and equity in liberal educational policies, 1945–1988', in S. Middleton, J. Codd and A. Jones (eds) *New Zealand Education Policy Today*, Wellington, New Zealand: Allen & Unwin.

Midgeley, M. (1994) *The Ethical Primate: Humans, Freedom and Morality*, London: Routledge.

Mies, M. (1984) 'Towards a methodology for feminist research', in E. Albach (ed.) *German Feminism: Readings in Politics and Literature*, Albany: State University of New York Press.

Miller, D. (1995) *On Nationality*, Oxford: Oxford University Press.

Mills, M. and Lingard, B. (1997) 'Masculinity politics, myths and boys' schooling: a review essay', *British Journal of Educational Studies* 45, 3: 276–292.

Moles, O.C. (ed.) (1990) *Student Discipline Strategies: Research and Practice*, Albany: State University of New York Press.

Morris, A. (1997) 'Same mission, same methods, same results: academic and religious outcomes from different models of Catholic schools', *British Journal of Educational Studies* 45, 4: 378–391.

Mortimore, P. and Whitty, G. (1997) *Can School Improvement Overcome the Effects of Disadvantage?* London: Institute of Education.

Mortimore, P., Sammons, P., Stoll, L., Lewis, D. and Ecob, R. (1988) *School Matters*, Berkeley, Calif.: University of California Press.

Murphy, A. (2000) 'Unravelling a loaded dice: an analysis of the state's response to the educational needs of young people in residential care who attended mainstream school', Unpublished report, Department of Social Policy and Social Work, UCD.

Murphy, R. and Torrance, H. (1988) *The Changing Face of Educational Assessment*, Milton Keynes: Open University Press.

Murray, C. and Hernstein, R.J. (1994) *The Bell Curve*, New York: Free Press.

Nash, R. (2001) 'Class, "ability" and attainment: a problem for the sociology of education', *British Journal of Sociology of Education* 22, 2: 189–202.

National Anti-Poverty Strategy (1997) *Sharing in Progress: National Anti-Poverty Strategy*, Dublin: Government Publications Office.

Ngan-Ling Chow, E., Wilkinson, D., Zinn, M.B. (eds) (1996) *Race, Class and Gender: Common Bonds, Different Voices*, London: Sage.

Nielsen, K. (1985) *Equality and Liberty: A Defense of Radical Egalitarianism*, Totowa, NJ: Rowman & Allanheld.

Nieto, S. (1994) 'Lessons from students on creating a chance to dream', *Harvard Educational Review* 64, 4: 392–426.

Noddings, N. (1992) *The Challenge to Care in Schools*, New York: Teachers College Press.

Nolan B., O'Connell, P.J. and Whelan, C.T. (2000) *Bust to Boom? The Irish Experience of Growth and Inequality*, Dublin: Institute of Public Administration.

Nozick, R. (1974) *Anarchy, State and Utopia*, Oxford: Basil Blackwell.

Nussbaum, M. (1995a) 'Human capabilities, female human beings', in M. Nussbaum and J. Glover (eds) *Women, Culture and Development: A Study of Human Capabilities*, Oxford: Oxford University Press.

—— (1995b) 'Emotions and women's capabilities', in M. Nussbaum and J. Glover (eds), *Women, Culture and Development: A Study of Human Capabilities*, Oxford: Oxford University Press.

Oakes, J. (1985) *Keeping Track: How Schools Structure Inequality*, London: Yale University Press.

—— (1991) *Multiplying Inequalities: the Effects of Race, Social Class, and Tracking on Opportunities to Learn Mathematics and Science*, Santa Monica, Calif.: RAND.

Oakes, J. and Guiton, G. (1995) 'Matchmaking: the dynamics of high school tracking decisions', *American Educational Research Journal* 32, 1: 3–33.

O'Carroll, I. and Szalacha, L. (2000) *A Queer Quandary: The Challenges of Including Sexual Difference Within the Relationships and Sexuality Education Programme*, Report compiled for Lesbian Education Awareness.

O'Connor, A. (1987) 'The revolution in girls' secondary education in Ireland, 1860–1910', in M. Cullen (ed.) *Girls Don't Do Honours: Irish Women in Education in the 19th and 20th Centuries*, Dublin: WEB.

O'Connor, P. (1998) *Emerging Voices: Women in Contemporary Irish Society*, Dublin: IPA.

O'Flynn, G. (1987) 'Our age of innocence', in M. Cullen (ed.) *Girls Don't Do Honours: Irish Women in Education in the 19th and 20th Centuries*, Dublin: WEB.

Oliver, M. (1992) 'Changing the social relations of research production', *Disability, Handicap and Society* 7: 101–114.

O'Neill, J. (1994) *The Missing Child in Liberal Theory: Towards a Covenant Theory of Family, Community, Welfare and the Civic State*, Toronto: University of Toronto Press.

Osborn, M. and Broadfoot, A.L. (1992) 'A lesson in progress: primary classrooms observed in England and France', *Oxford Review of Education* 18, 1: 3–15.

Oyler, C. (1996) *Making Room for Students: Sharing Teacher Authority in Room 104*, New York: Teachers' College Columbia University.

Packwood, T. (1988) 'The school as a hierarchy', in A. Westoby (ed.) *Culture and Power in Educational Organizations*, Milton Keynes: Open University Press.

Pakulski, J. and Waters, M. (1996) 'The reshaping and dissolution of social class in advanced society', *Theory and Society* 25: 667–691.

Parekh, B. (1996) 'Minority practices and principles of toleration', *International Migration Review* 30: 251–284.

—— (2000) *Rethinking Multiculturalism: Cultural Diversity and Political Theory*, London: Macmillan.

Parker, L.H. and Rennie, L.J. (1997) 'Teachers' perceptions of the sex implementation of single-sex classes in coeducational schools', *Australian Journal of Education* 41, 2: 119–133.

Phelan, A.M. (2001) 'Power and place in teaching and teacher education', *Teaching and Teacher Education* 17: 583–597.

Phillips, A. (1995) *The Politics of Presence*, Oxford: Oxford University Press.

—— (1999) *Which Equalities Matter*, Cambridge: Polity Press.

Pink, W.T. and Noblit, G.W. (eds) (1995) *Continuity and Contradiction: the Futures of the Sociology of Education*, New Jersey: Hampton Press.

Pollard, A. (1987) *The Social World of the Primary School*, London: Cassell.

—— (ed.) (1996) *Readings for Reflective Teaching in the Primary School*, London: Cassell.

Pollard, A. and Tann, S. (1993) *Reflective Teaching in the Primary School, a Handbook*, second edition, London: Cassell.

—— (1997) *Reflective Teaching in the Primary School: a Handbook for the Classroom*, third edition, London: Cassell.

Pomeroy, E. (1999) 'The teacher–student relationship in secondary school: insights from excluded students', *British Journal of Sociology of Education* 20, 4: 465–482.

Popkewitz, T.S. and Fendler, L. (1999) *Critical Theories in Education*, New York: Routledge.

Preedy, M., Glatter, R. and Levacic, R. (eds) (1997) *Educational Management: Strategy, Quality and Resources*, Buckingham: Open University Press.

Prout, A. and James, A. (1990) 'A new paradigm for the sociology of childhood?' in A. James and A. Prout (eds) *Constructing and Reconstructing Childhood: Contemporary Issues in the Sociological Study of Childhood*, London: Falmer Press.

Pye, J. (1988) *Invisible Children: Who Are the Real Losers at School?*, London: Cassell.

Qvortrup, J. (1993) 'Nine theses about "childhood as a social phenomenon"', in J. Qvortrup (ed.) *Childhood as a Social Phenomenon: Lessons from an International Project, Eurosocial Report No. 47*, Vienna: European Centre for Social Welfare Policy and Research.

—— (1994) *Childhood Matters: Social Theory, Practice and Politics*, Aldershot: Avebury.

Rawls, J. (1971) *A Theory of Justice*, Oxford: Oxford University Press.

—— (1993) *Political Liberalism*, New York: Columbia University Press.

Reason, P. (ed.) (1988) *Human Inquiry in Action: Developments in New Paradigm Research*, London: Sage.

Reay, D. (1996) 'Contextualising choice: social power and parental involvement', *British Educational Research Journal* 22, 5: 581–596.

—— (1998) 'Setting the agenda: the growing impact of market forces on pupil grouping in British secondary schooling', *Journal of Curriculum Studies* 30, 5: 545–558.

—— (2000) 'A useful extension of Bourdieu's conceptual framework? Emotional capital as a way of understanding mothers' involvement in their children's education', *Sociological Review* 48, 4: 568–585.

Reay, D. and Ball, S.J. (1997) '"Spoilt for choice": the working classes and educational markets', *Oxford Review of Education* 23, 1: 89–101.

Rees, D.I., Argys, L.M. and Brewer, D.J. (1996) 'Tracking in the United States: descriptive statistics from the NELS', *Economics of Education Review* 15, 1: 83–89.

Rees, D.I., Brewer, D.J. and Argyss, L.M. (2000) 'How should we measure the effect of ability grouping on student performance?' *Economics of Education Review* 19: 17–20.

Reynolds, D. (1994) 'School effectiveness and quality in education', in P. Ribnew and E. Burridge (eds) *Improving Education: Promoting Quality in Schools*, London: Cassell.

Richie, S.M., Rigano, D.L. and Lowry, R.J. (2000) 'Shifting power relations in the "getting of wisdom"', *Teaching and Teacher Education* 16: 165–177.

Rieser, R. (2000) 'Special educational needs or inclusive education: the challenge of disability discrimination in schooling', in M. Cole (ed.) *Education, Equality and Human Rights*, London: Routledge/Falmer.

Riordan, C. (1990) *Girls and Boys in School: Together or Separate?* New York: Teachers College Press.

Robertson, J. (1996) *Effective Classroom Control: Understanding Teacher–Student Relationships*, third edition, London: Hodder & Stoughton.

Rogers, B. (1997) *The Language of Discipline: a Practical Approach to Effective Classroom Management*, second edition, Plymouth: Northcote House.

Rose, K. (1994) *Diverse Communities: the Evolution of Lesbian and Gay Politics in Ireland*, Cork: Cork University Press.

Rout, B. (1992) 'Being "staunch": boys hassling girls', in S. Middleton and A. Jones (eds) *Women and Education in Aotearoa 2*, Wellington: Bridget Williams Books, 169–180.

Rudduck, J., Chaplan, R. and Wallace, G. (eds) (1996) *School Improvement: What Can Pupils Tell us?* London: David Fulton.

Rutter, M., Maughan, B., Mortimore, P., Ouston, J. and Smith, A. (1979) *Fifteen Thousand Hours: Secondary Schools and Their Effects on Children*, London: Open Books.

Ryan, C. (1999) 'Early school leaving: a sharing of responsibiliity', *Issues in Education* 4: 45–54.

Sadker, M. and Sadker, L. (1985) 'Sexism in the classroom of the eighties', *Psychology Today*, March, 54–57.

Sammons, P., Thomas S. and Mortimore, P. (1997) *Forging Links: Effective Schools and Effective Departments*, London: Paul Chapman.

Sayer, A. (1995) *Radical Political Economy: A Critique*, Oxford: Basil Blackwell.

—— (2000a) *Realism and Social Science*, London: Sage.

—— (2000b) 'Moral economy and political economy', *Studies in Political Economy* 61, Spring: 79–103.

Seale, C. (ed.) (1999) *Researching Society and Culture*, London: Sage.

Sen, A. (1992) *Inequality Reexamined*, Oxford: Clarendon Press.

Shavit, Y. and Blossfeld, H.P. (eds) (1993) *Persistent Inequality: Changing Educational Attainment in Thirteen Countries*, Oxford: Westview Press.

Shilling, C. (1993) 'The demise of the sociology of education in Britain? extended review', *British Journal of Sociology of Education* 14, 1: 105–112.

Signorella, M.L., Frieze, I.H. and Hershey, S.W. (1996) 'Single-sex versus mixed-sex classes and gender schemata in children and adolescents', *Psychology of Women Quarterly* 20, 4: 599–607.

Sikes, P.J., Measor, L. and Woods, P. (1985) *Teacher Careers: Crises and Continuities*, London: Falmer Press.

Simon, B. (1978) *Intelligence, Psychology and Education*, second edition, London: Lawrence Wishart.

Skeggs, B. (1997) *Formations of Class and Gender: Becoming Respectable*, London: Sage.

Skelton, C. (1997) 'Primary boys and hegemonic masculinities', *British Journal of Sociology of Education* 18, 3: 349–369.

Slee, R. (1995) *Changing Theories and Practices of Discipline*, London: Falmer Press.

—— (1997) 'Imported or important theory? Sociological interrogations of disablement and special education', *British Journal of Sociology of Education* 18, 3: 407–419.

—— (1998) 'Inclusive education? This must signify "new times" in educational research', *British Journal of Educational Studies* 46, 4: 440–454.

Smith, D.E. (1987) *The Everyday World as Problematic: a Feminist Sociology*, Boston: Northeastern University Press.

Smith, D.J. and Tomlinson, S. (1989) *The School Effect: A Study of Multi-Racial Comprehensives*, London: Policy Studies Institute.

Smyth, E. (1999) *Do Schools Differ? Academic and Personal Development among Pupils in the Second-Level Sector*, Dublin: Oak Tree Press.

Smyth, E. and Hannan, D.F. (2000) 'Education and Equality', in B. Nolan, P.J. O'Connell and C.T. Whelan (eds) *Bust to Boom: The Irish Experience of Growth and Inequality*, Dublin: Institute of Public Administration.

Smyth, J. and Hattam, R. (2001) 'Voiced research as a sociology for understanding "dropping out" of school', *British Journal of Sociology of Education* 22, 3: 401–415.

Sociology of Education (1996) Special Issue on Sociology and Educational Policy.

Sorenson, A.B. and Hallinan, M.T. (1986) 'Effects of ability grouping on growth in academic achievement', *American Educational Research Journal* 23, 4: 519–542.

Spender, D. (1982) *Invisible Women: The Schooling Scandal*, London: Writers and Readers.

Stanworth, M. (1983) *Gender and Schooling: a Study of Sexual Divisions in the Classroom*, London: Hutchinson.

Steedman, J. (1983) *Examination Results in Mixed and Single-Sex Schools*, Manchester: Equal Opportunities Commission.

Sternberg, R.J. (1998) 'How intelligent is intelligence testing?', *Scientific American* 9, 4: 12–17.

Sukhnandan, L. with Lee, B. (1998) *Streaming, Setting and Grouping by Ability: a Review of the Literature*, Slough: NFER.

Swain, J. (2000) '"The money's good, the fame's good, the girls are good": the role of playground football in the construction of young boys' masculinity in a junior school', *British Journal of Sociology of Education* 21, 1: 95–109.

Swift, A. (2000) 'Class analysis from a normative perspective', *British Journal of Sociology* 33, 4: 663–679.

Tawney, R.H. (1964) *Equality*, London: Allen and Unwin.

Taylor, C. (1985) 'Interpretation and the Sciences of Man', in *Philosophy and the Human Sciences: Philosophical Papers 2*, Cambridge: Cambridge University Press.

—— (1992) *Multiculturalism and 'The Politics of Recognition'*, Princeton, NJ: Princeton University Press.

Taylor, N. (1993) 'Ability grouping and its effect on pupil behaviour: a case study of a Midlands comprehensive school', *Education Today* 43, 2: 14–17.

Thomas, S., Pan, H., Goldstein, H. (1994) *Report of Analysis of 1992 Examination Results*, AMA and Institute of Education, University of London.

Thorne, B. (1993) *Gender Play: Girls and Boys in School*, Buckingham: Open University Press.

Tirri, K. (1999) 'Teachers' perceptions of moral dilemmas at school', *Journal of Moral Education* 28: 31–47.

Tirri, K. and Puolinatha, J. (2000) 'Teacher authority in schools: a case study from Finland', *Journal of Education for Teaching* 26, 2: 157–165.

Tobin, K. (1993) 'Target students', in B. Fraser (ed.) *Research Implications for Science and Mathematics Teachers, Volume 1*, Perth: Curtin University of Technology, National Key Centre for School Science and Mathematics.

Torres, C. (1990) *The Politics of Nonformal Education in Latin America*, New York: Praeger.

—— (1995) *Social Theory and Education: a Critique of Theories of Social and Cultural Change*, Albany: State University of New York Press.

Tovey, H. and Share, P. (2000) *A Sociology of Ireland*, Dublin: Gill and Macmillan.

Travers, C.J. and Cooper, C. (1996) *Teachers under Pressure: Stress in the Teaching Profession*, London: Routledge.

Tyler, W. (1988) *School Organisation: A Sociological Perspective*, London: Croom Helm.

van Veen, K., Sleegers, P., Bergen, T. and Klaasen, C. (2001) 'Professional orientations of school teachers towards their work', *Teaching and Teacher Education* 17: 175–194.

Walker, J. (1988) *Louts and Legends: Male Youth in Inner City Schools*, Sydney: Allen and Unwin.

Walkerdine, V. (1990) *The Mastery of Reason: Cognitive Development and the Production of Rationality*, London: Routledge.

Waller, W. (1932) *The Sociology of Teaching*, New York: John Wiley & Sons.

Walzer, M. (1985) *Spheres of Justice*, Oxford: Blackwell.

Wang, M.C. and Haertal, G.D. (1995) 'Educational resilience', in M.C. Wang, M.C. Reynolds and H.J. Walberg (eds) *Handbook of Special and Remedial Education Research and Practice*, Oxford: Pergamon.

Warren, L. and O'Connor, E. (1999) *Stepping Out of the Shadows: Women in Educational Management in Ireland*, Dublin: Oak Tree Press.

Warrington, M., Younger, M. and Williams, J. (2000) 'Student attitudes, image and the gender gap', *British Educational Research Journal* 26, 3: 393–408.

Waters, J. (2000) 'Big mac feminism', *Irish Times Education and Living Supplement*, 23 October.

Watkinson, A.M. (1996) 'Suffer the little children who come into schools', in J.R. Epp and A.M. Watkinson (eds) *Systemic Violence*, London: Falmer Press.

Weick, K.E. (1988) 'Educational organizations as loosely coupled systems', in A. Westoby (ed.) *Culture and Power in Educational Organizations*, Milton Keynes: Open University Press.

Weiler, K. (1988) *Women Teaching for Change: Gender, Class and Power*, New York: Bergin and Garvey.

Weiner, G. (1994) *Feminisms in Education: an Introduction*, Buckingham: Open University Press.

Weiss, L. (1995) 'Qualitative research in sociology of education: reflections on the 1970s and beyond', in W.T. Pink and G.W. Noblit (eds) *Continuity and Contradiction: the Futures of the Sociology of Education*, New Jersey: Hampton Press.

Welland, T. (2001) 'Living in the "empire of the gaze": time, enclosure and surveillance in a theological college', *Sociological Review*, 49, 1:117–135.

Wells, A.S. and Serna, I. (1996) 'The politics of culture: understanding local political resistance to detracking in racially mixed schools', *Harvard Educational Review* 66, 1: 93–118.

Wesselingh, A. (1996) 'The Dutch sociology of education: its origins, significance and future', *British Journal of Sociology of Education* 17: 212–226.

Westoby, A. (ed.) (1988) *Culture and Power in Educational Organisations*, Milton Keynes: Open University Press.

Wexler, P. (1987) *Social Analysis of Education: After the New Sociology*, London: Routledge & Kegan Paul.

Whitty, G. and Power, S. (2000) 'Marketization and privatization in mass education systems', *International Journal of Educational Development* 20: 93–107.

Whitty, G., Power, S. and Halpin, D. (1998) *Devolution and Choice in Education: The School, the State and the Market*, Buckingham: Open University Press.

Willis, P. (1977) *Learning to Labour: How Working Class Kids Get Working Class Jobs*, Westmead, UK: Saxon House.

Wilson, J. and Cowell, B. (1990) *Children and Discipline: a Teacher's Guide*, London: Cassell.

Wolfenden, S. (1994) *Managing Behaviour: a Practical Framework for Schools, New Edition*, Stafford: NASEN.

Woods, P. (ed.) (1980) *Pupil Strategies: an Exploration in the Sociology of the School*, London: Croom Helm.

—— (1984) 'The meaning of staffroom humour', in A. Hargreaves and P. Woods (eds) *Classrooms and Staffrooms: the Sociology of Teachers and Teaching*, Milton Keynes: Open University Press.

—— (1990) *The Happiest Days? How Pupils Cope with School*, London: Falmer Press.

Woulfe, E. (2002) 'State policy and educational inequality in secondary schools: a study of 13 schools'. Unpublished Master of Equality Studies thesis, University College Dublin.

Yoneyama, S. (2000) 'Student discourse on Tokokyohi (school phobia/refusal) in Japan: burnout or empowerment', *British Journal of Sociology of Education* 21, 1: 77–94.

Young, I.M. (1990) *Justice and the Politics of Difference*, Princeton, NJ: Princeton University Press.

—— (2000) *Inclusion and Democracy*, Oxford: Oxford University Press.

Younger, M. and Warrington, M. (1996) 'Differential achievement of girls and boys at GCSE: some observations from the perspective of one school', *British Journal of Sociology of Education* 17, 3: 299–313.

Znaniecki, F. (1973) *Modern Nationalities: A Sociological Study*, Westport, Conn.: Greenwood Press.

Index

Page numbers in *italics* represent tables. Page numbers in **bold** represent figures.
Page numbers followed by n represent notes